LIVE FROM RADIO RINKSIDE
The Bob Chase Story

Bob Chase as told to Blake Sebring

First published by AuthorHouse 1/16/2009

DEDICATION

Thanks to Sheryl Krieg, Murph Chase, Chuck Bailey, Mike Emrick, Mike and Dave Franke, Scott Sproat and Angel Knuth

Cover painting by Andy "Belfour" Nichols

MORE BOOKS BY BLAKE SEBRING

Tales of the Komets

Legends of the Komets

The Biggest Mistake I Never Made (with Lloy Ball)

On to The Show: Fort Wayne's lasting impact on the NHL and the hockey world

The Lake Effect

Homecoming Game

Fort Wayne Sports History

Lethal Ghost

FOREWORD

Dwight D. Eisenhower was beginning his first term as President, a kid from Oklahoma named Mantle was taking over where Joe DiMaggio had finished in center field for the New York Yankees, and there was a hockey team playing in a 2-year-old arena. The team was the Fort Wayne Komets. Clad in maroon and white, they were offering something new and exciting and curious to people in basketball-crazed Indiana – ice hockey inside the Allen County Memorial Coliseum.

It was at this same point in history that a tall, athletic gentleman from the upper peninsula of Michigan came to the city. Though he had played hockey there, he wasn't coming to be a Komet. Bob Chase and a powerful 50,000-watt radio station with the call letters WOWO were about to become as entrenched in the mid-century life of Fort Wayne as multi-tiered Wolf and Dessauer; G C Murphy (where you could buy donuts after watching a machine make them), and Myers and McCarthy. The latter was the only store in downtown Fort Wayne where you could get your black Komet spaceman tie. I know 'cause I got one for Christmas one year.

Over the years that followed, the broadcasting giant whose voice with such excitement carried the Komets exploits from tiny Hobart Arena in Troy, Ohio; rickety Oak Creek Ice Arena in Des Moines; and the modern Salt Palace in Salt Lake City and became recognized as one of sports' most enduring. There is no announcer in hockey who has been affiliated with the same team for so many years as Bob Chase: 1953 to present.

Envying Bob Chase's voice (a resonant bass) and height (6'5"), I grew up in LaFontaine, Indiana – population 627 by the 1950

1

census. By the time Bob was in his fifth season as voice of the Komets, I was newly hooked. (Somehow I got thru the first four grades of elementary school without hockey). I was one of the many Komet fans who "watched" games through his eyes from Louisville and Indianapolis and Dayton and Muskegon.

Considering the many provinces and states that could receive WOWO most of those years, it's safe to say that no individual has talked to more radio rinksiders about this sport than Bob Chase. And, there is no hockey announcer who has more memories or better stories. I am trusting that somewhere in the pages that follow you will hear about: a) borrowing a dollar from his mother and meeting his future wife, b) the night the Zamboni failed in Grand Rapids and the tow truck did, too; and c) the intermission at the Coliseum one night where – on a wager – the question was "would Chase Chase Stone or would Stone Stone Chase?"

Open the pages and perhaps you can remember some cold Saturday night when you walked through the steel doors of the cavernous Coliseum to hear teenagers calling out, "Komet Hockey Lucky Number Souvenir Program!!" you could smell the hot dogs in the concourse between the upper and lower arena seats, and as you got closer to one of the many entrances, pick up the sound of the Coliseum organ played by Norm Carroll or Jack Loos.

These are great times in the lives of hockey fans. And, so is the one you are about to have by reading about this man, his life, his family and his team.

As a student at Manchester College, and a Komet fanatic for 10 years by then, I first got to meet Bob when he agreed to do an interview for a class project. It was mid-day at the WOWO studios on Washington Street and the friendliness I felt on the air was evident in person. You're darned right I was nervous. But, not only did he talk on tape for 20 minutes, he also got the engineering staff to transfer one of his great calls of a playoff game (Fort Wayne vs. Dayton) onto tape for me. I still have it.

You see, Bob Chase was my icon. And, the icon of several other announcers I have met since. He conveyed the excitement of the game like no other "voice."

He used English well and spoke in terms that we could understand. But, more than anything, every year since that day in 1967 when he made time for a college student, I can say that not only do I know a broadcasting legend and call him a friend – but his stature grows with each season. He's in his 80s and still broadcasting! There's hope for all of us!

And, when he was inducted into the Komets Hall of Fame in 2003, they invited me to be there. It was then that I saw the love the Komets fans had for him, the respect the players still hold and the wonderful life he and his beloved Murph had fashioned together with those grown-up kids.

From Bob Chase, you learn a passion for hockey, priorities for family and a joy in the everyday. And he was the first sportscaster I ever listened to who would have something special to say in signing off the traditional Komet games on Thanksgiving, Christmas, and New Years. One of many influences I've tried to incorporate into my own work. That night, after there were congratulatory notes from NHL Commissioner Gary Bettman and broadcasters' association president Chuck Kaiton (Carolina Hurricanes announcer), he was offered the microphone. So much was written that day and said on the ice that night. But, true to form, he said, "I read some wonderful newspaper items today and I told Murph, 'ya know we ought to go out to the Coliseum and see who this guy is they're writing about.'"

Well, if you didn't know, you get to find out who this guy is for yourself in this book.

Mike Emrick
2008

CHAPTER 1
IT'S TOO MUCH FUN TO RETIRE

I'm happy that I can't look into the future because in 1950 when I took my first radio job, I never could have dreamed it would lead to the life and career I've had. In retrospect, it still seems like a fantasy, 58 years of marriage to Murph, 55 years of Komets hockey, 30 years of the Indianapolis 500, 20 years of high school and college sports and countless other unbelievable experiences from a career in radio. I still shake my head when I think about that because I don't know how I got here. All these doors just kept opening for me.

This year I'll pass Foster Hewitt's record for the longest affiliation by an announcer with one hockey team, as I continue with my 56th season calling the Komets. Foster was the Toronto Maple Leafs announcer for 55 years. When I started in this business, I never thought I'd make it a career, and never in my wildest dreams did I think I'd have a long career as a sportscaster.

I have a nice family, a decent life, a fun job and time to enjoy life with family and friends. Being rich was never one of the priorities of my life, and I've never regretted any of the opportunities I passed by either in the sports field or other general areas of radio where I might have been more materially wealthy. Sometimes I'll sit in the living room and I'll look around at Murph and think, "Man, we have had a great life, haven't we?" The kids collaborate that whenever they come home, call or write us. I never thought life could be this good.

I don't know what kind of a life I'd have had without Murph. There would be no way my life could have been as totally fulfilling as this is. The thing about it is, it doesn't quit. It stays that way, and we still have fun. The other day we were walking out of one of the stores hand in hand, and I said, "Who'd have thought two old people 82 and 84 years old would walk down the street holding hands." It's just a natural thing that we do.

Health-wise, we've been blessed. She's the iron horse, and my problems have been minimal aside from my heart condition. Other than that, I have never had any major health issues of any kind. The smartest thing I did besides marrying my wife was coming out of the Mecca in Milwaukee one November night in 1981, sitting in the front of the bus lighting up a cigarette, inhaling it and my throat was so raw I felt like I was swallowing razor blades. I said to myself, "You idiot, now is the time to do it." I took my cigarettes, my lighter and everything out of my pockets, threw them in the waste basket and never had another cigarette.

It's self-rewarding to think that I finally got enough discipline, enough gumption to finally do something I should have done a long time ago. I had smoked all my life from the time I was 14 or 15. Even after the war I was two to three packs a day. I wasn't just carrying them around, I was inhaling them. People used to hate to see me coming because if I was through a pack of cigarettes and I knew they smoked, baby I was bumming until I got to my next pack. I was totally addicted.

After I quit, I went through literal hell for about six months, but I knew if I ever surrendered a moment that I'd be right back on it again because I had tried to quit before. There were days when I must have been an awful guy to live with. I can be sympathetic with those people who have been addicted to other measures like alcohol and drugs and what an incredible fight it has to be to quit. I loved smoking. I liked the taste of the tobacco and it was really a good experience. When I really analyzed what I was doing to myself, I like to live a lot more than smoke.

When I graduated from college, the phrase "radio career" wasn't even in my vocabulary. Radio was just a secondary outlet until my other options came through. The longer I stayed in radio, I guess I found that I had a talent and ability for it and became much at ease with it. I began to get a lot of reaction from people who listened, including my mom and dad. My dad could be very critical and when he was complimentary, you know you deserved it. He liked what I was doing and was very proud of me, and that made me really feel good.

I think the key to the thing was where I went to work. At home in Marquette with WDMJ it was a means to an end, and it was an easy living. All you had to do was open your mouth. Then when I got to Fort Wayne, I realized then I was in a serious business. Fortunately, I had the basic talent and the presence and the personality to absorb what I was learning, and boy was I learning things.

I wrote home and said to mom and dad, I don't think I could have gone to NBC New York and been part of a staff any greater than this one here. They were amazing people, headed by a guy who will always be a legend in my mind, Jay Gould. Jay had this deep-rooted philosophy and a lot of people never understood him. He was so intelligent and brilliant that you really had to ruminate on what he said before you realized what he was trying to tell you.

Bob Sievers wasn't there when I first came to work. He had been recalled to the Korean War and was at Great Lakes Naval Station. He was a whole different genre. He wasn't a philosopher, what you saw is what you got with Bob.

It isn't only hockey, it's the radio business. Hockey to me is the ice cream. The main course is going to work in the morning and doing morning sports. I regret I'm not as active overall in the business as I was. I'm not committed for eight to nine hours a day in the office anymore. I don't do the creative things that I used to do and excel at because the business has changed. People don't go out and market and promote and do all the things in this business that they used to do. The radio business per se, being on the air, to me is really a gratifying situation especially when you can reap the reaction you get from being there and the morality that you put into it and it's accepted by the people who listen. When I go to work every day, I can hardly wait to get there. I could spend countless hours on the air that I don't have and be more profound about the world. I fortunately have an outlet with my commentaries twice a week and they have been an invaluable outlet to me to keep my fire alive, and I appreciate the fact that the station allows me to do this. They have put no restrictions on me whatsoever, trusting in my judgment and it's been a good mix.

I look forward every day going to work in radio. Radio is fascinating, even though now it's almost an afterthought. There's still so much potential. I still hope somebody wakes up to know we are a sleeping giant. The frustration comes from broadcasting within the station in the limited areas that we now are involved in. We don't have that depth we used to have.

My blowoff where I can really let her fly and enjoy it is with hockey. I don't know what I would do if I couldn't do hockey. Retirement is something I think about a lot, but I keep thinking, "Holy crow, what would I do if I retired? I'd miss this so much that I don't know how long I'd last without it. Murph probably couldn't stand me. The whole package is, this is the business which I dearly love, and I'll do it as long as I can still do it and they still want me to do it and Murph wants me to do it. She understands and sees what it means to me. The kids love to have me do it. They listen from all over the world on their computers. I've made so many friends that I'll never meet. It's an experience.

Not only do I like what I'm doing at age 82, but I also look at it in another way. I really go full-tilt from October through May, morning, noon and nighttime, too, thousands of miles on the road, bus rides into the night until four or five in the morning. I like it because you are isolated in a whole different atmosphere that you have to experience it to know what it really means.

I'm also privileged to be involved with a great bunch of young people. The morality and the quality of people who represent the Fort Wayne Komets are impeccable. They can only be that way because they wouldn't accept anything but that kind of people to be in their organization. So it's fun, plus they're all my kids. I've been through how many generations now, and why do I stay young? Thank God the kids accept me and I'm just one of the guys. They kid me and give me the business, and have a lot of fun with me and I have a lot of fun with them. I'm not a stranger to them. We don't have any social contact outside of the game, but they respect me and I respect them and we have a good rapport. It makes it easy to go to work and it isn't work. That's just a term.

One thing I've never done in my life has been to take a job because it's going to pay me X number of dollars. The dollars come when you negotiate for the job you are working on. Maybe it isn't always what you expect but I earn what I negotiate for and that's only for survival. The rest of it is love. I'm sure I wouldn't have the health that I have or the longevity nor would Murph except for the fact that we just love what I'm doing and she's a part of every bit of it. If you have a job all your life and you went to work and you could hardly wait for the day to be over so you could get out of there, and you can hardly wait for the day when you can tell them to stuff it, you haven't lived. You are just suffering your way through life. They're going to have to lock me out one of these days because I won't quit.

To me, hockey is really unique and I've been fortunate enough to play about every sport. I never played rugby, lacrosse or soccer, but about everything else I've tried. I've never been exceptional at any of them but passable enough to get by. I was a good enough athlete to play high school and college sports, and a little semi-pro stuff. There's something that is so different about hockey from the rest of them. I would almost call it an individual team sport. A coach of a hockey team has a really strange responsibility because he has to take talent and individual psyche and be able to match it up with people who can play together and be successful. Hockey players are all in their own way eccentrics, but they are all there with a common bond, like I'm there with the same bond because hockey is different from my way of thinking than any sport. You just have to make so many more sacrifices. Yes, I see football and baseball, but the actual physicality of the sport and what you put into it is so demanding that if you let up on it at any point for any moment it's pretty obvious you aren't doing your job. That's why I like hockey more than any other sport. There's no place you can coast except back to the bench. A lot of people who coasted with incredible talent went to the bench and never got back off. A lot of guys with no talent at all except the knowledge of how to scramble over the boards one way or the other are still playing because they know what it takes to win.

You don't go through bad years as much as you go through sad years. There's no such thing as a bad year because you're still part of the game, you're enjoying it and you're sharing it with the people who play it. Believe me, when it's not a good year, your agonies, my agonies are the same as the guys who play it. I don't get the bumps and bruises, I don't end up with the ego problems because I'm not in the game every night, but I'm still representing it and drawing word pictures of it. There are seasons that get very long. There are games that get very, very long, but when it's all over, you look back and say, that's one game. Tomorrow night is another game. It's not going to be the same as that, and the same thing goes for seasons. That was last season, so let's close the door on that and open another one. Some years you can anticipate you are going to have good years, and other years you look forward to with trepidation because you know it just isn't going to be that good. I've been very fortunate in Fort Wayne because rarely we've had consecutive down years of catastrophic proportions. There's always been that dedication, that ability or that magic to somehow recover and get back on the upswing right away. You don't have to worry because it ain't ever going to get that bad. That's a total reflection on team organization and ownership. I think probably the pattern was built back in the late 1950s when Ken Ullyot came to town. He put a purpose and a morality and profile on the sport here that rubbed off on everybody that it's been handed off to. It's so fitting that the people who own the team now were little kids at the time when this team's personality was being formed so they knew and expected that when they were fans and now they won't take anything less as owners. Fans can be extremely fortunate that kind of morality gets passed on because you can see in a lot of franchises in sports, if there is no morality, no image or no standards, it can go from the sublime to the ridiculous at every level.

I get a lot of people who say, "When in the world are you going to hang it up?" and I truthfully can't tell you. Sometimes, probably more so in the spring of a bad year when the season is over, now I know summer is around the corner and I look at that fifth-wheel and I want to travel. Murph and I love to travel. Now we're in our own world. I look forward to that with such intensity that you can't believe it. Those are the times occasionally when I think maybe out of the frustration of this year that I just ought to quit. Then I think, "No, I don't want to stop on a low." When I quit, whenever I quit, it's going to be on a high. I thought once before about quitting on a championship, and I didn't quit because frankly, I'm not ready to quit. As long as the people I work for are supportive and encourage me to keep going and are honest enough with me to let me know when the time has come when they don't think I can hack it... I want them to be honest with me because I'm not going to be a pouter. If I get to the point where it's going downhill to a point where it's beginning to reflect on my ability and on the product, I don't want any part of that.

I don't know when it's going to be. I just hope that I can maintain the quality. I've got a cheerleader here in Murph and if I start getting a little sloppy, and start to fold a little bit, we're such great friends, she would very honestly tell me. She tells me things now, which she has done forever, about little things I've said on the broadcast. She's my greatest critic, and I respect her so much because she is as great a fan as I am. If she tells me, "Bob, you know maybe it's about time we need to think about taking the trail," I'll give it a great deal of thought because I respect her and she deserves what she wants. She's tolerated me for many, many years, and she's still happy. I don't ever want to detract from her happiness. We've only got another 20 or 30 years together.

CHAPTER 2
WHEN EVERYBODY HAD THE SAME THING – NOTHING

My dad's name was Gunnard Wallenstein and my mom was Hazel Anderson, and they were married in early 1925. My dad was a semi-pro football player as well as an electrician for the Cleveland Cliffs Iron Company. The way they met was my mother had dated a guy in Marquette who was also a semi-pro football player, and they went up and played the Ishpeming Hematites. Her boyfriend was a halfback and at the line of scrimmage he met Pop, and Pop just creamed him, at which point my mother had an intense dislike for my father. Then she met him, and once they met they started to like each other more and more and finally were married.

At that time my mother was a nurse and my dad was an electrician, and here comes me. I was born January 22, 1926. I have a five years younger sister Marian who still lives in Marquette and is married to Arthur Mackey.

Mom was almost exclusively a private-duty nurse, and she would spend many months with patients whom she would give specific care to. My dad was an electrician who wired mine shafts, working with all kinds of heavy voltage stuff. My father was the one who laid the first marine electric cable in the upper peninsula of Michigan from Grand Island to Munising, which ironically is Murph's home town. He was also a pro football player who played for the Green Bay Packers in 1920 and 1921, and he was also one of the nation's top ski jumpers. He was 6-4, 220 pounds, a big man, and Mom was 5-10, about 170. I grew up in the Depression so every kid did about the same thing – nothing. Whatever you got you earned or you made or your mom or your dad made or helped you get it. There were no luxuries. If you happened to have a bicycle, you were darned lucky because bikes cost $10, $15 and your parents didn't have $10, $15 to buy you a bike, so Shank's Mare was the major means of transportation – that's walking.

Everybody was in the same boat. No one had anything, and no one really cared because we were all there. We made our own fun. That's where sandlot sports were really sandlot sports. When it became spring you played baseball, and there were always vacant lots you could play in. Nobody seemed to worry if you were hurting their property or anything, they'd let you play or whatever the case, they'd let you play on those lots. You'd play baseball all spring and all summer, and then in the fall you'd play football, and as soon as the ponds froze over you'd play hockey.

I lived a mile off the main highway at this hydro-plant on the south side of Marquette so if I wanted to go play, the nearest place was a mile and a quarter away. The only way to get there was to walk. And of course we lived on the shore of Lake Superior on the south side of Marquette and there were beautiful beaches there. The water was colder than ice, but we didn't care, we'd swim day in and day out. We'd play baseball for an hour or two, get hot, jump in the water for an hour or two and go back and play baseball again.

That was kind of our life, and if you were going to get anything out of life you had to find something to do so when I was 11 or 12 I had a small Milwaukee Journal paper route. The route encompassed about three miles, and I think I might have had 20 or 22 subscribers. I made two cents a paper, not to mention the fact that when I'd leave home I had to walk four miles to get to where they'd leave your papers. On a Sunday I'd get up at

6:30 a.m. and go up to the gas station and get there by 8. In the wintertime I'd pull my sled and do my papers, and I'd get home by 9:30 or 10. You didn't have showers in those days – you took a bath every Saturday night whether you wanted it or not – so I'd clean up, put on my clothes and go to church. I'd get to church by 11. Everybody kind of smelled the same way so we sort of ignored each other. Then I'd walk home from church.

Then as I got older and had more friends around the city, and I wasn't restricted to just one street, I got to know more people and occasionally one of them would be able to drive their parents' car which meant that I could get a ride home, or if I was going someplace with the gang they would come and pick me up. We were always good kids, and we never had any major problems of any kind. In those days morality was something you accepted as part of your life. It was just the way you grew up. Those who were immoral in obvious manner were rather ostracized. Either they came to you or they ended up being troubled kids.

My childhood was really pretty bland because there wasn't much trouble you could get into. Those were the days of John Dillinger and those guys. This one place of a friend of mine, they had about three old cars in the back yard, and we played cops and robbers all the time. Rather than cap guns, which we couldn't afford, we made rubber band guns. We had some incredible days.

Once it got to fall and then winter the ponds would freeze over. There were two ponds on my way home off the main highway, the big pond and the cookie pond, and the cookie pond would always freeze first because it was shallower. There were probably 25 or 30 of us, and we used that pond as our hockey rink.

I got an old pair of my dad's skates that were about six sizes too big to begin with, and I put extra socks on, I stuffed the toes but you spent all day on your ankles. The only other solution you had were clamp skates. The only problem was you'd get that key and tighten it down, and if for some reason or other the side of your sole slipped out, then you had to leave the game, unscrew the whole darn thing and start all over again. Clamp skates might cost a buck and a half where shoe skates might have cost you $8 or $9.

We played from the time we were little kids, and then I went to South Marquette on the big rink. They had about two baseball fields on it and the city would flood in the fall and really take good care of it. You'd go up there and half the guys you'd never seen in your life before, but you'd bring your skates and your stick and maybe if you had a puck you'd bring it. Or maybe Dad would cut birch pucks which were just trees that were the right size and you'd cut them to the size of pucks and point them black. The nice thing about them was with the rubber pucks when you shot them into a snow bank you couldn't find them, but the birch pucks were light enough that you could find them.

There really weren't any organized games. They might end up with one later when a couple guys would start choosing sides, there'd maybe be 12 guys.

There was no park board hockey, but there was a city team that played out at a rink called the Palestra. If the guys from the city who plowed the rinks saw a good kid or two, they'd come over and say "Hey, Buddy, stop at the Palestra Saturday morning and see so and so." That's where the big team skates. There was private team in town called the Wild Geese. The man who sponsored them was named Max Reynolds, a huge stockholder in DuPont, and he was at least a millionaire in the days when millionaires were like God. A couple of guys who worked for him would scout the Palestra group, and if they thought you were good enough they'd invite you over to play on his rink. If you got an invitation to go over there, man, you were in the hoopy doopy.

I'll never forget, I got the invitation to go over there, and the first day I'm not chosen for a team but I'm handed a bell. I'm going to officiate, but I didn't know anything about the rules for hockey. We had just played pond hockey, keep-away, and you just learned how to control things. I don't have a clue what I'm supposed to be doing, but I've got this bell in my hand. Everybody is screaming, "That was offsides you dummy...," so a fella comes over to me and says, "Slim, you ever played hockey before?" and I said, "In South Marquette on the pond and stuff, and I was over at the Palestra a couple of times." He says, "C'mere, give the bell to him," and I start watching and he explains some of the basic rules. I'm 10, 11 years old and all of a sudden it made sense what was going on. So a couple of days later I'm back and now I can ring the bell and all of that stuff. Eventually I get to play for the Wild Geese. I made a few trips, but then it got expensive and my mom and dad couldn't afford it so I just went back and played in a minor league at the Palestra.

When I was 16, the Marquette Sentinels, which were the semi-pro team, asked me to try out and I made the team as an alternate. I was having lots of problems then because the high school coaches were madder than sin that I'm trying to play hockey when I should be playing basketball and football. I had to kind of split my time, and I didn't play as much hockey as I wanted to.

There were no places to go for entertainment because there was one theatre in town, and the only time you went to theatre at all was if you managed to pick up 10 cents during the week, and you could go to the Saturday morning serials which were Flash Gordon, Roy Rogers, Tom Mix and all that kind of stuff. There was a fella who lived on Lake Street, which is where I had to walk to get anywhere, by the name of Eddie Foy and he cooked for the Michigan State Police. Their post was about half a mile down the road from where I lived, and all these troopers would come in there, and you got to see these guys as heroes. If you could split wood for Eddie on Saturday morning or maybe Friday night, and carry about 15 gallons of water... see there were no plumbing or taps, you pumped that rascal and you took two pails at a time and you carried them in and filled up the reservoirs and stuff, but you got 10 cents and you could go to the movies the next day.

But other than that, one of the major items that took up a lot of our lives was my father helped us build a camp which was near the hydro-plant where I lived, maybe three-quarters of a mile up a hill. There was a log cabin. He'd go around and he'd blaze trees for us so we would cut the right ones because this was all part of Cleveland Cliffs Iron Company land. We'd get them cut and we'd use a two-man cross cut and we'd saw them to the right lengths, and we'd take alike a piece of wood, tie a string on it, and two of us would put a yoke on the log, and then we'd drag it down to the campsite where Dad would help us measure and notch these things to build them. Then the Marquette branch prison was across the river from the hydro-plant I lived at. They had this gigantic dump where they threw all their trash, and we'd walk through the woods to that dump and there was a lot of corrugated metal. They had a prison farm, and when they would re-roof the farm buildings, they'd take that corrugated metal and throw it over to that dump. We'd go over, and the stuff that looked good, we'd drag it all the way through the woods, all the way up to the camp, probably a mile and a half, and then

Dad would help us put it up and make a roof out of it. We had a nice little camp, two bunks. Another one of the men and the power plant took a 50-gallon drum and made a stove out of it.

When we were there, we'd start trapping woodchucks, squirrels and stuff. We had a huge big cage for the woodchucks, and we'd feed them lettuce and stuff. Everybody had gardens and we'd take the scrap out of the gardens. The squirrels, we'd put a wheel up for them so they could run and exercise. We'd have those squirrels so tame they'd sit on your shoulders and you could feed them. In the fall when we went back to school we'd open the cages and they'd all go back. Some of those woodchucks hung around three, four years. They got so friendly you didn't have to cage them.

Our staple in those days was Van Camp's Pork and Beans. Anybody could afford a nickel's worth of Van Camp's Pork and Beans, and we'd build a fire in the stove, punch a hole in the top of the can and set it there until the beans got hot. Open the thing, get a goldang spoon and we lived on that stuff. On several occasions, somebody forgot to punch a hole in the top of the can and there would be a huge pow! There would be beans all over the camp.

These are the kind of things that took up our time. There were about eight guys in this camp, and this was the focal point of our lives. You had to be good because if you screwed up there and did something you shouldn't have, you were knocked out of the camp. I was the youngest guy all the time. If you wanted something, you worked for it.

The cabin was probably 12 feet by 12 feet. It was dug halfway into a hillside and had a slanting roof on it for water to run off. There was a great big window in the front, and then the door. We had kerosene lamps because they'd never let us use Coleman lamps because they were too dangerous. It was an honor to be able to sleep in the cabin. That was big stuff. Even though I lived there within a half-mile of the cabin, I couldn't go up there and sleep. There was a lock on the cabin, and the key was a half-mile away at the hydro-plant. Sometimes, if I got permission, I could go sleep at the cabin.

I also ski-jumped in the winter. I think the longest one I ever had was 185 feet. You start when you were a little kid with no brains. Ski jumping was a way of life in the Upper Peninsula. My father had been a very, very good ski jumper, and he encouraged us all. There were a lot of hills and areas up there that made it very easy to build small ski slides. We'd build a small ski slide where you could jump 25, 30 feet with no problem whatsoever, and they weren't even engineered. We just bullied our way in and made the jump. Then Dad helped us build a couple of hills where you could jump 90 to 120 feet.

When you build a ski hill and jump, you are never more than 10 feet off the ground. You might think you are way up in the air, but the force of gravity and the speed to leave the takeoff point provide you with an arc and gravity pulls you, and then the slope of the landing is configured so you never get too high off the ground.

One time I got knocked out flatter than a pancake. It was the first time I ever rode the big hill (Kirlin Hill). The landing hadn't been groomed, and there had been a little warm weather so it was glazed. I think I was 14 and there were three of us, and I had just gotten a new pair of Northland Jumping Skis for Christmas which in those days must have cost $35. We got up on the hill and everybody looked at it, and we rode the landing a couple of times. The hill was capable of about 240 feet, and the landing was pretty quick. I didn't go all the way to the top because there were intermediate places where you could control your distance. I hadn't ridden in the chute, but it turned out no one had. It was very icy and it turned out I got a lot more speed than I thought I was going to get.

In ski jumping timing is everything, and I had mistimed it completely. Consequently, when I got airborne, my balance wasn't even close to right, and I started to get nose heavy and realized I was going to have a problem. I think I remember the contact when I first hit. The next thing I remember is when I woke up, and it was like looking out of a globe, and all these trees were just spinning around. I'd been out for about 10 minutes. I had hit and I bounced and hit again and landed right on my head. The guys with me didn't know anything about first aid or what to do.

I broke my ski which really worried me. I thought, "If I go home and show this to Dad, all hell's going to break loose." I went out on one ski and got back to the road, and this one kid drove me home. That was my first experience with a big hill and it just positively flattened me.

Dad didn't say much. I told him what I had done, and he just sort of chuckled. Knowing what it meant to buy those skis for me… the fact that I used them and had enough courage to do what I did, gained me a lot of esteem in his eyes.

I was still hurting pretty bad, but I think he would have liked to have been there to see me to help me a little bit. Had he been there, I wouldn't have jumped because he wouldn't have let me. That's how dumb I was at that time.

They had to order me another ski, and two weeks later I rode the big hill again. Dad was there this time, and I survived this one.

CHAPTER 3
HIGH SCHOOL HOPES

I went to Marquette Graveraet High School. At that time there were three high schools in Marquette, Graveraet, Bishop Baraga and John D. Pierce High School which was affiliated with the Northern State Teachers College and eventually became Northern Michigan University. When I was playing ball, I ended up at 6-4, which was pretty tall, and I used to get a lot of ridicule on the road. There weren't very many guys who were 6-4 in those days. We had one other kid who graduated when I was a sophomore who was 6-6, and he was the biggest kid in the Upper Peninsula at that time.

I played football. I was an end both ways, and occasionally they played me at fullback so when we needed two or three yards, I'd get the grunt. I played three years. I played basketball for three years as a center, and in track, I ran the mile and did some high jumping back when I used to be able to high jump 5-2, and that was really big stuff.

I was pretty good at both football and basketball. Mind you, I was playing basketball when you were winning games by scores like 35-31, 26-24. If you had 8 to 10 points you were having a heck of a night with all set shots, no one-hand stuff, no jumpers and there was a center jump after every score. I was a pretty fair rebounder and I was always pretty good on jump balls. I served the city pretty well.

We had pretty good teams. We were one of the bigger high schools in the Upper Peninsula. At the time it was a city of

18,000, and we were the queen city of the north. Nobody was close to us so we had a pretty good choice of people, plus we had a pretty good school system and attracted some of the better teachers and/or coaches who came into the U.P.

Once I got to high school, I played football. I can remember late in my junior year we were playing Ishpeming and we'd had a snow storm. They had plowed the field off, and it was a playable field, but it was very hard, and we're all wearing canvas gloves because it was so cold, probably 20, 25 degrees. About every 10 minutes you had to change gloves, and pretty soon there were no more gloves to change into. We didn't have warm-up jackets, we used blankets we had brought from home. I'll never forget it. That's probably the worst memory I've ever had of playing football.

In basketball, we won a state championship in 1943, my senior year. Coming into that season, we didn't know how good we were at the time. We had four of the starting five back from a team that had gotten eliminated in the regional championship game the year before.

My senior year I developed a hook shot which was the only one-handed shot you could take in those days because everything was a two-hand set. We got through our regional and beat a team called Menominee for the right to go down to state. It was our first trip over the straits of Mackinac, and we played in Jenison Fieldhouse in East Lansing. Our first game we beat a team from Muskegon. Next, we eliminated a team from Grayling to go to the championship game. For the first time in our history, we played against an all-black team from River Rouge. We'd only ever seen one or two black people before.

Our coach was Roger Keast, the last four-sport man to graduate from Michigan State and he really pumped us up for this game. They jumped ahead of us by four or five points, but we stayed with it. I got 14 points, and we won the game 41-37, and our little guard Ray Beauchamp was the MVP.

My scoring average in high school was 11 or 12 points. For the style of basketball we played, that was quite an accomplishment. One night you might have a game of 15 or 16, and the next night you might have four. It was just how the game was played at that time.

Hockey was kind of my cheat sport. I would play it even though I wasn't supposed to. I played center, and then I went to defense when I got bigger. The game was so much different. It was strictly a game of carry and possession, and you couldn't dump it at the blue line, you had to carry it across, and there was no red line at that time either. It was just a very deliberate, slow game and it was totally a skill game. When I was 16 and playing on the Sentinels, I was playing against guys who were 21, 25, 30 years old. I was not a star by any means, but I was adequate. I was not a first-liner and rarely started, but I learned the game quickly.

I played enough as a youngster, and then I played briefly after the war. We used to be the Marquette Sentinels. Dow Chemical had a big plant in Marquette where they made Sentinel anti-freeze for cars, and they sponsored us. When Dow Chemical pulled out, we opened the next season with no sponsorship, and you would play three or four games and our business manager ran the box office. We would split the pot so we called ourselves the Marquette Millionaires.

CHAPTER 4
A SAILOR'S LIFE FOR ME

When I was 15, my friend Dan Hornbogen and I had done a little pulpwood logging deal, and once we got that cutting done, there wasn't much going on. Living on Lake Superior and being a Sea Scout, I took every opportunity to go out and work on the fish boats and doing anything I could to get out on the lake. There was a guy, a security man at the docks, and he was a good friend to all of us and was always scouting for us. His name was Ned Watson and he was part Indian so everybody called him Chief. One day the phone rang and he said, "Wally, how'd you like to go sailing on the Great Lakes? I have a job for you." Where? "Well, it's on a Canadian ship. You can't sail on a U.S. boat yet because you're not old enough. If your mom and dad think it's OK, I can tell the captain before he sails, and you'll have to meet the ship in Sault Saint Marie." I talked to my Mom and Dad, and mother just said "No way." My dad knew what it was. He said, "Let the kid go, if it doesn't work out, I guarantee you he'll be back in a bloody week." She still wasn't very keen about it, but finally agreed so I called Chief back, but the Goderich had just sailed but he could still get the captain on the radio phone.

It belonged to the Canada Steamship Lines.

He called me back about 15 minutes later and said the ship will be at Algoma Steel in the Canadian Soo, short for Sault Saint Marie. They were going to be in there the next day so I had to get to Sault Saint Marie, cross the border and report to Algoma Steel to get on the ship. Under no circumstances could I tell the folks at the border that I was going to go to work over there. I just so happened that I had a friend named Owen Steere who had a summer home on the Canadian side who was also working on the boat. His dad was a huge business broker, and they had a summer home up on Whitefish Bay.

So my dad drove me to the intersection of US 41 and M-28 which was south of Marquette about five miles. Me and my suitcase got out and Dad said, "Good luck," and I got my thumb out. About the third or fourth car stopped and he was going as far as Munising. Pretty soon I get another ride and this guy went as far as Seney, a little logging town which had about eight houses, a sawmill, piles of logs about a mile high, one gas station and one street light hanging in the middle of an intersection. We get there and it's about 9:30 p.m. and I'm still 70 miles away and the cars are few and far between. It's close to 11 p.m. and the gas station is still open so I go over to talk to the guy. I say, "I'm trying to get a ride to the Soo," but he's closing in about 15 minutes.

Lo and behold before he closes, this big truck comes in, and man, I'm up on the running board almost before he stops. He says, "Do you see that sign right there?" It says, "No riders." He must have looked at me and he said, "How far are you going?" I have to get to Sault Saint Marie and I have to cross the border at 7 a.m. He says, "I'm going right to the Soo. That sign is not my doing. That's a government sign, and we're not supposed to pick up riders because of the stuff we're carrying, but I'm sure you're harmless. C'mon, get in." We get to the Soo, we're getting close and he asked me some more questions about what I was doing. It's about 4 a.m. Where do I go? "I tell you what I'm going to do, this next corner I gotta let you off. If I get caught with you, I'll lose my job." I thanked him and went over to this little park and I'm laying on this park table, and there's nobody around and all of a sudden, boom, boom, boom, all these searchlights come on. It's 1942 and the Soo locks were fortified with anti-aircraft batteries because it was one place to kill all the shipping down to the steel mills on the lower lakes. I'm lying on my back there and I was just fascinated because they were sending aircraft over and the searchlights would zero in on the aircraft during this drill and then the batteries would zero in on the apex. There would be about eight beams that would lock in on them.

Finally, it got daylight and there was a little diner on the corner so I got something to eat. It was like 6 a.m. and the first ferry didn't run until 7 a.m. I got on the ferry at 7 a.m. and on the other side went through customs. "Well, son, where are you going?"' I'm going up to visit the Steeres. "OK, when you get up there, be sure to say hi to Mr. Steere for us, my name is Hank." As soon as I get through there I catch a cab to Algoma Steel at 8 a.m. The security guy knew I was coming and OK'd me to go through to the dock. I climb on the ship and I go up to meet the captain. Owen and I were going to get the afternoon off, and his little brother Pete was coming down to get us in the launch. About the time we're going over to the launch, somebody says, "Hey slim, the old man wants to see you up in his cabin." I go up and knock on the door and who is sitting next to the captain but the customs officer Hank, and I just about pooped my drawers. "Son, do you realize what you've just done? Do you realize this is wartime? You illegally crossed the border and made false statements. That is a case for high prosecution. Right now we can impound you and you're going to be up at our provincial prison in Ottawa making little ones out of big ones for about a year." All of a sudden, the captain says, "Relax, he's just scaring the crap out of you. But don't ever do that again." We talked and he and the captain were good friends. He said fine and dandy. Had I not been a friend of the Steeres I wouldn't have made it. I find out about a month later, the captain is coming into Marquette and my friend Chief is bringing him carton after carton of American cigarettes, which he puts aboard ship, and guess who is getting them? Hank at the border. They had a real conspiracy going.

We only sailed between Algoma and Marquette most of the time and loaded ore and came back. That would have been from about June through Labor Day, and then I had to come home and go to school. I was getting frantic notes from Mom and from the coach at school telling me they had already started, but I was having a hell of a good time and figured I'd stay as long as I could.

It was an old ship, 485 feet, built in the late 1800s. It had been sunk about five times. Because of WWII they needed every hull they could find to haul ore, and they had resurrected her again. Her top speed was about 9-10 knots. It was a beat up old bugger, but she floated. Late in the year, we get a notice we have to go Fort William and Port Arthur which is now known as Thunder Bay. All the grain from western Canada came in there and they had these grain elevators all over the place. We get up there and we had to wash the ship down inside to carry the grain because we carried both coal and iron ore. All the way up we work our buns off with these pressure hoses, crawling all over the place, hosing it down to get her clean. We get in there and here come the provincial inspectors. We failed the inspection and we had to do it all over again. We must have worked about 30 hours before we passed inspection.
I didn't know where we were going, but we were going all the way to Kingston, Ontario, and it took us six days to get there. I was getting so far away from home, and every time we stop to get a mail stop, it's "Darn it, get your butt home." I'm 15 years old, and I had never traveled before. I figured the safest thing for me was to ride that bugger all the way back to the Soo. I got off and Mr. Steere drove me home.

The next year I was 16 and I was old enough to work on this side, so I went down to the Soo right after school and went to the union hall. Those where the days you didn't know what the next ship was going to be because anything that floated could be used to haul ore. They called my name and they told me to report to Dock 2. U.S. Steel Company had the greatest fleet on the Great Lakes, and what do I end up on but the John Hulst, one of the newest ships in the Great Lakes. It was 700 feet, all welded, just a beautiful boat. I get on board and also find the third engineer is from Marquette, Ford Flannigan, and his father owned one of the greatest bars in Marquette.

That summer I sailed with captain Almon T. Patchett. He'd retired about 3-4 years before, but the war came along and they needed all the experience they could find so he was commissioned as a Coast Guard commander and given this new ship.

As time went on, I'd always go up to the wheelhouse on Sundays and whenever I could I'd ask if I could steer. They'd take it off the automatic pilot and I'd steer. I'd do this every weekend and sometimes in the evening after a day's work. I had done this quite a bit and one Sunday we're coming up Lake Michigan and we get into the straights of Mackinaw. I'd been steering about two hours, and the wheelsman comes up and says, "Let me know when you want me to take over." The captain tells him to get down and run my winch. Now it suddenly dawns on me, oh, crap. The captain said, "Son, you want to learn how to steer a ship, I'm going to teach you how to steer a ship today." We went into the straights and there was a little town called Detour. Now I know I'm in for it. All he told me was, "If you do as I say, we're never going to have a problem." I'm thinking I'm just going to bring him into the coal dock, and when he told me 10 degrees right rudder amidships blah,

blah. We go into the coal dock and just flat nailed it. It was so smooth, you couldn't even feel the ship when it hit the pilings. I can look down on the deck, and they're all giving me a hand. I'm thinking, "Oh, God, am I glad that's over." I say, "Thank you very much, sir, I'll go down on deck," and he said, "You will like hell."

What do I do now? He says, "I told you, you're going to learn to steer son." We backed out of there and I steered that sucker all the way up the St. Mary's River on a Sunday afternoon. My knees were shaking. I got her all the way up and I never missed a beat. By the end of the season, I was steering.

The second season I went on the Hulst again and then I enlisted. The captain wanted me to stay aboard and told me if I would stay he was sure he could get me an exemption. I didn't want to take a chance on it because I didn't want to go into the Army. They were incredible experiences. Captain Patchett was one of the wildest guys who ever captained a ship in the Great Lakes. He never slowed down for anything or anybody. When ships were moving, they would give five quick whistles and he'd been around so long he could tell by the echoes of that horn when he was getting close to another ship. I remember one day we had a whiteout and I'm up on the forecastle. You're right up in the bow and all of a sudden what do I see but a bowsprit coming right at me. I just turned around and I yelled, "Vessel dead ahead!" We stopped and the bowsprit is over my head here. As we get a little closer, I hear this guy from the other ship, "Patchett you dumb SOB!" He just knew how to handle a ship, but he'd scare you once in a while.

He was an eccentric old codger. When I first got there, about three or four days in they say "Captain wants to see you." Here he is sitting in this big wicker chair in the back of the chart room, and he'd say, "You like what you're doing?" The ship was pitching all over the place and he used to bring the young guys up there to get them seasick. I had never been seasick in my life and we talked up there for about 45 minutes. He said to me, "You ever get sick?" No, sir, I never have. He said, "You're doing a good job." A couple days later, he calls me up there again, and he's sitting in the chair. "You don't look as if you're old enough to shave." I say I don't shave very much. "You ever use a straight razor? Well, you're going to learn." He takes his hat off and puts it on the chart table and says, "You see that? I shave my head 20 times a summer. You're going to shave this head and if there's one nick in there you're going to pay for it." I lather him up, and you can't believe how scared I was, but I got the sucker done and I didn't put any nicks in it.

Another thing he did was he ended up with the damndest bunch of animals. He had about 10 rabbits aboard ship, and they'd be hopping all over the place at sea. All of a sudden we'd be coming into a storm and everybody and his brother was chasing these rabbits down to put them in cages so they wouldn't wash overboard. Then in his quarters in the bathtub, he had a pet alligator about three to four feet long. One day we go into Two Harbors, Minnesota, and all of a sudden I'm on deck at the time he walks out from the pilot house. "Slim, come here. See that guy over there. He's got something for me and I want you to go get it." I report to the guy and he gives me a box with a woodchuck in it. Guess who's feeding the sucker, me. It was a mean little sucker, but I'd feed it and water it. And this one trip we get down below and I go to feed the woodchuck and I couldn't find him. We were crawling all over the place, but we couldn't find it. Two months later we start shifting these timbers and we find out what had happened. It was a little rough and a couple of timbers had rolled off the pile and smashed the woodchuck.

He was an amazing guy, though. When he'd go in a storm and at that time I was on the deck watch, we had these big rods for measuring the ballast tanks. You'd go down, chalk the rod, send it down and pull it up and whatever the mark was you'd measure it. He'd want the ballast tanks at a certain depth. One day the watchman told me, "Don't go out there." We had a lifeline running down the middle of the ship but you didn't have life preservers. Pretty soon I'd hear, "Slim, where the hell are you?" I said, captain, the watchman said I shouldn't go out there. "Who the hell is running this ship? Not the watchman, I'll tell you that! Get out and sound those tanks. I'll give you five minutes to get out and sound them, and if I have to come down there, you're getting off at the first stop." He meant it, and out I got. I had a party, but I didn't get blown over.

He was a nice, nice guy. He'd sit up in the wheelhouse when there was a storm and he'd sit there and eat Bermuda onions like apples. The pilothouse would be all closed up because you'd get seawater and cold air in there. He was a character.

Those were the kind of things you could do during that time if you wanted to. All those experiences were there that you couldn't buy, and I was so fortunate to have the chance to do them. It was like being a soldier of fortune. I was available and I was fortunate enough to be in the right place at the right time, and my parents were pretty well condescending about such stuff.

Then when I got off that doober it was time to finish school and join the Navy.

CHAPTER 5
AHEAD OF MY TIME

I graduated high school and enlisted in June of 1943 when I was age 17 and five months. The reason I graduated at age 17 was when I went to kindergarten, I went into the room and sat down and I couldn't get my knees under the chair. The simplest solution was, "Well, he won't fit here, let's try him in first grade."

I knew when I turned 18 I was going to be drafted because the war was far from over in those days. I had been a Sea Scout growing up, I had sailed on the Great Lakes for two years, I lived on the water, worked with the guys on the fish boats; I mean I was Navy man all the way.

I went to boot camp in Farragut, Idaho at a brand new Naval Training Station just opened in the Rocky Mountains, probably 6,800-7,000 feet up. On a cloudy day, you'd be out on parade marching right through the clouds. The mountains above you were just so spectacular, I thought I'd gone to heaven at age 17.

When I graduated boot camp, they took the top 10 percent of the class to service school where you could come out with a rating or specialty, and I went to quartermaster service school. I ended with a quartermaster third class ranking, which meant you were a petty officer above just a seaman following service school.

While waiting to be assigned, there was field day meaning it was a Saturday when everybody scrubbed the barracks and did all the polishing and all that stuff which I didn't want to do. I had seen a message up on the board about exams going on for a naval aviation program. So I go to the exams, it took maybe four or five hours, and I missed the field day so everybody is giving me static when I get back.

The moment of reality arrived. Everybody was going somewhere, and every day you'd look at the draft list to see where you were going. The amphibious forces were getting everybody because they were getting ready for the march across the Pacific. One day I look and bingo! There's my name on a draft, and I'm going to Shoemaker, California, the home of the amphibious forces Pacific. They were going to teach me to drive a landing craft so to speak, and I was going to be carrying guys ashore and then backing off and going for more if I survived.

I accepted my fate and started to pack my gear when this guy comes along and says, "You lucky SOB, how did you get the draft you got?" It turns out I had passed my Naval Flight exam, and he had seen another list where I had been assigned to a college in New York state. When I see this thing, I go up to the officer in charge of my company and I ask him what's going on. He made a couple of calls and said your college draft takes precedence.

I reported to Hobart College in Geneva, New York, in October 1943. I was in class studying mathematics and different things that would give me the information I needed to learn navigation and eventually get involved in flight. I put two semesters in there and then went to Durham, North Carolina for a semester at Duke. From there I went to Pensacola, Florida, in June of 1944 and that's where I got my primary in advanced flight and eventually my transition flight.

I had three weeks of primary where they taught you to fly. You had 10 hours to solo, meaning if you couldn't solo in 10 hours, you were washed out of the program. I was a natural, and I soloed in an hour and 45 minutes. I had never flown a plane before.

When I was a little kid, Quaker Oats had a deal going where you could learn to fly by saving Quaker Oats labels and they'd send you this book on how to fly. This was a little stick-figure book, a very rough, cartoony type thing, but it showed you the stick and the pedals and described each thing. When you wanted to go up, you pulled back and when you wanted to go down you pushed forward, when you want to go left you push in your left pedal and push the stick to the left. I just devoured this book. I had that whole thing so committed to memory, I knew if I ever got a chance, I could fly. The minute I got into the airplane, that book and me and the airplane suddenly became one.

I had to do some other solo work, and it took me five hours total in the J3 Cub. Then I went to a transition plane, an open-cockpit biplane. Those were the days when you had the helmet, the goggles and the silk scarf. After 10 hours in that one, most of it cross country, I went into a Steerman, which was another biplane. That had a big engine, 450 horsepower, and that's when we started actual serious training. They were a tough airplane because they were very critical. People got killed in them. Then I graduated to the AT6, our transition to fighter aircraft.

By the time I got there, the fighter aircraft really wasn't built for someone of my size. I was 6-6 and 210 pounds and getting bigger, which meant I ended up getting involved in bigger aircraft, twin-engine control craft, the PBY, the Mariner. I didn't get any combat flying at all.

At that time an opportunity came for me to volunteer for a

mission that nobody knew anything about. They only wanted regular Navy personnel. I volunteered and didn't hear anything for about three or four weeks and all of a sudden I get orders in December of 1944 to report to Washington, D.C. That's how I got involved in Naval Intelligence and Communications Security, which was fascinating.

After I got my security clearance, I spent five weeks in intense training on all the encoding machines that the United States military had. They were the world's most sophisticated encoding machines. We were assigned to an underground radio station on the island of Oahu in Hawaii. We'd monitor all of the fleet files that came from San Francisco to Hawaii to the Philippines or Guam. We would also go aboard group flagships to monitor their radio shacks. We became privy to many of the top secret operations of the war in the Pacific.

I got into a couple of skirmishes in the Philippines Sea while we were aboard a carrier group. We were doing a destroyer group in Okinawa when they started Kamikaze-ing us, but we were involved only in the security part of that. We saw some combat but we were never part of the actual fighting.

When the war ended in the Pacific VJ day was pretty well just another working day. The war had ended, but we were still in areas where the word never got down that the war was over. A lot of guys were killed after VJ day because the word never got down to the Japanese troops.

Because I enlisted as a regular Navy person, I wasn't discharged until February 1, 1947. I had 60 days separation and I came home in time for Christmas in 1946. When I got home from the Navy, everybody was younger than me in college. Here I am the old dog and all these kids are 17 and 18 again. I'd been at school four days and I'm walking down the hall one day and this big guy comes up to me and looks at me and says, "Where the hell did you come from?" I said I just enrolled. "Where you been?" I've just been discharged from the Navy. "Where do you live?" In Marquette here. "Play basketball?" I said, Yeah, I did. He said "Practice is 4 o'clock, I want to see you there." He was the basketball coach.

I go down there at 4 o'clock and I didn't have anything with me so he gave me some shoes and stuff. We finished practice and I took a shower and here I am on the north side of Marquette and I'm living at home on the south side of Marquette which is at least six and a half miles away. No car. When I hitchhiked, I never stopped. I walked and hitchhiked, and if I got a ride I was lucky. I just stuck my thumb out about three times, and this car pulls up and this guy goes, "Now where the hell are you going?" It was Coach. He said, "Get in here." He drives me in this extra mile off the main highway to my place, and I thanked him for it. The next night I bring my own gear out, and I practiced Wednesday and Thursday and I'm in the starting lineup on Friday.

The quick return from the service and my immediate re-enrollment in school gave me no time to rehabilitate. I needed some space to just lay back and relax, so in the summer of 1947, these two friends and I, bought an Army surplus jeep. We rebuilt it, and one night under cover of darkness slipped out of Marquette and crossed the Canadian border and went up through Blind River to Hudson Bay. We got there in the middle of fly season, got eaten alive and left three days later.

We were gone for six and a half weeks total, with $200 apiece in our pockets. Our travels took us around the top of Lake Superior, and we took the old Trans-Canada Highway all the way west to the Big Bend country. We got to Calgary. We had never heard of Calgary or the Stampede, at that time a little local celebration. We decided to treat ourselves so we went to this bar to have a beer. At the same time, we asked around if there are any woods in the area so we could find a place to sleep. At the bar, this guy next to us asks, "Where are you guys from?" We hadn't shaved in weeks. We told him where we came from and that we were going to Big Bend country. He tells us about the Stampede, and we figure we'll stay a day or two. He invited us to follow him about five miles outside Calgary where he owned a big farm. He gave us a hay mow to sleep on, his wife made us breakfast every day and we could wash there and clean up. We stayed there three days. That's the only time we slept under a roof the whole trip.

I was still restless. I was majoring in business but wasn't really ready to finish college so I took a year and a half off in 1949 to figure out what I wanted to do with myself. I worked for a bottled gas company driving their big semi truck and played hard.

About that time Murph came into my life.

CHAPTER 6
MEETING MURPH

I first met Murph – actually I didn't meet her but I wanted to – in July of 1948. The buddies who went with me on the trip from 1947, used to run racing boats, and Munising, Michigan, always used to have a big Fourth of July celebration. We entered two of our little Class C hydros with outboards on them, and they've got these big ChrisCrafts and Hackercrafts and they're all saying, "Oh, my gosh, those poor guys with those little boats. They're just not going to get anything done." But they didn't know how fast Hydros can run. The water in Munising Bay was rougher than a cob, it was a big, big bay. Lo and behold if we don't sweep everything. The committee got so goldang mad they weren't going to pay us, but they eventually did.

After the races were over, we always had a deal, we'd go and get a few beers, and one guy would get the short straw and he'd drive so everybody else could go party. I had the short straw that night so we went to the dance hall on the outskirts of Munising. When we walked in, my best friend Dave Bennett saw Murph and said, "Hey, Wally, do you see that girl over there?" Yes, I did. Dave's dad was a doctor who worked with Murph who had just graduated from nursing school and thought the world of her.

I'm not a pushy type but did ask if she'd like to dance, and she just flat said no. She was with her two best friends, her girlfriend and her husband. That's the last of that, I thought, but a month or two later my mom was doing special duty at St. Luke's Hospital. I went to visit her one night and lo and behold who is at the nurse's station but Murph. She smiled when I came up. She knew my mom who came out and introduced us. That's when I found out Murph had graduated from St. Luke's Hospital School of Nursing, the same school my mother graduated from in 1918.

One thing led to another and I would go up and see Mom more often in the hopes I could see Murph again. She lived at the nurses home and was kind of one of the supervisors for the students. Eventually, I took her out for a soda or something and that date led to another and eventually we went to a hockey game and a relationship continued to develop.

Appropriately, our first date was a hockey game. I took her home and went to give her a goodnight kiss and pecked her right on the top of the nose. I figured that was it, I'd blown it and she'd never want to go out with me again. I've improved a little bit since then.'

I later asked her if she remembered my invitation to dance that Fourth of July in Munising, and she told me that at that moment the only think on her mind was her nurse's education and she was going to spend her life making her son's life as good as it could be. She was not interested in getting married or in men at the time.

Murph was the second of five girls in her family and graduated from Mather High School in Munising, Michigan, in 1941. She had been married, but her husband, Melvin Belfry, had been killed in a car accident in 1944. They had a son Mike who was about a year old at that time.

My mom loved Murph, and Murph loved my mom. If she hadn't liked mom, I don't think she would have paid any attention to me.

Mike was a catalyst to our relationship. Different guys had dated her a bit and she had taken them down to Munising to visit, and one of the things that was so important to her was, what was Mike's reaction to all these people? When he went thumbs down, it was see you later, that's it. When I met Mike, we went out into the woods and fished and things like that. Mike and I kind of hit it off. I didn't push myself on him. After a couple of times, it was obvious Mike and I were pretty compatible. He was four or five by then.

Everything was just right. Murph and I liked the same things. We had a lot of common bonds. We liked the outdoors, we liked the hike, we liked to hunt, we liked to swim, and we had mutual friends who were good people. We enjoyed each other and were compatible with each other's friends and families. It just worked out unbelievably well. It didn't take long to realize this was no ordinary lady.

The fact that I flew was a different dimension. I had a friend at the airport and I used to help him with his flight school, and I would sometimes fly Murph down to Munising for the day, about 45 miles from Marquette.

When I first started to court Murph, we'd go down for the weekend, and I didn't have any extra money. I had enough if we went out to get a couple of drinks and get something to eat if we went out dancing, but I sure didn't have any money to get a hotel room. Outside the city on the higher ground where the airport was, there were a lot of pine forests. So after the date, I had a car, I'd drive out and throw out a sleeping bag on the ground, sleep for the night and I'd get up the next morning. There were places where you could go and wash up.

One morning, as I'm sleeping in the woods, I hear something. I sit straight up and I'm looking right down the barrel of a rifle. This guy had been trapping coyotes, a coyote had pulled a peg and had the trap on him, and this guy had a dog and they were tracking the coyote. The coyote had apparently practically walked over my feet while I was sleeping, and the dog was on him. The dog made some quick reaction, and when he whined, apparently I woke up and when I sat up, this guy thought it was the coyote. He scared the hell out of me.

About a week later, Murph's dad heard this story from the trapper, and when she found out I was sleeping in the outdoors I was invited to stay at her house. It was part of our courtship.

In the fall of 1949, without any specific life objective, I proposed to Murph and she accepted, but sort of conditionally. She then made the wisest decision of my life. In her answer, she said, "Yes, but I do believe you should go back and finish your education, would you promise me that?"

We got married April 6, 1950, and I went back to school.

While I was going to school the second time, I took the summers off to work and make money. That's when I got involved in the LS&I Railroad. Murph was the operating room supervisor so she'd go to work at about 6-6:30 in the morning. I would get up and I'd have early classes to go to. Then, when I'd finish class, I worked on the railroad in the spring and the summer.

We didn't have a peaches and cream early life. We had our problems, mostly because of me, but they weren't major. It was a period of unrest for me but we lived through it because we were determined to live through it. That's a message that I have for anybody who wants to listen. Anybody can take the easy way out of something and end a relationship just because you are sick and tired of it or you are inconvenienced by it or whatever the case is, which means you lose the opportunity to have the experience of a lifetime by staying together, having children and weathering the storms and watching your whole dream develop. I thank the Lord that I had enough guidance and she had the tolerance to keep it going at a time we needed it to where we are today. I wouldn't change anything.

CHAPTER 7
HEARING RADIO'S CALL

That's when I finally got invited to go to work at the radio station which worked much better because I could go to school, I could work at the radio station and I could do some sports. That was the last job I had while I was in Marquette until I came to Fort Wayne.

The funny part is that none of this was any part of a plan. In the beginning, when I was going to school and stuff, I was not prepared to be a broadcaster and never gave it a thought. Then while I was working at a radio station in Marquette, they'd asked me to come over there and work because I had a bit of a reputation. I started doing hockey and other sports. It was a means to an end because I was going to college. I think I might have made 60, 65 bucks a week. I started in 1949. It fit in with my school pretty well and it was a winter job. I worked on the railroad, but they closed down in winter because it was an iron ore carrying railroad. Once the shipping was done, so was the railroad. There might have been 20 jobs for the year in the wintertime, but I was so far down on the seniority, I never had a chance for them. This came along and I was invited to try it.

You were everything. It was hi, would you run and do that newscast, OK, Wally will do that. Oh, by the way, I've got an hour this afternoon from 1 to 2, get some records and go on in. It was that kind of thing. But it was all independent. There was a little network, but very little. This was a commercial radio station, WDMJ. It was owned by the Daily Mining Journal, the Marquette local paper.

I had started with my exposure to doing some sports, which they'd asked me to try hockey after they found out I'd played. It was kind of fun doing it. I apparently had a little bit of a gift for gab, and I was fortunate that people knew me in town, and I knew a lot of people listened. It was the only station in town. I envisioned I was talking to a lot of people I knew which was kind of fun. That, of course, as I found out later was the objective of a good broadcaster, to find people to speak to, one on one. I talked to Murph a lot, when the kids grew up even down here, I talked to the kids a lot from the microphone to the house, or my comments were directed with their knowledge. So a lot of other people at the same time thought, Gee, he's talking to me. It's a secret to broadcasting success.

I didn't have a plan for anything. I had graduated from college. The job I had wanted hadn't materialized and that would have been staying in the Upper Peninsula and being an economic advisor for the Cleveland-Cliffs Iron Company on the economics of mining a ton of ore up on the range because they were having all kinds of labor problems. The mines were getting deeper and deeper. It cost more and more to mine a ton of ore, the strikes were getting more violent up there… they were having major problems, so here's the old cavalier Robert, I'm going to be the guy who's going to be the savior and explain to all these miners what it's all about. In the meantime, that job did not materialize because there was a strike going on and that's why I wasn't hired at the time. During that strike, a man who was 63 years old had to cross a picket line at a mine shaft in order to go down into a mine and start the pumps to keep the water levels safe so they would be able to mine when they got back. His own son who was on the line jumped him and beat the living daylights out of him to show what a great union man he was. I'm looking at that and thinking, Is this what I'm getting into? Is this the mentality of the people I have to work with? Not that I'm that superior, but I'm thinking if that's the way it goes when son beats up on father, that was it for me right there. I figured well I'll find something else somewhere.

I was relatively well known as an athlete. After the war when I came back, when I quit playing sports, the people at the radio station had known who I was. The guy who was the manager of the station had also broadcast some hockey so he was familiar with me through that, said, "Did you ever try broadcasting? C'mon down to the station, we'll talk." I went down and we talked and I went on a microphone and did a couple of things. Then he said, "You know I think you could do well." I'm thinking, "Yeah, sure." My moment there was still graduating and going into this Cleveland Cliff's Iron Company program, an educational program for miners. Had it not been for the strike of the miners, I would have either done something like that or been dead now from trying to cross the picket lines, but here I am in limbo.

I had called some games at home before that, but they were basically exhibition games between our Marquette team and other teams that we could get in for games. We played a team from the Soo one day, and I did the game and we sent it down the line to WSOO. They had Bruce Martyn doing their games, but he had moved on to WSAM in Saginaw so I went over and did the games there. In fact, Bruce came back and did color for me for a few games, and later on, he went into the Red Wings organization.

The first major game I did was the Soo Greyhounds of the Northern Ontario League and the Cincinnati Mohawks of the International Hockey League playing for the North American Amateur Hockey Championships at Pullar Stadium in Sault Ste. Marie.

Despite all that, I still wasn't convinced that was going to be my career by any means.

I had the greatest advisor in the world in my dad. He heard me do games on WDMJ in Marquette, and he'd say to me, "Bucko, for heavens sakes when I'm listening to the games, the one thing I'd like to know is what's the score? Don't keep it a secret." There were other little things that he would just comment on as time went by to help make me more aware of what people wanted to hear.

It came kind of naturally because I was still a player and through my eyes, I was still in the game and it made it easier for me to do the games. I was always pretty objective, as I am yet today. I rarely get involved and be critical. Some of the things I would refer to were different, but that was small-town radio. It was kind of funny and people used to like it because I'd say something, and they'd say the next day, "I know just what you were talking about!"

Before I came to Fort Wayne, I probably had done about 35 games over a period of two years. I had done some high school basketball and high school football and a little college basketball. I was in an element that I was well aware of having played a lot of sports and enjoying them. It kind of helped me put myself in the mood of the games. Maybe if I hadn't played I'd have been a little more reticent to express myself. It came kind of almost too easy.

Coming to Fort Wayne was a case of right place, right time. This friend of mine gets married, I'm in his wedding party. He was married at 11 o'clock so I buzz off and do a noon newscast, and then go out to the reception. His aunt was from Fort Wayne, and while riding to the reception, she heard me on the air. When she got back to Fort Wayne she called the station manager who was a good friend of hers and said "I heard this guy in Marquette, Michigan, I think you better talk to him. They called out of the blue. The fella says, "We've got a good report, send us tape, will you." I say, "OK, fine."

I dismissed it completely and I go back to my job and spun my records and worked my job. About three days later, the phone rings and it's the same guy saying, I'm still waiting for that tape! All of a sudden I heard the station manager on the extension listening to my conversation which ticked me off. He's eavesdropping on my private conversation, so I said to the man, "I just sent that last night, it should be there in a day or two." Then I promptly recorded what I was doing, put it on tape and sent it out. A week later they call and say come down for an interview which I did. I got in on a Saturday in the middle of June, met with the people, had the audition and went back home. They call me and say, "Hey, hey, hey, come to work." On July 1, I was here.

I really had no formal training in broadcasting until I came to Fort Wayne and went to work for Westinghouse, and they were the greatest broadcast training ground in the world. Again, it wasn't something I had really thought was going to be a career, but when I got here, after about a month I realized this could be. Then I began to realize what an incredible organization Westinghouse was. They were the hallmark of broadcasting, bar none, and as I grew into this thing and got to know the people, apparently I had a gift for the business that I wasn't even aware of. I had many compliments and a lot of opportunity to learn. I figured, oh, what the heck, it's better than working, so here I go.

CHAPTER 8
IN THE NAME OF CHANGE

The minute I was hired, before I ever went on the air, Guy Harris, the program manager said, "One thing you are going to have to do is change that name." My hackles went up, and I said, "Oh, no, I don't, that's my name and I'm proud of it!" He says, "It's too long. It has to be short and catchy. That's the only reason."

Then he began to tell me all these different people who changed their names, so I accepted that. He said, "Go home and talk it over with the wife and let me know in a day or two what you want to be called." I said, "Well, what the heck, I've got it already. I'll keep the name Bob and just call myself Bob Chase." He said, "Where the hell did you come up with that?" I said, "Be careful, that's my wife's maiden name." From that moment on, before I ever hit the air I became Bob Chase. My wife was pleased, my father-in-law was proud as a peacock because all he had was five girls, so I was his boy.

When I first changed my name, there were times I'd finish off a show and all of a sudden my name would pop out. It was just automatic because at home I always use my own name. I explained it to my folks. I told them and I told the station I would never ever legally change my name. I'm extremely proud of the heritage our family has.

I came down here July 1, and then Murph came down October 1 and Mike came down December 15, and we were a family again. That's the way it stayed for a couple of years. In fact, we were concerned for a while that we were not going to be able to have children. Everything seemed to be healthy on both sides, but we just couldn't kill a rabbit. All of a sudden, bingo, everything worked out wonderful and that was Kurt who was born in 1955. Karen came along in 1958 and David in 1962. With Michael, we had our family of four.

The kids were all Wallensteins, and I think that gave them anonymity that was good for them. They lived their own lives in school, and their friends all got to know who their dad was, but I think it gave them an advantage to be themselves which was great.

Nobody down here ever called me Wally because nobody knew me as that. When I go home, my friends still call me Wally. All my kids were called Wally.

CHAPTER 9
TAILING THE KOMETS

When I got here, July 1, 1953, the guy who was WOWO's sports director at the time was Ernie Ashley. He did Big Ten football and he did Komet hockey. All of a sudden it's fall, and Ernie goes down to Bloomington to do IU football, so the program director says to me, "I notice from your resume you've done some hockey. We're doing these Komet games and I want you to do the games until Ernie comes back from Bloomington. You start it, and Ernie will come back and join you on the Saturday games."

Apparently, they liked what I did a lot. Ernie, even though he was from Minnesota, hadn't done much hockey. Because he was from Minnesota, they assumed he knew hockey. After about five weeks, people are starting to talk about this guy who is doing the Saturday games, at which point Ernie starts to come back a little quicker. The engineer who went with Ernie to Bloomington liked me so what he would do on the way back was driving very slowly to make sure Ernie couldn't get back so I could get the games going. So Ernie started driving his car to Indianapolis and he'd pick it up there and race home. He'd walk in the building, sit down in his seat, grab the mike and away he'd go. It was just, "Hi folks, thanks, Bob, I'm back and ta da da da and away we'd go."

Apparently, Ernie had been putting out a few feelers to try and find a bigger market for himself, and about Christmas time it turned out he had a chance to go as a program director at a station in Springfield, Ohio. It was a management position, and that's what Ernie wanted, so he's gone. All of a sudden, it's January, and guess who's doing Komets hockey?

CHAPTER 10
HYPING HOOSIER HYSTERIA

Ernie had also broadcast whatever other sports there were, so comes March, here's IHSAA basketball tournament. In those days we would go to Kendallville and do the sectionals there because they fed into the Fort Wayne Regional. Len Davis and Hilliard Gates and anybody who had a microphone and could talk was doing the Fort Wayne Sectionals.

That was my first spring to do basketball and it was 1954 and history tells in 1954 the championship game of the IHSAA Tournament at Butler Fieldhouse was won by Milan. There I am, the first time I've ever done a high school championship and what do I get – the epic of all-time. I didn't know it at the time because I couldn't quite believe this was Indiana basketball because I was used to class basketball in Michigan, and I'd experienced what it was like not only to play high school ball but also to win a championship. At the time I did it, the Indiana tournament didn't seem like anything special to me. I was always for class basketball because I had grown up with it and I could see what it meant for kids who worked hard for four years to believe they still had a good chance of winning a championship. I was always appalled to think they would match up of some of the teams they matched up. Here were these little schools with no possible chance of winning because they might have had 30 guys to choose from going against schools of 3,000.

For the most part, the format proved that until Milan came

along and punched a hole in it. I had never ever seen a high school or a college game that was so blatantly delayed by one man, Bobby Plump. He's standing at center court holding the basketball for four and a half minutes of play. I'm like, This is Indiana? Wow. I couldn't believe in a championship game that one guy would stand there with the ball under his arm and not even move. Nobody came to get him, and it was totally mind-boggling. They'd make a few moves and nothing would happen. There was no movement in the game, and I couldn't understand it. They didn't even move the ball around the perimeter, they just stood there.

I filled the time as best I could. Fortunately I had Cal Stewart with me who was doing my color, and he was very glib as well. We were somehow able to fill the time. We're pulling through every reference we had to keep it alive. It got to the point where I just had to say I had never experienced anything like this in my lifetime.

Lo and behold, what happens to it but it becomes immortalized. When the movie "Hoosiers" came out, the movie was better than the game. They couldn't afford 4½ minutes of nothing in the movie. It didn't mean anything to me at the time except I didn't think it was a very good game.

CHAPTER 11
KEEPING MY DAY JOB

When I started at WOWO, I was a staff announcer and that meant you had a schedule you went by and you did station breaks and all that kind of good stuff. You had a few little record shows you'd do on the weekend and stuff like that, but it was strictly a journeyman job when I first got started until Ernie left. I was still a desk jockey as a staff announcer and a sports announcer so I had daily sportscasts I was responsible for.

Those were back in the days when sportscasts were 15 minutes to a half hour when you could really do a sportscast with a lot of interviews and things like that.

The first thing I realized was how big WOWO was because when you got there, you'd look at this big map of the world up on the wall, and there were little pins stuck in it all over the place. I asked what those were for, and they said, "That's where we've gotten letters for WOWO's reception." South America was very, very strong, England, France, Germany, Africa, Australia. It was so mind-boggling when you turned a microphone on the responsibility that you had because of the territory that was covered. You were in awe of the fact that you were working for a radio station of that caliber. As I've said so many times, Westinghouse being the owner of that, it couldn't get any better than it was. It was better than working for NBC or CBS. It was a thrill and a privilege that will forever be in my life.

In 1954 Westinghouse began to clean out all their soap operas and drop NBC and ABC networks because they realized there was a lot more lucrative income in the local markets, but they were all plugged up because they had nothing but network stuff on. As soon as they could phase out contracts, they'd end up with a half hour of radio time, maybe from 11 to 11:30 in the morning. Their big wheels came in, and every time a half hour would open up, guess what, there'd be Bob and I'd be filling in with music. I'd get a half hour here and an hour there.

Finally, when they got it all cleared out and began putting people in place, Westinghouse said, "OK, buddy you're the guy who sort of blazed the trail. You get the choice. Do you want morning or afternoon drive?" I said afternoon drive and I was never sorry for it because this was a real factory town and between 3 and 5 p.m., this town was like an anthill with all the factories changing. We called it "The Bob Chase Show" and I was on from 3-7 in the evenings, and there would be newsbreaks in there along the way. There would be the 6 p.m. news slot which would last a half hour and then I'd come back and finish it off until 7 p.m.

I had a very successful run as a jock in town. At one time I had a 78 share of the audience at 4 p.m., one of the highest ratings in the country at the time. We were all powerful. Westinghouse made us that way because they were a scientific company who knew how to prepare broadcasts to air and catch the ear of the public. With the 50,000-watt signal, we were all over North America, and everybody knew WOWO. At one point and time, Bob Sievers was the No. 5 disc jockey in all of the United States. I was 11th at the time. That's the kind of broadcasting excellence that Westinghouse knew how to develop.

When I started my show, I understood what my responsibilities were and the important thing in those days you had to focus on music and timing. It wasn't just grab some records and run, there's an incredible science when you are programming music on radio. At that point, you didn't have a lot of time to talk because you were so loaded with commercials. When jockeying was big in the early 1950s, record companies were turning out records that were like three minutes, three and a half minutes long or better. All of a sudden they realized, if they wanted to get their records played, they better be two minutes to two minutes and 15 seconds or you couldn't afford to play them.

At that time you still didn't have a lot of time to talk, but I managed to work my way around it in a way that almost got me in trouble. If I had a problem or had something in my craw, I would say, "Boy, just got a letter from down in Huntington yesterday, and they're talking about such and such. They're saying, this is right, that's wrong. I don't know, how do you feel about that?" So I'd let it go, and one day the general manager said to me, "Chase I've been listening to you on the air reading those letters. That's fine, but I'm the only person who editorializes on this station, and you better remember that." Well, if he'd have ever asked me for an actual letter, I'd have been gone. I did get some letters, but it was one way I could relieve my mind of some issues.

If I was going to go on the road for a hockey game, I would come in at 11 a.m. and do the show on tape. Then I'd be gone so my show would play. We were in the air seven days a week. We weren't in the studio seven days on the week because on Sunday we had a group called the Fabulous Four and we would do four hours of music from Noon to 4 p.m., an hour apiece which we taped on Friday or Saturday. The Fabulous Four were myself, Jack Underwood, Marv Hunter and Cal Stewart. I left the Fabulous Four in 1967 when I was named marketing and promotion manager, and I think it lasted until 1971.

Whatever I did, I was always very fortunate because I had my family at home. From Mike on down to David, I bracketed about every age group imaginable in youth so I knew their likes and dislikes and I was cool, man. I knew all the lingo, and it helped me immensely in how to play my music, when to play certain kinds of music when I knew the kids were listening, and I knew there were times when I knew the kids weren't listening so I got back into the adult music.

One of the things back in the early days of record spinning, you didn't have to be a rock jock, a country jock, pop jock. You were an entertainer, and you had a music library full of the greatest artists in the world. During one program in a four-hour basis, I might play rock and roll, Bill Haley kind of stuff for 15,

20 records, I might play Frank Sinatra, Perry Como all this kind of thing, and female artists and groups, big bands and country and western. There was something there for everybody, and everybody liked all music. They weren't forced to segment at that point. I would even get into at certain times more than kind of album type of music. You had to justify when you played it, why did you play it? I had to be able to explain it to the program director.

If I had a program on Monday, I had to have my sheets for Wednesday's show turned in before I went on the air on Monday, the reason being they always wanted to know what you were playing because it was the payola days, when they were paying jocks big bucks, and they wanted to see if there was any kind of pattern going on to what you did. Were you being influenced by anyone to play their music? We were in an unusual position because WOWO was one of the test-market positions in the United States because of our isolation in a small market and our amazing power all over the country. A lot of products were advertised on our station before they ever went national, and a lot of music was the same way. We were the second station in North America to have a Beatles record. These were the kind of things that we enjoyed the privileges we had. You better not violate the privilege or the honor of working for this company will be short-lived and if you got fired by Westinghouse people really took a look at you.

There was a lot that went into building a program. You'd sit there at the turntable and listen to music. You took a lot of time to build a program, and you did the same thing every day, and I was always doing sports. Maybe I'd go off the air at 7 p.m., and then I'd come on again a half hour later from Kendallville or Huntington or Marion doing a ballgame. I'd go in and tape the whole show, and everything was as if it were live.

On the weekends, I also did a show on Saturday afternoon from Noon to 6 p.m. in the summer times. I did what we called "Parade of Bands" stuff. There were so many great bands in those days and they had so many great solo artists who were stars in their own right. I might do a half hour of Benny Goodman and a half hour of Nelson Riddle and come back with Harry James.

As for the new stuff, we had a music board and they would judge the music every week that we were going to keep in the system. We didn't care about the Billboard charts. Yes, we kept a lot of that, but some of the Billboard stuff wasn't desirable and we didn't play it. It never hurt us a bit.

Those were the kind of things that gave me an appreciation for the industry. You look at guys today like Howard Stern and Don Imus, these guys wouldn't have been able to push mops to wipe the floor when real radio was going. They couldn't cut it. Now it's all specialized, little niche radio going on all over the place and it's all chopped up. I have a very strong feeling that the kind of programming that made radio great could again make it great if somebody had the courage to do it.

I did the show from 1954 to about 1967, and that's when I went to administrative side of the company but I still stayed on in sports.

WOWO just had incredible power to pull people in. I used to do vacation relief when I was the assistant program director, filling in for everybody else. My favorite shift was the all-night show starting at midnight. You were heard all over the world. One night I get a phone call. This sultry-voiced gal starts kidding me and finally she says, "I'm sorry but we have to go back to work."

They were long-distance operators in Baltimore, Maryland, and they were listening to the radio in their lounge. I mentioned that on the air, and half an hour later, a woman calls and thanks me very much because they had a new baby who was colicky and she was walking the floor with the baby in Dallas Texas. All of a sudden the phone rings and this guy says with a real southern drawl. He says, "Tell you what I do, I'm an all-night guard at a peanut warehouse on the Georgia-Alabama border." He had the wildest old drawl you ever heard in your life. Then I got a call, and a man goes, "If you can guess where I'm from you get the grand prize." This guy was on a yacht in the Caribbean sailing along.

Security guards from the U.S. embassies in South America used to call us. We were a worldwide signal and it was just unbelievable who we heard from. It was a tremendous responsibility when you started to realize the power of that radio station and the loyalty with which people listened. That was built by people like Bob Sievers, Jay Gould and Jane Weston who was our women's service director. They built credibility into the radio station that still exists almost out of myth. When you come into an atmosphere like that, it's mind-boggling.

CHAPTER 12
WE'RE TALKING TO...

I had a wonderful time on the show and got to meet and interview some wonderful people. The record companies would call your program director and say, "Hey, I've got the possibility of da, da, da, da... would you like to have one of them?" So then Guy would say, "Hey, we got a chance to get so and so," and then we'd try to get whoever fit the mood of the show I was doing at the time. We would wire tape the interviews and then play them on the show. If someone was in town, then the promoter would bring them into the studio and we would do them live. It was tough to do them live during the week because you were so limited to the amount of time you had. You had to be able to control it. Maybe you'd have to break an interview up that was seven minutes long, and you'd have to do 2:15 segments, and you had to plan on that when you were doing the interview to make sure it fit.

I think the first interview I did anywhere on the air was with Gordie Howe, and that was in the Upper Peninsula. One of the first ones I did down here was Polly Bergen.

I guess one of the most important persons I interviewed early on was Richard Nixon. The national plowing contest was going on in Roan, Indiana, and he came in as the vice president at the time. I think Harold Ickes was the Secretary of Agriculture, and I interviewed him. When Nixon came along, nobody knew if they were going to get him or not, and all of a sudden, boom, he shows up, and Jay Gould had done a piece with him and Jay brought him over to me. When I saw him coming, I'm going, "Oh, brother, now what do I say?" I survived.

I never did interview a president, but I've done vice presidents. I never caught them when they were presidents. Maybe I was the reason they were elected at the time. The funny story with Dan Quayle was he was at Orchard Ridge that year for the Mad Anthonys and he was the Red Coat celebrity. He was pretty much covered by security and I managed to sneak through on the driving range, and I said to him, "Mr. Vice President, can I talk to you?" He looked around and "Oh, my gosh, Bob, c'mon over." So the Secret Service people were kind of looking. They weren't sure, but if Dan Quayle said so, I guess it's all right. So in that interview, we talked about music, Indiana, WOWO, and his life, and he said, "You know, I'll never ever forget you because of all the record hops you used to do at Hiers Park. Do you ever remember a snotty-nosed kid about 10 or 11 who kept bugging you all night to play Bill Haley's `Rock Around the Clock' one more time?" I said, "As a matter of fact I do," and it was him.

When the Beatles made their first tour in 1964, we took a group to Indianapolis as a part of a promotion. We got into what amounted to their post-concert deal. We got five minutes to do something with them, and you had to make your choice because they only had so much time available. When you filled out your interview card and your affiliation, you had to come up with a guy, and I picked Ringo Starr. He didn't say much. They were still almost in awe of themselves because they were hot where they were in Liverpool and throughout that area, but when they came here they knew it was going to be big but they couldn't even anticipate how big it really was.

I interviewed Bob Hope several times at Mad Anthony tournaments. He was always a very delightful guy. I didn't know what to expect with him, and basically, you feed him a line and he's gone. You just hope you can hang on and follow him. He was very kind, very gracious, truly, truly a very funny man. He didn't need writers, he had such a wealth of experience, but he could get very serious when he wanted to. He was quite pleased to be there because of the big league nature of that entire tournament and thought it was one of his favorite celebrity tournaments.

Anita Bryant was almost a regular with us. She listened to us all over the country, and she'd call in. Sometimes she'd be traveling late at night with her husband, and she might just call to talk with Marv Hunter for a while. Other people did that, too in the record business. Maybe they'd call my show in the afternoon if they were going across the toll road. We were a very important station in the lives of talent.

One of the most interesting stories was a total surprise to me. On Nov. 26, 1956, Tommy Dorsey died at 4:20 in the afternoon, and at 6 p.m. we had a half-hour news spread. I was the jock from 3 to 7 so I would also read the introductions and the formats to the news people. I read the introduction to the news at 6 p.m., and that's the lead story. Then the story says, "Be sure to stay tuned to WOWO because Wednesday night at 8 p.m. Bob Chase will narrate a two-hour documentary on the life and music of Tommy Dorsey." That's the first I heard of it, but here across the glass was the program director Guy Harris just laughing his hind end off and I'm going, "Now what do I do?"

Guy says, "OK, boys, let's roll up our sleeves and go. We're committed to this." So we agree we've got to find all the people around Dorsey's life that we can. I remembered that Toots Shore's in New York was a great place that Tommy Dorsey loved. I called Toots Shore and I talked to him and explained who I was and what we were about to do. He gave me a little thing himself, and then he said, "Just a moment, I'll see if I can get some other people for you here who are friends of Tommy's." So pretty soon he comes back, "Mr., Chase?" I say, "Yes." "Just a moment." Pretty soon this voice comes on and says, "Hello." I say, "Yes, I'm Bob Chase," and he says, "I'm Nat Cole," and I about fell off the chair. I do this beautiful interview with Nat Cole, and Toots Shore comes back and says, "Was that OK?" I say, "Sir you blew me right off my feet. I can't believe this." He says, "Is there anybody that you would specifically like to have?" I said, "I guess if it's anybody, it's Frank Sinatra. I just think he would add too much to it." He was Tommy's vocalist before he broke out on his own. He says, "Can I have your phone number there? I'll call you back in a few minutes." The phone rings and here's Toots Shore again, and he says, "OK, Bob, now here's the number to call, and you call between 8:30 and 8:45. If you miss the window, forget it. That's the time you can talk to Frank Sinatra."

So I thanked him and 8:30 comes around and I'm dialing the number and Frank Sinatra answers the phone. Toots Shore had it all set up. It was a great interview, a great time, and that was really before Sinatra was really up there. He was big and he was important, but he got more important as time went on. He was an incredible interview, very polite, very nice.

The highlight entertainment interview of my life probably was Elvis, no doubt about it. He came here to the coliseum on March 31, 1957, and this was the smallest venue he played in all of his early tours. He was hot off the Ed Sullivan Show and controversy was just surrounding him with all his gyrations and everything else. The people who brought him in here were the people who owned the hockey club, Ernie Berg and Harold Van Orman, so naturally, I got the pole position. He only allowed two interviews and Ann Colone got one and I got one. Chivalry wasn't dead at that time, we had 15 minutes so I said, "Annie, go ahead, you're first." Annie talked and talked and talked and even Elvis was getting a little edgy. She finally winds it up and I've got about four and a half minutes left. So Elvis says to Colonel Parker who is standing there, "Can we give him some more time?" and the Colonel says, "If you want to, yes. Go ahead, Mr. Chase."

It was a great interview and Presley was so humble it was scary. He was just totally polite, expressed himself very well, and it was just a bit of a surprise because I thought he might be difficult to interview. Instead, he was almost too easy because he responded so well.

We talked a little bit about religion because he had come from a Gospel background. He was a deeply religious guy, he wasn't a junkie. He was a classy young kid. Then we talked about his style, and he said, basically his style was a religious style, and it was. The revival stuff was in that kind of tempo and their backgrounds and arranging were that way. The church people in the South were very expressive in their music and physical in their music. He brought that to the world stage, and the people out of the South in those days when there was little television or little knowledge of how they celebrated religion weren't used to this. This became a cult of its own, offensive initially to a lot of people. Even Ed Sullivan wouldn't let a camera go to his waist, but when you see what has gone on since then, Elvis was not a trailblazer, he was a saint. It was a real top thrill in my life.

I began to thank him for making Fort Wayne a stop at a time when he was the hottest talent in the world. We were so pleased he was coming and I was so thrilled to have a chance to interview him, and he said to me, "Mr. Chase, I just want you to know we're happy to be in Fort Wayne. I've heard an awful lot about you and the Bob Chase Show and it's really a privilege to be interviewed by you." Oh, boy!

The interview was about six minutes, but the story doesn't end there.

We had a fellow on our air Jim O'Brien who went to Cleveland from WOWO to become the program director for the all-sports station in Cleveland. He called me one day when the Rock and Roll Hall of Fame was in its construction stage yet and said, "By the way, you wouldn't happen to have that interview you did with Elvis?" I said, "Yeah, Jimmy, I've got it, but it isn't the original. I don't know where that went." I had no idea where the original ended up, but a listener had taped the interview, and years later they were clearing out their attic and found it. He called me and said, "Bob I don't know if you'd like this or not, but we ran across your interview with Elvis. We were cleaning up, and we were listening to some tapes, and lo and behold there it was." I made a copy and sent it to Jim O'Brien and he and his engineering group enhanced it.

Then he called and asked if I still had the picture that we had taken at the time. He said, "If you can send me a picture, I think we're going to be able to get this into the Rock and Roll Hall of Fame." I sent the picture up and, yes, it did get into the Rock and Roll Hall of Fame. There was the picture, and a little story and when you punched the button you could hear the interview. It stayed in the Rock and Roll Hall of Fame for about six or seven months. Then the Presley group came up from Memphis and at that point, they had to OK every single Presley item once it became an official deal, and the first thing that went was my interview because it wasn't sanctioned.

Another interesting time was President Kennedy's assassination. I think that was one of the most emotional things I've ever done. I didn't believe in this day and age in the United States of America that kind of thing could happen. I was still an idealist, and it was inconceivable and especially John Kennedy because, to me, he was the epitome of what America should look like – young and vibrate and expressive. He was an exciting president to me.

We were in a staff meeting at the time, and our news director Hal Cessna hears the bells were going crazy on the AP and UPI machines so he left the meeting and went to the newsroom and he was gone for a little while. He came back, and Hal was a very quiet, very under control person and he was a tremendous newsperson. He just walked in and said, "Excuse me, gentlemen, but I think you are going to want to hear what I have to say. President Kennedy has just been assassinated." Then he started to choke up. Jack Underwood was on the air at the time and he got so emotional he couldn't continue. Everyone one of us were emotional. Cal Stewart had it going for a while and then Cal couldn't handle it any longer, and then I took over and I went for a long period of time and then Hal Cessna came back and did some more.

We immediately went into dirge music. All regular programming stopped. The Washington Bureau went online with all Westinghouse stations, and then we did other things as we saw fit, whatever news areas we had, biographical stuff, local reaction when we had it, state reaction and this kind of stuff. We just fanned out our contacts wherever they were and used them when we had a chance. When Westinghouse news wasn't on the air, we did what we could. We had so much background that was coming through from AP and UPI that we no problem filling airtime and it was all so fresh and new because it just kept coming and coming. We just continued that for many, many hours and then it settled down a little bit as time elapsed. We stayed in dirge mood with no music whatsoever for at least 24 hours.

CHAPTER 13
MEETING THE BEST AND THE BRIGHTEST

I also always did a lot of sports interviews. Back in the good old days, I interviewed just about anybody who ever went through the Mad Anthony charity golf tournaments. I interviewed Jack Nicklaus and he was just out of Ohio State at the time. Jack was still rather new at what he was doing but very articulate. He had a heck of a day that day, and I think he had shot a 64.

Lee Trevino was one of the funnier ones I ever did. He had a runner who would keep him in beer so every place that Lee went he had a cold beer. He still hit the ball terrifically well. He was playing with Tommy Bolt, and here he is on the green at 18 in two shots. He's got a long putt for an eagle, and if he makes it he's got Bolt closed out. Here's Bolt under a great big pine tree in two, and he's trying to see how he's going to get out of there. In the meantime, Lee is up on the green joking with the gallery and having a great time. He was so funny. So Bolt finally gets set up and takes his shot and holes it out for an eagle, at which point everybody goes crazy. Trevino missed the eagle putt and Bolt wins.

Trevino was not lewd or anything. He was a little gamey on some of his remarks, and some of the people decided they never wanted him back again. The thing is he donated his whole purse to the charity, what they paid him to come in. We never got Lee back which was just a shame, because he was just a people person. He talked to everybody. He was just a fun guy to interview.

CHAPTER 14
FLYING THROUGH THE BIG TEN

During the falls, I broadcast 14 years of Big Ten football, starting in 1957. Paul Haberley ran one of the local banks, and he and Tom Longsworth, the radio sales manager, were very, very close. One day Paul said, "What are the chances of you guys doing Big Ten football again? Tell you what, if you guys give me a prospective Big Ten schedule, get it priced out, let's go have lunch and talk about it and I want Bob to do it." I had done football before but not Big Ten football. So we met and agreed to do a rotating schedule. The only game we were obligated to do was the Old Oaken Bucket game. It also gave us an opportunity to take Notre Dame games away from South

Bend because Mutual had the exclusive contract for games there so whenever Notre Dame went to Purdue, Northwestern or Michigan State where we had a chance to get to them we would do that. We also always did the Michigan-Michigan State game. The one game I never got to do was the Michigan-Ohio State game because it was always the same day as the Indiana-Purdue game.

When we'd get into hockey season, rather than driving we'd leave at 8:30 a.m. and I'd fly up wherever the game was, and then I'd fly home at night and do the hockey game. When we had the long distance runs like to Champaign and Iowa City we took a twin engine. We could get up and hum about 230 or 235 so we could get back in time for the hockey games.

Maybe the most famous game we did was the Notre Dame-Michigan State game from 1966 which turned out to be for the national championship. Don Chevilet was my color man, and that was a real charged game because there was a lot on the line that day. It was a hard-fought game and that was Michigan State back in the days of Duffy Daugherty. He had some of the quickest, most disciplined teams you'd ever see. He could play with anybody the way he coached because he had a light line and they never went straight up, they cross blocked and took you on at an angle. They'd have sort of an unbalanced alignment on the line, and when they would take you they had guys who were 220 pounds handling guys who were 260 270 just because they knew how to do it.

I think that was the year for Michigan State. They had these signs that said, "Kill, Bubba, Kill," for Bubba Smith. Then I remember one year they had this sign that said, "Hail Mary Full of Grace, Notre Dame is in second place." It was amazing right after the game is over this big banner came out.

This time the game ended 10-10, and Notre Dame sat on the ball at the end and you wondered what they were doing.

We had to do a hockey game that night so we flew up there. We had some weather and stuff so a pilot went with us. Gunnar Elliott was a seasoned campaigner when it came to press boxes and broadcasts and all the other stuff, and he used to tell me, "If you get to someplace and you want to make sure you got a cab, when you go from the airport to the stadium, you tell the cabbie, `You be right here at the end of the game and I'll give you tip.' Then rip a $20 in half and give him one half. I guarantee you he'll be there at the end of the game." So Chevy and I come out of the tower and the press box at Michigan State and the cabbie is right there. Who is trying to talk the cabbie into taking him to the airport but Johnny Lujack who was broadcasting for Notre Dame that day. Lujack is trying to talk him into taking him back to the airport because he had something to do that night in Chicago and he had to get back to the airport to catch a plane. We come over, and he says, "Is this your cab?" and I say, "Yeah it is, Luj, why?" He says, "Jeez, this guy won't budge, what did you do?" So he says he's going to the airport and so are we so I invite him to come along. We get in the cab and I give the cabbie the other half of the $20 and Lujack goes, "What's that for?" I say, "That's his tip, that's why you couldn't get him." The cabbie shows him the other half, and "Luj says that's a hell of an idea. I'll never forget that one." So Luj pays the cab fare back to the airport.

CHAPTER 15
COVERING "THE SPECTACLE"

I started covering the Indianapolis 500 in 1955. I had met Dick McGeorge who was a big wheel for Champion Spark Plugs and did all their racing public relations. I got to talking to Dick about a lot of things and we decided one year we were going to do some 500 coverage. I was in my first year of what we called 500 Countdown. I was going to spend the month of May down there, and then we were going to edit it all out to do seven hours of radio from 10 p.m. at night until 5 a.m. the night before the race.

Dick said he'd sponsor that seven hours. He ended up getting me Champion Sparkplug credentials, and I had pit passes. At 5 a.m., Billy Wolf, who was the engineer, and I would jump in the wagon and I'd sleep in the back seat. We'd get down there 7:30-8 a.m. We'd file reports, and I'd file them on behalf of Westinghouse News Bureau in Washington, D.C. and we'd do progress reports on different lap times. It was off the top of our heads so I'd ad-lib stuff. There was a bank of pay phones right next to the pits, inside the fence, so I'd hang a sign an "Out of Order" sign on the one phone. Nobody seemed to want to test it, so I'd run over there, look around, and pull the sign and make my call. I had a phone whenever I needed it.

Whoever was available, anybody who was anybody, I interviewed. From the oldtimers of the day, the Roger Wards, Parnelli Jones kind of guys, AJ Foyt was just a rookie – all those people were just part of the standard interview process. I did the entire thing from 1955 to 1979 when it was getting to the point where it was very difficult to work there any more. The fellow who was running the racetrack at that time was strictly a TV man and they didn't want anything to do with radio for a while.

When it came to auto racing, I met the greatest of the great. I interviewed literally hundreds of them over the years and made good friends of many of them, among them Parnelli Jones. I got to know Eddie Sachs and he was one of the funniest guys I ever knew. He was one of the first guys to start driving the rear-engine four-wheelers. He found a new groove in the racetrack for those cars. He made a wider attack when he went into the corners. He wasn't the usual guy who would go diving into the turn, drift into the wall and then dive into the corner and drift out to the wall. He made a wider attack when he cut into the corners and he put a new groove into the track and as the racecars advanced they all started to use it. He was a crowd favorite, always a grandstander. The one year he said to me, "You know what, they laugh at me but I'm winning this thing this year." I said, "OK, tell me how you're going to do it." He said, "Don't say anything, but I found out how to cheat in the corners." That was a year he ran into a wreck and burned to death on the front straightaway.

I saw all these guys come in as rookies. A.J. Foyt was an unusual guy because once he got his car qualified, he would dedicate as much time as he could to getting everybody else up and running. He was just a magical guy with cars. He always turned his own wrenches and he just knew how to tweak little things and make things happen. This one day I'm in the pits, and A.J. is coming down the pits, and I say "A.J., Bob Chase, I'd like to have a chance to talk to you." "Oh, I don't have any time to talk," and he was gone. I figured, "Well, the heck with you." The next day I see him going back and forth and I'm not paying any attention to him, and one day I'm sitting on the pit wall and it's kind of quiet. All of a sudden I hear, "Hey WOWO. You want to talk? C'mon let's go back to the barn."

We walk back to his garage and he says, "You probably think I'm a real asshole, but I'm not. I was so busy trying to get so and so's car going. I like to see these guys run. I wasn't trying to be mean, but I was all wrapped up in this stuff. I'm sorry about that." So we do this interview, and it was a great interview. He said to me, "Look if you come down and do this again, as long as I know you're around, just show up and I'll get to you as soon as I can. I promise I'll find you." I always got good interviews with him, no problem at all.

Parnelli Jones was one of the nicest guys I ever met. I used to have him on my show occasionally and we became friends, and when Parnelli retired, I was there. That year Joey Leonard was driving the old STP Wedge Cars and they were doing things around a race track that nobody else could do. Leonard says, "You think I can go fast if that guy right there would get off his dead fanny he would blow the doors off this place." Parnelli just says no thanks and that he's retired.

One year Eb Rose was selling his race car and he had it parked on the grass inside the pit wall. Elmer George wanted to buy it. Parnelli takes it out three, four laps and he's flying around the track. Elmer then takes it out and he's four or five mph slower. Then Parnelli takes it out again and he's got it right back up there. They said Parnelli Jones could take that racetrack and run anything you put him in faster than anyone else. He just knew how to run the track. One time George Snyder was following Parnelli around the track right on his tail, but when Parnelli came off he lost three mph. He just understood the track.

So two years after he retired my phone rings one day and it's Parnelli from California. "April 5, be at the Firestone Garage at the speedway. I've got something you have to see." I walk in that garage and what does he have, but the jet car. He'd been testing it in Phoenix and he announced he was coming out of retirement to run this car. He would have won the race except for that $6 bearing that broke with a few laps to go. He was on the pole and I was inside by Turn One and by the time he came around the short side he had a 10-car lead.

One of the most unusual guys I met down there was Donald Davidson. He was the English boy who committed the entire history of the 500 to memory. There's this big crowd out in the pits. This is Roger Ward, and he'd reel off Ward's entire history of anything he had raced in his entire life. They'd bring somebody else. Up. It was so fascinating. What an interesting guy he was. He was the kind of guy you'd love to have alongside you anywhere on the radio.

CHAPTER 16
BASEBALL BUDDIES

Through baseball, I made a good friend with Ernie Harwell. Back when Mr. Mac used to bring players in here for Mr. Mac Day, he brought the Detroit Tigers in. I got to know George Kell pretty well, and one spring we're coming back from Port Huron and Ken got us tickets and we'd go to the Olympia and watch a Red Wings game. Knowing Bruce Martyn, I'd go sit in the press box with him.

So I'm sitting in the press box and I felt this hand on my shoulder and this guy says, "Excuse me, but I'm going to have to use you." I look and here's George Kell. They had just gotten back from spring training. He said, "I'm glad I found you because I'm a southern boy to start with and we never see hockey because we're in the South training and we're gone by the time they start in the fall. You're going to have to tell me what this game is all about." We just had a wonderful evening. We left and something happened and I got a hold of Kell for some reason. He said, "If you are ever coming to Detroit for a game, let me know and I'll take care of you." As it so happened, Don Chevilet's uncle was the head groundskeeper at Tiger Stadium and he had the box directly behind the Tigers dugout.

We came up the one time and I called George one time and asked if there would be any chance to visit. He invites us up so Chevy and I go up and sit in the press box and I got to meet Ernie. Several other times that summer when we'd go up, George would always say, "Whenever you come up here, we'd love to have you come see us." I got to get a rapport with Ernie, and when George would do the middle innings, Ernie would sit there and shoot the breeze with me. One thing led to another and that fall some people in Fort Wayne had a little boy who was terminally ill, and they knew I knew Ernie Harwell. They wanted to know if it would be possible for some kind of Detroit Tigers' memorabilia to be obtained. I called Ernie and explained what had happened. He said, "Bob, don't worry about it," and about three, four days later here comes a glove, three or four balls, a Tigers jersey and a picture of all the Tigers for this little boy. Several other times I did things like that as well, and he always came through. One year for Penny Pitch Ernie sent me an autographed picture of the Tigers. We always stayed friends.

Strangely enough one of the bonds I made out of that was Charlie Maxwell. He lived in Paw Paw, Michigan, and they used to call him "Sunday Charlie" because he could hit home runs galore, but he always hit them on Sunday. I got to know him pretty well. One day we're up there with Kurt sitting in the box, and I had told Charlie we were coming and all of a sudden he comes around the corner and meets everybody. Then about the fifth inning, he comes back around the corner and says, "Kurt c'mere. Put out your glove," he plunks three balls in his glove and they were autographed.

Through that, I also met Al Kaline. I got to meet him on an exhibition day when they had a celebrity ballgame for a fundraiser. I met Kaline through Gordie Howe, who could really hit a baseball. Holy cow! He was knocking those balls out of the park as well as any of the Tigers. God, could he crush the ball.

I used to visit with Mickey Mantle and Billy Martin up at Shuck's Lounge in Kendallville where they came in for a smoker every year after the season. They were fun guys. Mickey was just the most laid-back guy. He'd just get the most pleasant glow when he had a few drinks in him. Martin, after about 10 drinks, was ready to fight anybody.

CHAPTER 17
MINING THE MID-SUMMER CLASSIC

Among some of my spontaneous sports adventures was covering the Major League Baseball All-Star game in 1975. NBC was carrying the game in Milwaukee, and WOWO being an NBC affiliate at the time carried the game and needed some pre- and post-game interviews. My son David and I hosted a contest on "Why I'd like to take my dad to the baseball all-star game." Once we got our winner, we flew to Milwaukee and had a nice dinner before the game and away we go. One of my assignments there was to get some background information from players to use as pre-game filler. Then I was going to do a live wrap-up after the game. The problem was they didn't have any credentials for me when I went up there. I was wearing my blazer with WOWO across the pocket, and I'm in the front lobby of County Stadium and I saw Mickey Mantle and some of the players go down this set of stairs. I figured that's where the players are going, I'd better go look and see what's going on.

I got to the bottom step and there was one runway to the left, and I knew that was the locker room, and one to the right which I knew had to be toward the field. I took the road to the right, climbed up the stairs and there I am, right at the fence on the field. I see an usher there, and he opens the gate and I walked onto the field. He never asked me for a credential or anything, probably figuring if I was coming up from downstairs I ought to be there.

I'm on the field and it's early pre-game but there are players all over the place. The batting cage is going, and there are TV crews out there and there's a whole bunch of stuff going on. I didn't know anybody or anything out there. As luck would have it, walking across the field heading toward the third-base dugout is Steve Garvey. I recognized him because that year he was a write-in winner so I stop him and explain who I am and what I want, and he says, "Bob, no problem at all." At that time there's an NBC crew on top of the dugout yelling, "Garvey, get over here." I said, "Steve, why don't you go ahead," and he says, "Oh, no, we'll finish this, they've got all day." We did just a wonderful interview. What a great guy he was. I thank him and he says, "By the way, do you need some other interviews." I say I'll find my way, but he takes me over to the batting cage, and says, "Who would you like? I'll bet you've never met Hank Aaron, have you? Hank, this is my friend Bob Chase from WOWO in Fort Wayne and he'd like to talk to you." We had a nice interview and Garvey is still standing there. "As long as we're here, I've got another one for you. Bob, this is Jimmy Wynn, the Toy Cannon." He was another nice guy and when I finished up, who's standing behind me but Garvey and Tommy Lasorda so I meet him and interview him. Steve says, "You got enough or you need somebody else?" I say, "Steve, I'm sorry, I just don't want to do this to you. I'm so beholden to you." He says, "Don't you worry about it, I'm happy to help you," and he skips off and goes over to the NBC crew.

Now I'm standing there talking to Lasorda and who walks up but Pete Rose. Lasorda says to me, "Do you know Pete?" I said,

"I'm kind of from his territory. I'm from Fort Wayne," and Pete says, "Fort Wayne? Oh, WOWO, I listen to your station a lot." Now I've got all these interviews and as I'm going back to go down the runway and over along the third base side is a catcher catching some American League pitchers. It's Bill Freehan. As a good Tigers fan, I'd follow him to the end of the earth. I introduce myself to him and I get an interview with him. Then that was it. I go down and call the station, I use some alligator clips on the phone and I record about three bits so they can put them on the air.

It was just incredible all these people I had met just through Steve Garvey. It's just like going to sports heaven and you're in the baseball section.

When we went back to the airport after the game, they are rolling the airplane out for me and the kids go into the restaurant and who is sitting there but Freehan. He was a replacement catcher in the game, and they never used him. He was so mad he couldn't see straight. He says, "The funny part is I won't forget you because you're the only one who even interviewed me. I'm not a bitcher, he said, but I can't believe I would take a weekday off like this and I only got to warm up a couple of pitchers and that was it. Next time, I don't think I even want to be part of an all-star game."

I remember Jimmy Wynn hit a home run and that ball was still going up when it went out of the park. It was like a line drive. Pete Rose hit a stand-up triple no problem. He hits the ball, goes around first and goes around second and gets 20 feet away from third base and takes this huge sliding dive and the dirt is flying all over the place. The ball is still in the outfield and the people booed him. Of course, it was an American League city at that point.

The folks at the station couldn't believe all the stuff I'd been able to do. That just epitomizes a lot of the things I've done in my sports life. I was just in the right place at the right time. I've had so many of those experiences like that in other sports.

CHAPTER 18
PITCHING PENNIES

When I came here in 1953, Penny Pitch had been pretty well established. Jay Gould and Bob Sievers had started it in the late 1940s when they received a letter from a woman who had a son who was a quadriplegic, and he said he was interested in becoming a writer. The letter said, "They have special typewriters, but we certainly can't afford one. We just wondered if there was some way you could help us." Jay and Bob picked it up, just between the two of them, and said let's just go on the air. With all the listeners we have, maybe if everybody sends a penny, think how much that could be. And it got to be more than a penny. People started sending pennies, nickels, dimes, whatever. They just did it for a couple of days the first time and they got $2,300. They had enough to buy the typewriter and some extras for the young man.

That worked out so well they had a promotional meeting at the station. Then they began to work it differently and to find a deserving family or families that it could really help By the time I got there in 1953, it was becoming a real tradition already. At the time when we would start Penny Pitch in mid-November, we would get envelope after envelope. The postal department would have to bring it up in boxes, and we would throw it in these big round garbage barrels. Maybe once a week we'd have a Penny Pitch party on the air, and we'd open these things. What we'd do is write to all the churches and the welfare people and ask if they had any deserving recipients for Penny Pitch.

Then we would sort out the run of the mill ones and if we had a couple of exceptional ones we would immediately go out and investigate them. We'd go to their church, their pastor, to their welfare people, whoever had authority and a feeling for their situation. Then when we'd get down to the last two or three families we'd go to their homes to see what their conditions were and what kind of families they had, and we'd elect to honor one or two families. The people that we worked with usually, maybe dad was a productive person who had an injury, maybe they had three or four kids and Mom was doing three or four jobs, their house was about ready to run out, their money had already run out, that kind of stuff. They were real genuine cases. We would say it's a family in northern Indiana and we'd tell these stories about them.

We'd receive around $100,000 a year. Then we set up a deal where we'd take an attorney and their pastor and we'd go to a bank and set the rules up. They would be given an allowance, but they couldn't get their hands on the money. In one instance, the father had suffered a serious injury, they had four kids, and the mother worked all kinds of jobs. We talked to them and we went into Angola and the real estate group there cooperated with us and found us a home. It needed some work but had four or five bedrooms. They got the house, the mother got a nice job working in a restaurant and the kids got some scholarship money they could get when they turned 18. Those are the kind of things we did.

One time we had a man and his wife in their high 80s. They were living on Social Security, but they had their house which was small had gotten into such disrepair they were going to condemn it. They had no money and no equity in the house to go into assisted living. They couldn't afford to redo their house, so we gathered together all the union people and put a whole new roof on the house, all new windows, renovated the whole thing inside, and gave them a new furnace. They got that and then we supplemented their Social Security income for the rest of their lives.

About two or three years after I got involved in it we were doing a Penny Pitch party and this lady said, "Bob, look what we have here." A Penny Pitch family from two years prior that we had helped sent us a check for $900. They knew what this had meant to them to keep their family together, to give them a new start, and they felt that rather than have Christmas that year, they gave all their money to Penny Pitch.

I was sales promotion and marketing manager at the station, I really believed in Penny Pitch. Times were so different, attitudes were so different, and you had an opportunity to be part of something special. It was something I dearly loved to do. We used to have these original penny pitch auctions. The phone company would set up a bank of phones and we'd do an all-night memorabilia auction. It was amazing the money we could raise, $22,000-$24,000 in one night.

The most we ever raised all together was somewhere around $115,000. We were constantly in the $60,000 to $80,000 range. That was a given. When I was there, I don't think we ever went lower than $50,000. Everybody would get involved. The schools would get involved and have a traveling trophy. We'd go give talks at all the grade schools and middle schools. It was just an incredible community effort.

We had a group of out of Huntertown and they rigged up a bathtub on wheels that they would pull around with a horse. And they would go all the way down the streets of Huntertown and all the little towns in between, they'd almost go door to door and people would throw their money in the bathtub. They'd pull it all the way down to People's Trust and Savings in downtown Fort Wayne and put it through the counters, and they'd come up with $2,000, $3,000, $4000 through the years.

Mike's Car Washes were incredible for us, and we raised thousands of dollars through them. One day I'm standing on the corner in downtown Fort Wayne with a Penny Pitch barrel at 6 a.m., and people would just pull over and throw their money in the barrel. This car comes along, and this man says, "Good morning, Bob," and I say, "Thank you and Merry Christmas," and I've got what he gave me in my hand, and I look and what do I see on the outside of this roll but a $100 bill. That's not a good hour of the morning to be standing in downtown Fort Wayne with $100 bills in your hand so I stuffed it in my coat pocket. We got the station wagon and took the barrel away and I reached in my pocket and pulled it out and there were nine $100 bills. It had come from Ed Dahm at the carwash. Ed and Mike Dahm had Mike's Carwash.

The stories were unbelievable. You could do a book on Penny Pitch. Everything was like magic. When you finished with it, you had such a warm feel good feeling. Man, it was a high.

CHAPTER 19
HOP AROUND THE CLOCK

In 1955 when the station was still pretty musical, Guy Harris was always looking for something different that would separate us from the others. He talked to the owners up at Cold Springs resort at Hamilton Lake and made a deal with them to go up and try this record hop. We didn't know what it was going to do. After World War II kids quit dancing, and we figured if we could get them started we could have some fun. We promoted it pretty well and the first night out we got up there and we got about 120 kids, and they were just sitting around looking at each other. We had a heck of a time getting them out onto the floor to dance, but we had four different times to see if we could make it work. The next time up we promote it and we give a free rose to all the girls and a boutonniere to all the guys, and we ended up with 200. Then we started doing things like group dancing, the bunny hop, snowball dancing and this kind of stuff, anything to get people on the floor. About the third time we tried it, we had some other gimmicks to try but now some of the grownups had heard about it and they showed up. They loved it and danced like crazy and then the kids started to dance and it began to move it along.

Then we talked to the record companies and they always had artists out and about making appearances so we started bringing people in who had a one-time hit or a couple of hits, and they would come up and mime a couple of songs and we'd give away their records. It just grew, and finally, the guys at Bledsoe's Beach at Lake James said they wanted one, too. We had established the one pretty well, and the first one was on a Friday night so we decided we'd try Bledsoes on Saturday night. We got a better crowd quicker because they knew what to expect so now we had Friday and Saturday and we kept alternating. The second year the hops grew to about 500, 600 kids per unit and by the third year at Bledsoes we were hauling in between 1,000 and 1,200 a hop. The one at Cold Springs we ended up with pretty close to 1,000 kids there as well because we had a lot of Ohio kids coming over as well. It just kept going and going, and it was just unbelievable how it grew. Then we branched out and did a hop at Lake Tippecanoe. A lot of times we'd do two hops the same night if they were far enough apart geographically. It was just amazing the people we drew to those things.

It lasted 15 years at least. Then, like everything we did, the other stations jumped on it and started doing it in their own way, but the WOWO record hops were the place to be. It happened there. We brought in a lot of pretty good artists. We tied a summer promotion around the ones at Bledsoe's and we called it Beach Ball which was a full weekend. We would have a hop both nights and on Saturday we'd have boat races, and on Sunday we'd have a boat parade, skydivers, parasailing and we did that for about seven years.

You loved it. You worked because you really like what you were doing, and you were always meeting new people. We were better recognized in the area than the local TV people because we were all over the area.

The promoters ran it with an iron hand at both places. You didn't mess around in those days. There were not conciliatory rules. You either went by the rules or they threw you out, and if they threw you out, you never got back in. We never had a problem. Maybe one of them would go and talk to the kids and usually, that was enough. The privilege of being there was enough to keep everybody in line.

That branched off into a lot of school record hops. One time I went down to Muncie to do a record hop for Muncie Central High School, and it just happened to be the night of the Muncie-Marion basketball game which is just an incredible rivalry. Pretty soon you see Marion kids coming in and Muncie kids coming in and I'm thinking, "Oh, brother, this is going to be a dandy." Then this little guy walks up to me, he might have been 5-9 or 5-10 and says "I'm so and so and I'm the juvenile officer for the Muncie Police Department. Don't worry about these kids. As long as I'm in there nobody is going to bother you. As long as I'm in here these are my rules and everybody plays by my rules or they are out." All of a sudden all these huge kids come over and start hugging the guy and rubbing his head. They were very respectful. About the only problems we had came from about six kids from Fort Wayne. He said to me, do you know these people? I said I know them and they've been trouble every place we've been, and I would rather they not even show up. He said, "They're gone," and they throw them out.

Then those same kids go after me at a record hop in Hartford City two weeks later and the kid comes at me with a knife. All of a sudden I saw the knife in his hand and I got so mad I went right over the record table after him. All of a sudden, he realizes, "Holy crap!" and he's out the door. Then I got some mail, and it said, "Don't worry, we'll get you. We know you're going to be in Decatur in two weeks." I knew this could be trouble. The Indiana State Police had a post at Baer Field and they had this big sergeant named Herzog and he was in charge of the post and he was a good guy. I called him one day, and I said, "I'm not sure but I could be having a problem." He says he'll take care of it. So we got to Decatur and the kids are there and they have that smirk on their faces. All of a sudden about 10:30 and there's this main door going into the dancehall area, and I looked at the whole door was filled with nothing but one huge Indiana State Police Officer. I looked at him and he gave me a wave and he calmly strolls around the edges and comes over to shake hands. He says, "I know who those kids are. They're over ta da da da," and I say, "Those are the ones." He says, "We might as well get rid of them now," so he walked over, and he told them, "OK, I'll give you a 15-minute head start. I want you to get back into your cars and head back to Fort Wayne. If I catch you anywhere in between, and I mean it, you're in the slammer. Now get out of here because you're going to create a problem for yourself, one you won't be able to get out of. I'm just trying to tell you, be smart, don't cross me." I never saw them again, ever.

We had some great times at those hops. We used to do one on Sylvain Lake up at Rome City on a huge aluminum raft. We'd take out 60 people at a time and we'd cruise the lake and dance. The thing was when they all started dancing to the beat, that was back in the days of the turntables and the turntable arm would start bouncing. So now what do we do? We got this huge tub like a washtub and put a floating inner tube in it and put the turntable on the inner tube and that solved the problem.

I still have people who come up to me and say, "Bob, I know you don't remember me, but when I was a kid I never missed your record hops at…" We made so many friends out of those things.

CHAPTER 20
MONKEYING AROUND IN THE CAGE

We used to do the craziest things for promotions. One time they decided to put a circus cage in front of the building at 124 West Washington, and they would put me and a bunch of monkeys in the cage. In order for me to get out, I had to get 1190 signatures. It was sort of a popularity test of sorts. Hey, if it was fun you did it. That's what made us who we were, we did the craziest stuff you ever saw in your life.

So I get in the cage and it dawns on me that 1,190 signatures are a lot of signatures. They had three or four of the girls with yellow pads, and I'm broadcasting my show from 3-7 p.m. from the monkey cage. By the time I get out there, there are cars lined up all the way up to Calhoun Street. It was at least a double line or better, and down around the corner going north, and I'm feeling much, much better. It took 25 minutes and I was out. They were signing signatures as quick as they could sign them and I got out of the monkey cage.

The monkeys were fine. I didn't know what they were going to do, but they had a separation between me and the monkeys so they didn't gang up on me. The people thought that was the funniest thing they ever saw. I went back upstairs and finished my show, much to the disgust of the promotions people who thought they'd have me in that cage at least for a couple of hours.

On this same day, I had one of those safari hats, and Bob Sievers was on the noon portion of his shift, so I walked into the station with this helmet on. As Bob normally would do, he says, "I see Bob Chase just walked in and it looks like he's ready to get into the cage with all those monkeys. Bob, come over here. Oh my gosh, what do they call those helmets again?" I said, "Bob they call it a pith helmet," and that was the end of Sievers. He starts laughing and says, "I don't know folks, but I hope I heard right."

We did all sorts of dumb things, but Bob was one of the gamest guys we ever saw. When I left the air staff and got into the promotions and stuff, I could think up all kinds of crazy stuff. At the Sports, Vacation and Boat Show one year they had an alligator wrestler with a three-legged alligator. So we dream up this deal where the fabulous four were going to wrestle alligators. So I go to the pet shop and we got four little alligators, about a foot long, and we threw them in the pool. We blew the whistle and the boys had to go after them. Sievers undaunted just jumped in and he just tracked his alligator down and had that little sucker before you knew it. Now here's Chevy standing on the edge of the pool and he's got on a wetsuit with a helmet and the whole thing. As the alligator go by he's reaching over trying to grab one. I happened to be right behind him, and as he went to reach, I pushed him and in he goes. Well, he really got upset. In those days Chevy used a little color back in his hair to make sure he kept it bright and nice. So water gets underneath his gizmo and here's his color back dripping down his cheek. He was really upset..

The hockey season used to open on Halloween weekend and we would do an opening night promotion. One year we decided the Fab Four – who at that time were Don Chevilet, Jack Underwood, John Cigna and Bob Sievers – would do an apple-bobbing contest, but to make it a little more difficult we had the big barrel with the apples at center ice and they had to get there by riding tricycles. The boys would start at one net on a whistle, ride to center ice, bob for an apple and then take off for the other end. Needless to say, once somebody started slopping up around the barrels full of apples it got wet and you had no traction. Everybody was trying their best to bob an apple, and they couldn't get the job done. Sievers came up to bob the apple and he dove right into the barrel. He was down practically to the bottom, fanny up in the air and up he comes with an apple and jumps on his tricycle and heads downs.

He was always the biggest trooper of all with all the dumb things we did. We had donkey races, and we'd give Bob the best donkey because we wanted him to win. We'd start on one and by the time he got to the other end he'd be so stiff half the time he'd fall off the donkey. We'd have a race deal at Baer field or Avilla and we'd always make sure Sievers had the best car because we always wanted him to win. We'd fix it so he got the lead and he always had a good car so nobody could quite catch him, but the one thing he didn't understand was that you had to go through the white flag to get to the checkered flag. As soon as they threw the white flag, Sievers drives off the course because he thought he'd won it. When the circus would come to town, we would meet them at the railroad yards and we would be part of their parade. I'd always have Seivers sitting on top of the biggest elephant they had. He said, "An elephant isn't a pretty thing to sit on. They are very bristly and picky, and you don't realize how high up you are until the elephant stands up." He never fell off an elephant. He was also our coach for the Air Aces basketball team.

We ran Rose Bowl tours for 30 years through Kelsey Travel. In the year Indiana went in 1968 we had 170 people and we had the plane almost to ourselves. Hilliard Gates went out to do the game for NBC radio and he was on our plane with us. We had more fun because Hilliard was very much composed and prim and proper. We were sitting in the back of this thing and there's a round lounge, and Hilliard was there and we were yakking and having a good time. So all of a sudden this diabolical idea hits me and I say, "By the way, we have a real celebrity in this crew. This guy, you don't very often meet people like this. This guy is the radio guy for NBC in the Rose Bowl, his name is Hilliard Gates." The first thing that happens is the stewardesses gave him a hug. He was about to fall right out of his chair. He really enjoyed it as time went by.

We put on one of the greatest air shows this town ever saw and couldn't fly. We went to Smith Field, and Duane Cole who was one of the world's champion acrobatic pilots lived in Fort Wayne. We got with him to put this show on and he had hundreds of friends in the business. We had the whole thing set up and he had different people coming in and we had an Air Guard flyover set up. Lo and behold the day arrives for it and it was a beautiful day except winds 30 to 40 mph and tornado warnings all over the place. So it's completely out of the question, and the air guard wouldn't even do a flyover, but we've got 25,000 people at Smith Field. It's wall to wall people and Duane goes up and with a friend of his of his and they did all kinds of aerobatics. They did a car to plane transfer where they fly over the car, a guy from the car crawls up a rope ladder and into the plane. Duane did his specialty which is what they call dead stick aerobatics. He goes to 5,000 feet and turns off the engine and starts doing maneuvers all the way to the ground. Even though we couldn't do a full show, nobody left disappointed because of the incredible show we had.

CHAPTER 21
A SPECIAL MEMORIAL DAY

On April 17, 1967, our oldest son Mike was hit bad in Vietnam, and it was really nip and tuck for six weeks, and we continue to thank the Lord for giving him back to us because he was about gone. I talked about it on the air because it helped really to talk about it, and so many people in town knew Mike because he was a heck of an athlete. Michael was an incredible peer person for all the kids. He was that much older than the rest of them as he was born in 1943. He was a complete, flat A scholar, wall to wall. He was a very good athlete, he was all-city in football and all-state in track.

They had this Memorial Day witness at the coliseum back in the days when many people used to come in here for the service inside the building. They asked me to be the guest speaker that year, and Jay Gould was the emcee. I always had tremendous respect for Jay. I had been there for a week, maybe a week and a half and Jay invited me to go down to the Roxie for breakfast. We're sitting there and he says, "You know, I really like what I see and hear with you. I just wanted to sit down and talk to you. I think what I see is you. That's good. You just be you and if people like you, you've got it made. If they don't like you, they'll turn you off. Don't try to be something you aren't. I am. I live in a glass house, I have no escape, and this will be my lot until I retire."

He got involved in a manpower freeze in World War II. He had a chance to go to Chicago and be the Master of Ceremonies at WGN on the Quiz Kids, but he couldn't go. Instead, he was stuck here on The Little Red Barn. Jay just stayed but that wasn't him, really. He was a musician, a poet, an author, another dimension of the amazing people who made WOWO what it was. He had a great influence on me.

So I worked and worked at this speech and tried to get an address together that I felt would be adequate to the situation. I'd work on it and then I would show it to Jay because he was an incredible author and writer. They used to call him the wordsmith. He'd say, "You're on the right track, just keep it going." One day I had written, I had edited and I turned it around and I didn't know where to go with it, and I said, "Jay, I just don't know what to do." He read it over and said, "Don't change a thing. That's what you want."

So we get here on stage on Memorial Day after the parade. There was a young marine there by the name of Doug Pickell who had been hit in Viet Nam and had lost his sight. He knew Mike, and here he is up on stage, and he's not worried about Doug Pickell, he's worried about Mike and how he's doing. I got so emotional over that and it's almost time for me to go. Jay was over two more from me, and I just stood up and I went to Jay with the script in my hand and I said Jay, I can't do it. He said, "Say's who?" and I said, "I know I can't do it, I'm just going to go to pieces." He says, "If you're going to go to pieces, you're going to do it up in front of everyone." Jay gets up and the first thing he does is he addressed his talk to the empty seats. You don't think that wasn't something!

Now, man, I'm tied up. And He introduced me and I took a great big deep breath, and I started. I didn't get very far, and here I go, and I'm starting to come apart. I was pretty well unraveled and I took another real big deep breath and I got my composure back. I finished it and a little wavery, but I got through the whole thing.

Here's the text of that speech:

"In 1944 a young Fort Wayne man of vision and dedication conceived an idea that now stands as a monument – a shrine, to those we honor today. Paul Gronauer was his name – a member of the Fort Wayne Junior Chamber of Commerce... His idea, erect a memorial to Fort Wayne and Allen County men who had laid down their lives in defense of freedom and their country. The junior chamber and then president, Raymon S. Perry, adopted the project, naming as chairman of that memorial committee one of their members – Mr. Don Myers.

The junior chamber waged a vigorous campaign to bring this project to reality and in November 1947, the issue was submitted to a referendum vote and was accepted by the citizens of Allen County by a 5 to 1 majority.

Ground was originally broken in January 1950, and 31 months later, the Allen County Memorial Coliseum was completed and dedicated. At this time plaques were placed in Memorial Hall honoring men of Allen County who had died in action in World War I and World War II. 108 names from World War I and 535 names from World War II were listed under the inscription... "This coliseum is dedicated as a living memorial in honor of these men of Allen County who gave their lives in World War I and World War II of our nation so that we might live."

The men of World War I, "The Great War," and those of World War II "The war to end all wars," fought and died to protect the honor of our nation in the cause of world freedom. Their background or race, creed, and color were as diverse as the world in which they lived. Nevertheless, they were Americans and in the traditions of our founding fathers, they acquitted themselves with honor and dedication to bring about a victorious and just end to the battles they were committed to in the struggle for right. Many of these brave soldiers were first-generation citizens of our nation, who coveted their birthright with a zeal never to be duplicated in generations to come. America, to them, was indeed the land of the free and the home of the brave.

Following World War II, political ideologies held the field of battle, subversion and intrigue replaced guns and bullets. Confrontations became a conference table and the roar of battle was replaced by the harangue of multi-lingual debates. Their spoils... millions of deprived people who until that time had gone unnoticed... now were to become pawns in the compelling goal of world domination.

Treaties affecting these unfortunate masses became battle lines for ideological warfare that soon became too hot for any arbitration other than physical force. Korea took its place prominently in the world history books, as a battleground between the factions of freedom on the one hand and those of suppression on the other.

As the major free world protector, the United States in honoring our obligations committed our young men to the defense and guarantees of freedom to South Korea. This strange land,

thousands of miles from our borders, became the personal concern of hundreds of thousands of young Americans.
In the conflict that followed, Allen County mourned the loss of 66 of her sons, who gave their lives unselfishly in the defense of freedom. With Korea as the benchmark for the tolerated boundaries of political and military intervention, a new type of war developed... to consume the prime youth of the world.

The next test of the rights of those seeking choice was Viet Nam. Young America again was in the foreground in defense of freedom, the cream of our youth, fighting and dying on strange battlefields in support of the ideals into which they were born and so fiercely dedicated to protecting. A half million of our leaders of tomorrow are representing the United States this very moment in Viet Nam... the finest group of soldiers to fight in defense of freedom in the history of our nation. Yet again, this brutal battleground is minimized as a conflict, not a war. Apathy to the commitment of our soldiers, sailors and airmen in these actions is most distressing. Honor is now measured by many in the ability to evade the responsibility of serving our flag. Concern for the future of freedom is waning.

Our current generation is the first product of comparative plenty. Sacrifice is no longer one of the stepping stones along the path to maturity. Consideration for fellow man has become less a factor in our moral makeup than ever before. If ever America needed to take stock of its moral and social fiber, it is now. We are more than at any other time on the threshold of decision.

Here at home, we have the time to ponder our future. In the steamy deltas and hot dusty highlands of Viet Nam, this present generation of Americans are demonstrating their faith and dedication to their flag and to the nation for which it stands... They have made their decision.

My family has had active personal involvement in two wars, and one conflict in defense of the principles of freedom over the past 50 years. My father in World War I, myself in World War II and our oldest son in this present Viet Nam conflict.

Today we pay homage to the memory of 108 valiant Allen County men who answered the call in World War I... 535 of the greatest fighting men the world has ever known lay down their lives in World War II... 66 Korean conflict servicemen who paid the supreme price of honor... 1 in the Berlin Airlift and now 27 of Allen County's finest young men have already given their lives in the Viet Nam conflict.

It is with deep humility and a fierce deep-rooted sense of patriotism I accepted this invitation to present this dedicatory address this day... Memorial Day... May 30th, 1967. But for the grace of God, and the modern miracles of medical technology, my son, Michael, would have been one of the honored dead we remember today. We are more fortunate than many, and share personally the grief of the tragedies of conflict... Losses that are beyond expression.

To the memory of those who have given their lives that we may live, a reverent thank you.

We dedicate this Viet Nam plaque today in their memory in the humble knowledge that they lay their lives down with honor while defending the principles of freedom set forth by our forefathers. May we also not forget those brave men who at this moment are still fighting for the very principles for which these men died. May peace with the fulfillment of their purpose be a speedy and rewarding reality.

Thank you.

Little known to me, Bob Jones who was our PR guy at the time was recording it, probably about eight minutes. All of a sudden here in July, the General Manager Carl Vandigrift calls me into his office and he's got this thing sitting there in a walnut stand with a flag behind it, this big medallion. He said, "You like that?" and I said, "Yeah, that's pretty. Where'd you get that?" He said, "I didn't get it, you did." He was a member of the historical group locally so they had sent it to him and it was the Freedom Foundation's medal for patriotic addresses. I didn't have a clue about anything like that. It was totally right out of the blue, one of the real emotional thrills of my lifetime.

CHAPTER 22
STARTING WITH THE KOMETS

When Ernie left right after Christmas there was only one left standing, and that was me. I never anticipated being where I was, that I would get where I wanted to be so quickly. It was like a miracle. I certainly had hoped at some point and time doing the sports once I got started there. Lo and behold I'd been there seven, eight months and, bingo, I've got the whole ball of wax. A little old boy from Marquette and suddenly I'm playing major market ball. I think the fact that t I had played the sports and played a lot of them and played intensely really helped me at each game because I understood the games and I was fortunate enough to be able to express myself through my eyes in a manner that people liked. Had it not been for that, I don't know where I'd be right now. I was just fortunate to be in the right place at the right time.

All through the football season, I had been doing the hockey, and when the football season was over that was it. I didn't even do color for him, he did it by himself. The WOWO management felt comfortable because they didn't have to go on a search to find somebody to replace him which was what worried me. They anointed me, and from then on away we go.

I had made friends with the players prior to the time I got the play-by-play job. I got to know some of the guys, especially George Drysdale and Eddie Long and a couple of the others. It was an easy transition for me to make with the players and the game. I had done enough of it before I got there not to make any mistakes or no more than normal. At that point when I had days off I would come out and skate with them just to practice, and Murph and I got into the social round and the whole thing. The earlier years were the off-ice fun times because we were all together and we were all about the same age. In the later years we were a little older, but not much, but to begin with we were really close. The guys would come over to the house for coffee before they would go to practice, and I'd go to practice skate with them, and maybe after if I wasn't working we'd go and have a beer or something. It was a whole different atmosphere than you have today, very laid back, but the guys were good hockey players still.

In those days they didn't have any rookies around, they were all basically veterans who had come out of major junior and had played some senior A in Ontario or in the west, and they had decided rather than play for a lunch bucket a couple times a week they'd come down here and play regularly. Some of them decided to be adventurous and come down to the "I" as it got going. Their presence really helped make it a good hockey league. People just didn't realize at the time the caliber of hockey they were seeing because with only six teams in the NHL there were a lot of marginal rejects who came down here and played, and there were some real talented players.

The old IHL was kind of disjointed in the beginning because

there wasn't a lot of supervision. Fred Huber was the league commissioner, and he had so many other irons in the fire, although he did a good job I thought in representing the league and giving it credibility, it was sort of an orphan league. The NHL didn't want us, the AHL wouldn't recognize us, people in Canada were thinking, "What in the world is this?" It started out as a border league and spread to the real IHL as more teams came into it. It wasn't really that recognized a league. If you don't make the AHL, you go home and play senior. When guys came down here, nobody knew much about the IHL until they got home and told people about it the next spring. Then it became to gather momentum, and they were saying, "Hey, it's not a bad place to play and you can make 100 bucks a week besides."

In the early days of the Komets, the first several years they had some incredible players but they didn't have enough. They'd have four or five guys who were really, really good and they would hold us in games until they ran out of gas where the other teams were three or four players deeper. When you only had 13, 14, 15 players on a team, that made a big difference.

One of those early Komets was George Drysdale, who was laid back just like he is today. I never saw George get excited about anything, really, but he was a heck of a hockey player. He could have played in any era because he was so fundamental. He was strong, had a good shot and he was a team leader and a good captain. The thing about George was when he got his chances he didn't too often miss.

Eddie Long came in here as a kid, and he was totally dedicated to his father. He just adored his dad, and Captain Long was an old army man, a real salty little rascal, but he was the nicest man you ever saw. Eddie evolved out of that, and then as he got exposed to more coaching, I think Doug McCaig helped him a lot because Doug gave him a different kind of confidence than he'd had prior.

Eddie was never one of these outstanding forceful front-runners to begin with. He just came to work, laced his gear on, worked his buns off and took his lumps and went home. I think he probably did more than anything else, he went home and called Captain Long, and said well Dad, and I got one or two or I didn't get any. Eddie's life revolved around his dad who was just a great man. I think Eddie still relies on the influence of his dad whom he loved very dearly. It was just an incredible relationship with his father.

He kept battling away and pretty soon he started putting the puck in the net with some regularity and he became our leading or near-leading scorer. He wasn't a fighter, but he'd get knocked all over the place and he just kept coming back for more. He got the respect of the people because he was here to play Komet hockey and he was very representative of what Komet hockey should be.

Those were the days of working the puck and carrying the puck in across the blue line, and there was no dump and run. They knew how to come out of their own end and how to pass. They were basically complete hockey players, again at a time when they came out of junior skilled enough that in today's world, most of them would be National Hockey Leaguers.

They were perceived as being a pretty nice bunch of guys. At that time the only household names in the sports market were the Zollner Pistons and the Komets initially had to fight for individual recognition. Team recognition happeend almost instantly because here comes this alien sport into the coliseum with all this action, banging around and the fighting. Then when these guys walk out of the dressing room everybody expects them to be like pro wrestlers and they were the nicest group of guys you could ever imagine, nice humble people, always attuned to their fans. Hockey players have always been that way, and I think the always will be. It began to grow. The problem was the first couple of years we just didn't have a team good enough to put up any good numbers.

When hockey first got started the old Crown Brewery was our sponsor for several years. The fan club started almost immediately. They had a real nice social room right at the Brewery and we'd have a lot of fan club meetings there. It was just a nice atmosphere to get to know each other in. They were really instrumental in humanizing the Komets and giving them a chance to meet people. It was a popular place to go because being a brewery, guess what? The price of the beer was unbeatable. They always had snacks, and the fan club maybe would bake eight or 10 dishes of goodies. It was a nice atmosphere to get going in.

The Pistons weren't much competition, quite frankly, not as much as you would have thought. They had already established their persona, and the basketball team never was what you might call a blue collar team. They had appealed to those people who could afford the season tickets to fill up the North Side gym, and a lot of people who would have liked to see them couldn't get tickets. Even though there wasn't that much to do, people found other things to do because basketball couldn't be in their routine because they couldn't get tickets. Once the Memorial Coliseum came in here, they all figured they were just going to knock the doors down and the place would bulge at the seams and it would be utopia, but it never was. The only crowds of substance were when the building first opened, but they tapered off quickly. If they ever got a crowd of 5,000 they were really living high on the hog, and that's the same 4,000 to 5,000 they had at the North Side gym.

They were kind of a different crew at that time. Personally, I thought they talked at a higher level than they should have to appeal to Fort Wayne fans who are the blue collar folks who live and die with you once you get their loyalty.

As a sports town, Fort Wayne has always had its good and bad times. Right now the Komets make it a good sports town. Let's face it, they have actually created an image and people are benefiting from it by association, being in the building and a lot of them haven't worked hard to make it happen. A lot of people say Fort Wayne is a fickle sports town. It's a little bit like Detroit. When you go to Detroit and you are a new team you have to earn the respect of that market, and once you do they embrace you, but until you do, sorry buddy, you just don't get it.

It took the Komets a long time to do that because there wasn't much to say about their early accomplishments. We had some good players but for one reason or another we just never got there. We played the first four years of our existence and never got to the playoffs. Then Doug McCaig comes along and whipped us into some kind of playoff shape, and unfortunately who do we start with but Cincinnati. We won a game and that's when it was two out of three in the first series, and we win the first game in Cincinnati. We're coming home and thinking, "Oh boy, oh boy, oh boy, if we can jump on them tomorrow night we're going to the next round." The thing is, we woke Cincinnati up. We had a goaltender named Jerry Fleury at the time and I don't think I've ever seen any better performance than I saw that night in Cincinnati. He was positively unbelievable and kept us in that game, but he left his game in Cincinnati. He could hardly stand up the next night, and there was only one goaltender. That was back in the day when you didn't have two goaltenders, but we had fun there for a night.

Doug McCaig was a good guy, a good coach, a tough guy, and it gave everybody confidence when McCaig was on the ice. Doug McCaig was the toughest gentleman in hockey, and that was the NHL giving him that title. As Frank Chadwick who was a longtime referee said in his book, he never saw Doug start a fight, he never saw Doug lose a fight and he fought them all. In this league, Doug rather than punching people he would just pick them up and shake them. He was incredible. He was the nicest, happiest, most easy-going, softest man in the world off the ice.

Back then the travel was primitive. When this club began, they had no bus service at all and the players would use their personal cars and would be paid a stipend based on mileage. There was no insurance or anything. The league accepted it, too, because they only thing they were worried about was if you showed up for games. You just had to hope that the people who used their cars had good ones. Within those first several years, two different times we had Denver in the league, and we drove to Denver through Omaha. That was a long, long trip. You'd come into the Rockies and get into those snow storms, and there were a few times when I didn't think we'd ever see the light of day again.

The fourth or fifth year they made a deal with Hefner Chevrolet where they leased four station wagons so that was what the Komets traveled in. They'd stay at Hefner until we made a trip, and the guys would pick them up and load them up and we'd go. We took off on the same route but nobody stayed together. Somebody would be a hot dog, some guys liked speed and some didn't worry about it. There were a few games where the first car that got there started the game because it was that close. They'd straggle in depending on weather and other things.

Eventually, we got our first bus from the Huntington Bus lines, and their busses were called flexible flyers. Huntington bus lines did not have first-class equipment. We'd sit in the back on the way home and play cards, and the engine was in the rear, and sometimes there was enough smoke in the back you thought you were in a fog bank. It just smelled, and you'd get off the bus and pert near have to shower before you went to bed. It was terrible. There were no bathroom facilities. It was, "Stop the bus," and sometimes it was pretty cold. There was some baggage space below, but thank God we only had 13 players.

They weren't held to any standard because again hockey was a curiosity. Here was something nobody had ever seen around here in the Midwest. A lot of people couldn't understand anything but basketball.

When I first began to work with the hockey club, Ernie Berg, who was the general manager and one of the owners, would invite me along on speaking engagements with the team on the mashed potatoes and chicken circuit and we'd talk hockey. One of my educational ploys was even in those days they had one of those magnet boards where you could set up plays on, but on the other side of that board, there was still a basketball board. I would ask, "OK, how many of you guys understand anything about hockey? Anybody here ever watch a basketball game?" And they'd get all excited. "OK, now, first of all, let's go to the basketball court," and so I'd put out the forwards, the center and the two guards and we'd talk about how you'd design a play in basketball, how everybody handled what they did. I'd say,

"OK, now remember that," and I'd flip the board over, and let's stick a basketball here on the hockey side. "Here are your two guards, we call them defensemen, here's your two forwards, we call them wingers and you still have a center so we're still even." I'd show them how you worked it out and how they shot and made plays and set up screens. Then they'd be, "What about that red line and the blue lines?" Then you'd have to work with them on that and explain the zone to zone attack. Some of them wanted to learn, and others just watched. I did an awful lot of that for a number of years. A lot of times it would just be myself and a one or two players.

CHAPTER 23
THE LORDS OF HOCKEY

With the advent of the Memorial Coliseum in 1952, Zollner Pistons fans were about to embark on a whole new era. Here was a big building a professional building, something they had always wished for and finally had. There was another group in the city interested in a sport called hockey which at the time was completely foreign to Fort Wayne and Indiana. Hockey was soon to prove it was going to be a major force in competing for the entertainment dollar in the entire market.

A couple of visionaries, Harold Van Orman, a local hotel magnate, and his sidekick, Ernie Berg, who at that time was a marketing man for a local gas distribution organization, decided they wanted to try hockey. The third member of that group was Ramon Perry who was the group's attorney and also had a modest investment in the franchise.

The story of their acquiring a franchise is a tale unto itself. They went to Toledo to meet the commissioner of the league, Andy Mulligan, to apply for a franchise. When Mulligan told them the franchise was going to cost $2,500, without missing a beat Van Orman pulled his wallet from his pocket, laid it on Mulligan's desk and said there it is. At which time Mulligan said thank you and issued them a franchise. Mr. Van Orman quickly picked up his wallet and put it back in his pocket and he and Ernie left Toledo assured they would have a franchise and also in great relief. Had Mulligan challenged Van Orman's wallet, he'd have found about $40 in it, not nearly $2,500.

The new ownership wisely decided they needed to educate the local fans on hockey and held two free preseason clinics at the coliseum. The local sports fans came out in such numbers that both clinics filled the building. When the first season started, and in the face of the NBA's Zollner Pistons, the Komets immediately began to out-draw professional basketball. Even with Van Orman, Perry and Berg running the team the first four years, they had little success on the ice. They had more than fair success at the box office, but mismanagement eventually almost cost them the franchise. In 1958 when faced with financial difficulty, they went in search of somebody to help resurrect the franchise and appealed to a friend of Van Orman's who ran a team in Troy, Ohio, by the name of Ken Wilson. In fact, they initially offered Wilson the job which he didn't accept but promised that he would produce a person who could help them out of their dilemma and at that time turned to his personal friend Ken Ullyot, introducing him to Van Orman and Berg to run the team.

Ullyot also at that time began to bring in talented players. He had a great scouting chain throughout his junior background. His brother in law Johnny Walker was the chief scout for the New York Rangers. He put together the base of that long successful run for many years.

When Ken showed up, he realized the potential here. He wanted some of the action and eventually bought out the rest of the owners. When he left, he gave it to Colin to run, but that was a very difficult time economically in Fort Wayne during the early 1980s..

Colin was undercapitalized and he couldn't maintain the team, but then local radio executive Bob Britt decides he's interested in buying the club. During the following year, it turned out that he didn't have the liquidity to keep the team going either so they went into bankruptcy. The team was about to fold, but as it was about to go under, David Welker entered. No one else was going to step forward and he did and he ran the team for several years before he got into a spat with the Memorial Coliseum. David pulled stakes and moved the franchise to Albany, N.Y., where he met complete resistance and the Choppers failed in half a season.

That's when the Franke brothers came in and purchased a defunct franchise that had belonged to Flint. The Frankes had been on the periphery of hockey here for a long time. There was never a meeting time that somebody advertised the club for sale that the Frankes weren't present. When their big chance came, they had a lot of community contacts and a lot of great ideas. They just openly said, "We're going to do this and do that, and have a sellout opening night." They began to market the daylights out of the hockey team and made it happen.

They really continued to be successful because of the way they forced themselves into the marketplace. They knocked on every door you could find and did all kinds of promotions. Part of that now includes Scott Sproat who was previously the boss of the Continental Basketball Association's Fury. After the Fury failed, Scott came over to the hockey team and that was a whole new evolution of Komet image again. He did things promotionally that would have never been allowed over the years because it was too daring. He's a magician. Then they put another ingredient in the thing when Icy shows up after Salt Lake disappeared.

CHAPTER 24
WALKS LIKE AN OLYMPIAN

I'd skated a lot with the team over the first couple of years I was here and made most of the practices so Ernie called me one day, and said, "I understand you have a friend on the Olympic team." Weldy Olson was a buddy from Marquette who he had played at Michigan State and he was playing on the U.S. Olympic team that was coming in to play an exhibition game against the Komets. So Ernie said, "How'd you like to play against the Olympic team?" I said, "Are you kidding me?" He said, "If you'd like to play, I've talked to Doug and he felt you wouldn't embarrass yourself at all. If you want to do that let's make a deal and I'll sign you to a contract."

 The station loved it because what better thing was there than to have Bob Chase the play-by-play man actually be a hockey player. Luckily, the game wasn't broadcast. We had 13, 14 players on the roster and the Olympic team brought in 20 guys so we dressed everybody we had, including me. I was the fourth defenseman. We had three defensemen, nine forwards and a goaltender.

The games were different in those days. It was all pass the puck and move the puck. I had skated with the team a year or two before that. When I found out I was going to play, I got serious and I got in shape. In fact, McCaig said to me, "I wish half my guys were in as good a shape as you are. You're taking this

serious." I said, "I'm just trying to preserve my own life, Dougy."
I always stayed in shape. I never really was one to get way out
of joint. I just enjoy feeling good, and I still try to stay in shape
today.

With less than a week to go before the game, I pulled my groin.
By that time, I'm committed and have already signed a contract
with the club. I just babied that sucker along.

One of our sales people at WOWO was really excited for me
and he was behind the goal in warm-ups so I went and talked to
him because there was no glass up in those days, just a screen.
He said, "Are you feeling OK? Man, you look like death warmed
over," and I said, "I'm still trying to swallow my heart."

It was a lot of fun. We're warming up at our usual end. I skated
out and saw Weldy at the other end. And all of a sudden this
stick hits me right between the legs, and I turn around and
there's Weldy. "What the Hell are you doing here?" I said, "I
came out for one reason, I'm going to line you up." We started
to laugh.

It was a thrill playing against the Olympians, but the one thing
I had said to Doug was, "Let me just sit here until we establish
something if we're going to get it done, and then after it loosens
up a little bit then find and dandy." He said, "Yeah that's good."
Then on the first player change, he taps me on the back and
says, "Over the boards." I said, "Doug..." and he growls, "Get
over there!" Here I am, boom, I'm in the middle of the hockey
game after three minutes. I really thought Doug would let me sit
there and absorb it a little bit.

I was right over the boards right off the bat. My partner was
George Stanutz and he was a good guy to play with because
he was an excellent defenseman, a great hockey player. In

today's world, he would have been an automatic NHLer. He was a big, rangy kid who skated like heck, could handle the puck beautifully. Stanutz told me, "Don't worry about it, Bob, I've got you covered." Also, George Stanutz was the only guy who rivaled Eddie Long and George Drysdale for having the biggest honker on the team.

Anyway, on my first shift we come down and get the pressure on them and I'm playing the right point and Jean-Paul Lambert is down right beside the net and I'm wide open on the point so he fires the puck back to me. I unloaded right away, and right at that moment Hartley crosses the net and tips it up and we're up 1-0. Ray Perry, who was another club owner also ran the PA, so here we are leading the Olympic team 1-0, and he says, "The Fort Wayne Komets goal by No. 10 Hartley MacLeod, assist to Jean-Paul Lambert. The other assist goes to No. 4, Bob Chase?!?" The crowd really got a kick out of it.

Then on my fifth or sixth shift out they gave Weldy a breakout and hit him about center-ice and they've got me trapped. George was somewhere, and I'm way back here on the dot so I try to head him off, but he beat me. He said hello, goodbye and put it home. Then he came around and jumped on me and knocked me down, just having fun. Nobody knew what was going on, and he even got a penalty for it. They didn't understand what good friends we were. We tried to explain it to the ref, but he thought we were making a travesty of the game.

The Komets all got a big kick out of it because they thought it was kind of cool that I'd actually do it. We beat them 6-4, and I happened to be on the ice for three goals against so Bud Gallmeier writes a story the next day talking about my debut as a Komet not being especially inspiring. "Chase would qualify for the hat trick in reverse. Of the four Olympic goals, three were scored when `High Pockets' was on the ice."

We had a little luncheon after the game, and Weldy and I were just yakking about home and his brothers. They were quite a family. At one time at Michigan Tech, three Olsons played on the same line. There were nine boys all together, and they also had a sister who played at a time when girls did not play. In later years they had a team, and they played around the Midwest as the Olson family. Some of their kids played, and they could field about 14, 15 Olsons and they were pretty good. One of the brothers, Eddie, coached here and should have had a shot at the NHL but he never got it because he was a US-born player. He led the AHL two straight years in scoring, but never even got an invite to a pro camp, so he came here and coached. He did have one distinction as the first American-born player to ever coach a Canadian pro hockey team, and he did that in Victoria.

That was my last game for a while, though I did play in Oldtimers games after we put that group together. Teddy Wright was my partner in the Oldtimers games, and sometimes I'd get two or three points per game because I'd get him the puck and watch him go.

CHAPTER 25
ULLYOT COMES TO TOWN

Despite some early success drawing crowds in their first season, after a while the Komets were just hanging on and they were going belly up before they brought Ken Ullyot here in 1958. They were either going to close the doors or find someone to help them put a hockey club together because they were going bankrupt because of mismanagement and the inability to understand how to organize a team.

They had no contacts to bring in good players, and they relied on whomever they hired as a coach to bring in whomever. As an instance, the first and second year they were in the IHL they ran ads in The Hockey News, saying "Hockey players wanted, call for more information." Then these guys would call and give their pedigree, and these guys here knew nothing about them. Honest to goodness there were people who came into training camp here who stood and hung onto the corner of the net to make sure they could stand there long enough for somebody to see them. There were several, you thought, "Man, I hope this guy doesn't get on the ice because they are going to kill him." There were some real jokes, but the owners didn't know any better because they were poor hockey people.

The only thing they knew was, "Man, if we get hockey in here we know it's going to go," and they were right but it took a while because they didn't really know what they were doing. They spent a lot of money on players and were spinning their wheels. Some of their first coaches were good guys, but they brought in their own people to play and lived and died with those people, and they died more than they lived. It was the same old story, bring in your friends and they'll eat off your back as long as you'll keep them. Some of them didn't. Eddie never did, George never did. Ivan Walmsley was always a hard worker, but a lot of them came in and just enjoyed the ride.

It's amazing in a way that hockey stayed here and persevered because of the terrible record we had. They had gotten down to the point where the team had not played well and nobody was coming to the games, quite frankly. The Pistons were still in town and they weren't drawing that well, either. Everybody hoped with the new building they could fill it up, but that didn't happen. A lot of our crowds were 2,200, 2,800, maybe 3,400. A big crowd was 4,100, 4,200 and we were doing well if we could get that. If we could end up with 5,000, oh, baby, we were flying tonight.

Then Ernie Berg called me one day in the summer of 1958 and said, "We have a fellow coming in that Kenny Wilson recommended. He said he's a hell of a hockey man and we need somebody badly."

Ken Ullyot really didn't look like you would expect a crusading hockey general manager to look like. He was extremely well groomed as he always is, he wore kind of brown-rimmed glasses and had his hair all combed down. He wasn't the big hulking guy, he looked more like a professor than a player and he was a professor as it turned out. Ken had spent his hockey life not only playing but observing. He watched how people did things, and he curried the favor of a lot of coaches and managers while he played for them because he was interested. He learned a lot of lessons many hockey players never did, and when he came here he had a lot of it he could apply. All he had to do was make a phone call if he needed help or ideas.

Ken didn't exhibit much personality when he first came. I think he was trying to get to know the community and people around him, and he really didn't let his guard down too much to start with.

The first thing he did was start to bring in bonafide hockey players. That's when a lot of the oldtimers who played prior to that left. One of the things he was really concerned about was Edgar Blondin because he was just an incredible crowd favorite because when Ken saw the makeup of things, he realized Edgar wasn't going to make his team. The question was, "How in the heck am I ever going to approach this thing? What are the fans going to think when the first thing I do is get rid of the most popular player we've got?''

We had training camp in Troy, Ohio, and Kenny's training camps were real training camps. Once you went over the boards, buddy, be ready to hang your hind end on the end of those suspenders and skate it off. Well, after about four or five days down there, Edgar spent everyday heaving over the rail. He finally went to Ken one day and said, "I appreciate the fact that you invited me to your camp, but I'm not going to make it so I'm going to retire." That was the greatest thing that could have happened as far as Ken was concerned, and Edgar made the right decision.

A lot of the guys didn't come back. It was sort of an amazing evolution when Ken came here because some of the people he felt were going to be problems as if by magic some of those people faded away.
He started bringing some of these people that nobody had ever heard of, and that changed the face of this hockey club. He brought skill into the game and right off the bat we started winning which is something we hadn't done consistently. That all of a sudden put a new image on the face of Komet hockey.

He knew a lot of people in Western Canada and began to bring players in here like Reggie Primeau, Lionel Repka, Sid Garant, Andy Voykin, Con Madigan, John Ferguson and Duane Rupp. From then on it was a whole different attitude. You remembered players who left here because of their accomplishments rather than their inability to do things. We ended up with some great hockey teams.

He brought in a lot of quality players with character. One thing about Ken, he didn't care if you were Wayne Gretzky, if you didn't have character and morality he didn't want you. He got a few of them in there who surprised him because they weren't what he expected and talent be darned, bingo they're gone. But he was smart enough to get somebody for them. He brought a number of people in here who were pretty good hockey players but they didn't fit the mode of what he wanted and they parted amicably.

I finally convinced Ken that WOWO was the place he had to be if he planned to tell the story of hockey to the market. He had been pressured pretty hard right off the bat by Hilliard Gates to go with WKJG because the Pistons had just left town. Hilliard had all the authority because he ran and owned the station and could offer Kenny anything he wanted where I was limited in what I could do. The station wasn't that excited about making any concessions because at that time the Komets were ready to go anywhere, and the station wasn't really that excited about it. We almost didn't get on the same page, but we finally got this thing together so we go to Orchard Ridge one noon to have lunch to consummate the deal. Don Rice from Rice Oldsmobile was going to be the major sponsor, Carl Vandegrift the GM of WOWO was there, and Ken. We were having a very cordial time and had lunch and everybody was pretty comfortable and Ken gets up and says, "That's the problem with you Americans. You sit down to have lunch and you waste two hours talking about nothing. I have things I have to do today. Thanks. See ya." When we got back to the station, Vandy said, "You know for two cents I'd jerk this thing. I can't believe somebody would do that. Doesn't he realize we're trying to help him?" I said, "Yeah, but you have to understand Ken," and he said, "I do not, Ken better understand us." There was the battle line I had to fight for four or five years, and it wasn't easy.

When Ken showed up, he transformed this franchise into really what it is today. He set the tone morally and ethically, and everybody inherited the traits and kept it going to the point where it became the flagship of the league. I'm trying to minimize anybody else in the league, but it's obvious. That's another fortunate part of being where I am here and have been since I started with that big 50,000-watts booming all over North America. That alone was a real establishing factor for accepting the IHL in a lot of areas because I was the only person at that time broadcasting and we were heard everywhere. I was the first guy to every broadcast, and it began to catch on. We sort of had the inside track about it and people began to talk. I always tried to keep the NHL presence involved in it by giving their scores. There were a lot of people who knew a lot of players in this league and had no other way of keeping up with them, so there I was.

CHAPTER 26
THE RIGHT-HAND MAN

When Ken was in Prince Albert, he met a man named Colin Lister who worked at the bank and became involved on the board of directors for the team Ken ran. Ken respected him for his honesty and efficiency to the point that he knew when he came here he had to have somebody inside that office he could implicitly trust. Financially, they were in one heck of a bind that they had to get out of before they could breathe. As it proved, he could not have found a wiser choice under any circumstances.

Colin was kind of the glue that held the team's image together. He was the only one who would go anywhere anytime at all to put on his Komet hat and talk hockey, bring players and do whatever he had to do to get into the community. He was the point man for everything that was done publicly in the early days. You just recognized Colin for the image of hockey because he wasted no time becoming involved.

Shortly thereafter Colin began to get into youth hockey. Once Dick Zimmerman and Colin got together, the rest is minor hockey history in town. Colin was the glue that kept hockey kind of together because he was the advance man and everybody loved him.

We spent a lot of time in schools. We'd bring a bag of equipment, and have our little talk. At that time a good friend of mine was the president of NBC and NBC had opened up their original television hockey with Peter Puck, so I called one day and wondered if I could get a copy of Peter Puck. He said well, we have a real problem with that. It's copyrighted and we have a lease agreement to use it on NBC. I explained what I wanted it for, and he said, "I'll tell you what I'm going to do. Do you have anybody there who knows how to transfer this film? What I'm going to do is send you this special deed and I want it back in a week." Here I am and I have Peter Puck going. The kids ate it up. We'd do Peter Puck and we'd have a couple of guys talk, and we'd see who the class character was or the guy who needed a boost, maybe the wallflower. We'd call him up and say, "OK buddy, you're going to be a hockey player today. Let's get dressed." Sometimes it would be funny because the little kids couldn't get it all on, it was too much. Then we'd take a picture of him with the players and we'd send him a picture later. Every kid in the class got one ticket so they would bring their parents.

Colin dedicated his life to youth. Hockey and baseball were his things, and I think about every available resource he had he put into those sports to the benefit of the kids. Any youngster who ever played or Colin and was in his organization played like a little Major Leaguer. He treated them so well. He was a moral inspiration to everyone, and I think everybody whose life he has touched has been a better person for it. I've seen kids, over the years when I was working in the office there, come up to talk to him and they confided in Colin a lot of times in a much deeper manner than they did even with their parents. There was a certain aura of trust and peace with that guy, so much so that he made you feel good just being around him. But, don't cross him. He could be one tough little rascal if you crossed him. He was always soft and kind but he could be just as sharp as he needed to to make sure he was the alpha in a situation.

Between hockey and baseball, I wouldn't begin to count the number of young men he's been a part of their lives. It was always a case where he was there for them when they needed him, and I know a lot of his personal funds and time went into helping not only the kids but also their parents as well. He absorbed a lot of costs for some of those kids to be able to play both hockey and baseball. He had a lot of support from the Zimmermans. They were kind of his surrogate mom and dad in the United States, all the Zimmermans from John and Minnie on to Dick and Floss. He was part o the Zimmerman family really for many, many years.

CHAPTER 27
THE BEST TEAM, THE WORST LOSS

The 1959-60 squad was just incredible. If it hadn't been for a couple of crazy bounces… We had everything to gain and just couldn't cash on it. It just wasn't meant to be I guess.

That team finished 50-16-2, and they dominated because of the system they played and the way Ken coached. They didn't have to be the best complete package but they had to be complete players so they could do what they had to do to make a team.

That's why they were hard to beat because they stayed within themselves, they were well disciplined and waited for their opportunities and when they got them buried them. It was fun to watch because it wasn't frantic hockey. The control that they had over the game, you never dumped the puck and chased it. They had a reason for everything they did.

The funny part of it is the year we lost it in the Turner Cup Finals to St. Paul. That was an amazing night, April 14, 1960, for Game 4. The Memorial Coliseum was pretty well filled because it was our first home game and we needed the win to tie the series. The darn thing goes to overtime and then one overtime after another. In the second overtime was when Ronson had the penalty shot, and everybody figured we were in great shape because he was unbelievable that season. When he went in on Glenn Ramsay, the puck bounced a little bit, and Lennie just flat missed it. That was it right there.

After that, it was just a stupid shot that hit somebody's stick and ricocheted up into the air and hit Komets goaltender Reno Zanier in the back and rolled down his back and into the net to give them the win. Everybody lost it for just a second, and then it was in the net. It was so anti-climactic the way they played the game to have it end on something sloppy like that. St. Paul was a good hockey club, and they had a great coach in Freddie Shero. The game finally ended at 1:25 a.m. in the fourth overtime.

The game went so long, people were leaving at 11:30 because it was a Monday night, but other people were coming in. The second shifters were getting off at Harvester and they all came running out. Some people who had left the game early came out of the bar and came back in. Hartley MacLeod was bartending at Neil's Oyster Bar so it's about midnight, and there are three or four people in the bar, and he shuts the bar down and says, "C'mon jump into the car and we'll go to the hockey game." Twenty after 1 in the morning the game finally finishes.

The Komets came back to win the next one, but there was really nothing to it because both teams were so gassed. Give the Komets credit because the came back and forced a seventh game before St. Paul won it. That's when it's tough to lose a championship in our own ice after you'd almost won it. They got a jump on us in that last game because of that.

That was the famous game where I had a little mishap thanks to George Drysdale. As the game wound on, I hadn't had a chance to get anything to drink so I asked George to get me something after the third overtime. George walked down to the press room and grabbed a bottle of soda, and as he's walked back up to the press box, he gets stopped by Jimmy Stovall who says, "What have you got there?" George tells him, and Jimmy goes, "I've got something that will keep him awake," and he has George pour the soda into a nearby trash can. Then Jimmy pulls out a flask and fills the bottle with that.

George comes back to the press box, hands me the bottle and says that's the only thing he could find. At this point, there are only about 30 seconds left until the start of the next overtime, so I tilt my head back to chug this thing. Then I realized about mid-gulp it wasn't soda. It took my breath away and tears came flying out of my eyes. I tried talking and nothing came out. At that moment I was in a total panic because my whole voice just left me. George is just sitting there giggling like crazy because he thought it was the funniest thing in the world. Finally, I got my control and started to talk about the game. It sure woke me up for the rest of the night because I didn't anticipate being there until 1:25 in the morning.

CHAPTER 28
THE SENSATIONAL 60'S

59-60 was a shock that it took a while to recover from and it was 62-63 before we got back into the championship round. That was after the departure of a number of the 59-60 team, either to a higher level, moving on to others or just sort of going into private business and fading out of the situation here.

No one would have thought when we made a trade to Indianapolis for Chuck Adamson that Chuck was going to be the goaltending force that he turned out to be. He was unbelievable. Not enough people give him enough credit for skills and abilities. He was just incredible and he brought us our first Turner Cup. He was the guy who back-stopped that team. He went into private business when he had the opportunity and he was just a good guy, a funny guy to be around. He sure knew how to stop the puck. I saw him on both ends of the spectrum. I saw the night he made eight saves on a night and I saw him on two occasions make 72 saves in a game, one of them against the Montreal Canadiens and he only lost 3-1. I'm sure Chuck had an ax to grind there because he belonged to the Montreal organization, and Toe Blake was with the team and Charlie wanted to let Toe Blake know, "Buddy, here was one you could have had." And even Blake after that game really tipped his hat to Chuck for the incredible job he did in goal. Mind you, it wasn't a National Hockey League game, but the Montreal Canadiens were all here, and they could play at about half speed and just tie up about anybody they wanted to. It was just amazing.

Chuck was well ahead of a lot of the other athletes because those were back in the days when you ate a steak and a baked potato, a piece of toast and a cup for your pre-game meal. Not

Charlie. When he came to the games, he'd gas up on pasta at home or on the road, everybody else would be doing their thing and Charlie would be shoveling down the spaghetti, and guys would be going, "How can you play on that? What kind of diet is that?". He was ahead of the curve again.

One of the rituals Charlie had was he was a lot like Robbie Irons because they both had unsettled stomachs before games. After warm-ups, Charlie would bow to the urge. It's a little gross, but one night it was an especially big night and Charlie was kind of pumped up and the urge got to him before he could get off the ice. And of course he wore a mask and it was a pretty gruesome looking thing.

CHAPTER 29
THE TURNER CUP

There was one special game that was the turning point in the whole history of the playoffs for the Komets. Charlie had been playing well but Muskegon was really putting it on us that night. The funny thing is we'd had some injuries and we brought in a kid named Gary Sharp from Greensboro of the Eastern League. Right off the bat, bingo, Sharpie scores and we're up 1-0. Then all of a sudden we dried up big-time. Lionel Repka was injured and it gets to 4-1 or 5-1 and Ken figures we have to go back home the next night and let's not take any more chances with Lionel. So he pulled him out of the lineup, and now it's 6-1 and it's still early in the second period.

All of a sudden early in the second period Lenny walks through the team and bingo. He got two goals before the end of the period and it ends up 6-4 after two, but we're still back of the eight ball and we're having a tough time getting it to go. In the third period Charlie is running all around and he's standing on his head and all of a sudden he's in the corner and there's a wide-open net and here comes the puck out of nowhere. As if by magic this great big long stick of Eddie Long's comes whipping through the goal crease and clears the puck. That to me was really the key because it would have been 7-4 at the time. Low and behold we keep nipping away and we work it up to 6-6 at the end of regulation. The line of Reggie Primeau, Norm Waslawski and Roger Maisonneuve just kept coming, and we won 7-6. When the whole thing was over, I went into the Mohawks' dressing room because they were expecting to come back to Fort Wayne the next night and win, and they were all sitting there in the state of shock 20 minutes after the game was over. They hadn't even taken their gear off yet. Joe Kiss who was one of their big tough guys was sitting just inside the door when I came around the corner to look, and his eyes were just as red as could be. He was crying like a baby because they never thought they were going to lose it. It was just one of those miracle finishes. Reggie, Norm and Roger were incredibly instrumental in that third period to get us back where we belonged, and Reggie won the faceoff back to Roger for the game-winner. My first comment when we won it in OT was, "The Mowhawks didn't survive the French and Indian War."

The thing is Minneapolis was a force to be reckoned with. One of their colorful players was Moe Bartoli. Ken told Ivan Prediger, "I don't care what happens, your man is Bartoli, don't you lose him! If you told Prediger to go and run through a wall, he'd be through the wall before you could say, "Ivan, wait a minute." Moe was a petty good hockey player but he wasn't full of physicality. Ivan ate up the job and was a possessed guy when he had to do something. It was so funny because the Minneapolis bench would be making a change, and sometimes Bartoli had to get up to get out of the way so somebody else could come off, and Ivan would be halfway off the bench before he realized Moe wasn't going on for that shift. Whatever happened to Bartoli, Prediger was on him all the time. It was one of the funniest things I've ever seen watching match-ups. They talked a lot, but they didn't talk trash talk but Ivan made sure Moe knew he was around. The thing about Moe was any place on the ice he was dangerous. He could really hammer the puck.

We played the first game against Minnesota here and then we didn't have ice so we had to go up there for the next three games. I'll never forget we're coming back from Minneapolis playing cards in the back of the bus and Jumbo Goodwin is sitting next to me and he keeps hitting me on the shoulder and saying "Chase, we're up 3-1! How about that?" It was almost a chant and everybody realized we were where we didn't think we'd be. Then we came back and got the ice and finished it here. They were happier than heck. We come back and won a championship with kind of a new cast of characters. We knew how close we'd been and didn't get there and they really relished the fact that they felt really vindicated. That turned the attitude around because know they believed they could really win.

CHAPTER 30
HELPING DOC GET STARTED

One day a young man of maybe 16 came down to the station at 124 West Washington one day in 1957 and said who he was and that he had been listening and he really wanted to become a sports broadcaster. So we had a long conversation about it, and he was such an intense, dedicated young guy that you had to like him right off the bat. He was just the perfect little man, really. He wasn't in awe of anybody, he was in pursuit of. That kid was Mike Emrick, who today is the dean of NHL broadcasters.

I told him that anytime he had a chance what he should do was get a little recorder and try doing the game, then c'mon up if he wanted and we'd talk it over. He was practically there the next day. He came back to the station and we listened to it. I gave him a few little hints and stuff to get it started, but holy crow, you could already tell he had so much enthusiasm for what he was doing. This just kept rolling and he got better and better at it.

He would sit up in the end of the press box, and before that he would sit up in the corners of the building talking into his tape recorder. He always felt he was going to disturb somebody in the press box, but he really didn't. In those days there was a lot of room up in the corners. He didn't do every game at that point, but he would show up on weekends and whenever he got a chance. Maybe he'd come out before a game and we'd run some stuff and go over some little things.

When he went to college, he continued to pursue the dream. At that point he ended up in Marion, Indiana, doing some on-air stuff, but he was pretty restless. I told him, Michael just keep your ear to the ground, something will show up someplace. Whatever it is, if it means you have to go in and wash underwear to get into a hockey club, do whatever it takes to get your foot in the door. He got his foot in the door in Port Huron, and he wasn't a broadcaster, he went in as PR man. I know he was a little frustrated, but the guy who was their radio man had been there for a quite a while. Finally, through misfortune, Mike got his chance when their play-by-play man was killed in a bus accident coming out of Des Moines. It was a bittersweet thing for Mike, but he was ready for it and did a nice job.

Bob McCammon was coaching there at the time and he knew Mike well. A little later McCammon was named coach of the

Flyers' American Hockey League team in Maine, and by that time Mike had been in Port Huron for two years so Bob took Mike with him. That's how Mike became the voice of an AHL team.

When Fred Shero left Philly in 1978, McCammon came in and he brought Mike with him. The people who owned the Flyers took an immediate liking to Michael. He was versatile and could do a lot of things so he did some of their play-by-play and was soon noticed because of his unusual style. He didn't have that old hackneyed Canadian, monotonous style. God bless those who broke trail for it all, they did some great work in their way, but because of Foster Hewitt, almost every Canadian broadcaster when he started as a kid adopted his style which was a classic style at the time, almost a monotone. Danny Gallivan broke the mold in Montreal but he did it in French so I couldn't understand what he was saying. But Mike was excitable and he really brought the thing to life as he still does today. He adds more to a hockey game, with peripheral information, and still maintains your interest in the game more than anyone I've ever heard and that makes him so great. He's an encyclopedia of information that he distributes in a timely fashion that is always apropos to the situation. He just as a wonderful ability to weave so much storyline into a game.

He was out of the game for a while, in a lull until they rediscovered him. He finished college and got his doctorate which is how he comes by his nickname "Doc.". He didn't do play-by-play for a while and even taught in college for a while. He was looking for an alternative direction, but he realized, as many people do, the love of what you really like to do overwhelms even your better judgments sometimes. Fortunately for the people who listen and watch, he got himself full-time back in the game. I don't know who Mike's agent is, but he can be very fortunate to have a property like Mike because Mike is so saleable and so genuine and sincere. I envy him for his traits. I wish I could emulate them as well as he does.

I don't know what Mike ever took from me. When you told Mike something, it was there in the encyclopedia. He took the best of what he felt were his abilities and put them into a style that he maintained. The style is still today the same as it was years and years ago, not only with hockey but whatever sport he does. His style follows through and the sincerity of it all shines through. It's like a good book. You can't put it down once you start reading it.

The thing about Mike he has never ever forgotten his original roots. He's never been on an ego trip of any kind. What you see is what you get, that's Mike Emrick. Any father would love to have him as a son and I'm sure any kids would love to have him as a father. He's an amazing guy, and he and his wife are two peas in a pod. It's a tough life to live, as I know, especially with Michael because he's all over the world all the time and to be able to maintain that home relationship, Mike can do it because he is that kind of an intelligent guy.

We stayed in contact, and Mike is a very loyal friend. You might not see Mike for six months but he's like a true friend is, you take up right from where you left off the last time you saw him. He doesn't know a stranger. He's such a wide-open, wonderful guy that he's easy to know and very, very easy to like.

One time I got to work with Mike again, and it was one of those unexpected things. They had asked me to come up and be part of the telecast of the United Hockey League All-Star Game in Muskegon in 2000. Terry Ficorelli was running the play-by-play, and I split some of that up with him and Mike was the master of ceremonies and he came up to join us in the booth. It was fun working with him. When you are with somebody who has that kind of ability, you just kind of sit back a little bit to feel it out to see where it was going. I didn't in any way want to step on Mike's toes. He was always so gracious, he was always trying to hand me a bit, which I took when I could, but he was the boss. I loved to work with him.

When the Komets and Mike Franke asked me if I would feel good about having a 50th-anniversary recognition in 2003, I was honored and a little overwhelmed and humbled. This thing came along and they couldn't get a date for it, and I didn't press the issue, but finally, Mike Franke said, "OK, we're going to do Bob Chase Night on March 8." He said, "You know why don't you? When this all began, one of the guys we talked to was Mike Emrick because we wanted him to send in a congratulatory telegram or do an audio or a video. At which point Mike said, 'No, I won't do it. Whenever it is, I want to emcee the ceremony.' '' At that point, they sent Mike the entire Komets hockey schedule of that year, and out of that entire winter, Mike had one Saturday night off and that was the night they chose for Bob Chase Night. He refused any kind of remuneration for it, and they finally paid for his transportation and he didn't even want them to do that. It was just a thrill of a night to see this little giant come all the way and take a whole weekend out of what was an incredibly intense schedule to do that for me. It was just a real unforgettable honor.

Then I turned the trick around two years ago when Port Huron inducted Mike into the Port Huron Hockey Hall of Fame. They had a surprise for Michael. When I did the introductions, I went one step further and I had them pull this shroud away from the press box in Port Huron to reveal it was being named "The Mike Emrick Press Box." That was one time when Mike was surprised, he really was, and he showed a lot of emotion. He holds his emotions better than I do, but you can very obviously hear and feel when he's touched by something. I just chuckled about that all night long. He didn't know it, and when that shroud came down you could have driven a truck into his mouth and down his throat.

CHAPTER 31
FROM BEHIND THE MASK
TO BEHIND THE MIKE

I always liked Robbie Irons as a player because he was just a good guy and he was always up front and never minced any words with anybody. You always knew where you stood, so I felt maybe he'd like to help on radio after he retired. We talked about it, and he hemmed and hawed but once he got up and got it started, he got into it. There was a point and time that his contributions were valuable enough to me that I didn't want to lose him. With that in mind, the Komets stepped forward to assure that he would continue to be my color man.

Robbie and I have been together now for more than 20 years. Robbie works well because he is always Robbie, and people who know him know what I mean by that because Robbie has always been his own man, and he broadcasts like that with me. Broadcasters appreciate color people who have opinions and views rather than just being an echo of what's gone on. The nice thing about Robbie, whenever there's a lull or when I throw it to him, we've gotten into a communications system now we don't even have to look at each other. When I stop, whatever the tone of my voice is, he knows, bingo, and away he goes. He also can see when it's time to be quiet and away we go. We rarely ever step on each other, and when we do it's basically out of excitement.

Robbie is not afraid to disagree with me. It isn't necessarily a disagreement as another view. He's never come out and said, "That's not right..." He expresses himself that if he wants to go in another direction, he knows how to segue to what he saw. He's never ever contradicted me, but he's skillfully turned the tide in his direction.

He adds a dimension that a play-by-play man can't. When you were watching the action, you have to watch the puck and who is around it. He picks up a lot of the peripheral action, and his depth as a former player has really been an asset. Robbie in his own way does a great job on play-by-play as well, and I was surprised at how well he picked it up. I would never be worried about leaving the job unattended if I was sick or something because Robbie could do it. Technically he doesn't have any technical background at all, and he doesn't want any. The longer he doesn't have to handle technical equipment and set up amplifiers and that kind of stuff, the more immune he is to the total job. I think he's pretty smart about that. He can plug in the power cord, but after that, he's lost.

Robbie has a way of taking the technical aspects of the game and making them easy for anyone to understand. That's what makes him so great. Those are the sides of the game that I have no way of bringing to people because I'm so busy chasing the biscuit. When something breaks down or something happens, he's right there. Rather than just extolling the virtues of a beautiful day, you need somebody who can break down the play and bring the insight to people they normally wouldn't get.

He's never supercritical of players. He always manages to hedge enough to let people know he understands what's going on in this world as well because he's been there. Over the years he's gotten more confident, with more flow and he's more at ease. I think he likes what he's doing now more than he did and looks forward to it. He came back year after year, and let's be brutally frank about it, as much as you like to do something, unless you can somehow get some reward for your talents and contributions, it's going to end someplace. Fortunately, the Frankes and the Komets saw his value to the broadcasts.

I wish he would go on the road because I think it would be a lot of fun, but Robbie always says, "No, slick, I've had my share of the bus rides. You can have them."

CHAPTER 32
THE SIDE MEN STEP FORWARD

Color people are really important to the broadcast, when you can get them. A side man has always been a home luxury basically because the entities that I work for didn't want to incur the extra expense of sending someone on the road.

George Drysdale worked with me for a long time. George is a great guy, a low key person. I like to have ex-hockey players as color people because they are all continuations of something rather than being just a mimic of me. The hockey players have always had their own take on each individual situation, and George was that way as well. George was kind of quiet guy who sat in the backgrounds and sometimes you had to poke him almost to get a reaction, but what he said was worth listening to. He has a great sense of humor, and if you could get George going, maybe on a description I gave in play-by-play, he'd sit there and just chuckle for five minutes. Half of it I'd let go through on the microphone because it was entertaining everybody knew Georgie. He was a very beloved guy long after he retired. The thing about George still today is he's not lost his charisma. Everybody likes him and George is exactly what you see is what you get. He's been a very valued friend off the ice, he and his wife Rosemarie, almost since we came to town. They were probably two of the first people we socially befriended when we first came to town.

George was kind of the first guy to do color commentary, but nobody ever set a pattern. Don Chevilet was a color person for me on all the things I did for a long time. Not only did Chevy do hockey, in fact, I think he even did a game or two when I had prior commitments. He worked on all my sports with me so we were kind of a tag team on staff for a number of years at WOWO.

Frank George was a WOWO newsperson and he was sports buff and he did color for me for a while. He was an Easterner with a Boston accent. He was kind of different because he took different tangents. He was a historian of the game, and he would talk about different things other than what was happening on the ice at the time. Not always but he did that quite a bit as well.

The most unusual color person I ever had was John Davis and we used to call him Digger O'Dell because he was an archeologist. He was a doctor of many things, a genius, a complete brain, he was a doctor of archeology who led digs all over the Middle East. He held the Hebrew chair at Grace College and was the president of Grace College. Through all that, John somehow found time to come to Fort Wayne and do games and occasionally when available when we were going West, he'd be standing alongside the road and we'd pick him up on the bus on the way through. He was just such an unusual guy to be around, he loved what he did. I had tried many different times to try to get him some kind of stipend so he could keep going, and they refused to pay John a penny. He was so valuable because of his overall depth of intelligence, and he would have been an incredible addition even to the station other than being my color person. John was my color person when we had the IHL all-star game in Milwaukee and played the U.S. Olympic team. That was a great thrill for John because he became a hockey buff the more he got with it and was on the bus with the guys. They began to call him Digger as soon as they found out he was an archeologist, and here he is the president of a divinity school.

We had a French defenseman by the name of Charlie LaBelle. He was positively a French Frenchman. He was standing in the bus one night on the way back from a game, and John had a bunch of papers in his lap so Charlie says, "What you do there, Doc, eh?" He says, "Well I'm correcting my exams for my Hebrew class." Charlie had never heard of the word Hebrew. Charlie wanted to know what it sounded like to speak Hebrew so John gave him a sample. So John says, "Charlie you teach me French, and I'll teach you Hebrew." It didn't get very far because John would give him phrases, and a Hebrew phrase with a French accent wasn't something you heard very often. Those there the kind of things we did.

John was a very valued person, and I'm really sorry that we couldn't have continued our professional friendship. He had gotten to the point where his responsibilities at school were so much that when he had an idle moment he really couldn't devote it to travel to a hockey game. His wife Caroline was one of the most beautiful people. They were just a great couple.

One time John was doing digs in the Middle East, and once you finish a dig you have to restore it as much as possible to its original state and he was very meticulous. He was such a hockey fan, that in one of the digs he buried a hockey program and a Komet hockey puck. He just thought that was the funniest thing since buttered toast, thinking how some archeologist a 100 years from now would open a tomb and find and what's he going to find but a Komet program and a Komet puck. We haven't had a report on it yet so apparently, they haven't come across it.

He was just a great guy, and he was really the last full-time color person I had before Robbie and I got together.

Then, unfortunately, Robbie with his work couldn't be involved in road games. There were a few times on the weekend I'd say, "I've got a seat next to me," but he always said, "You can have those bus trips. I had enough of those to last me a lifetime." Maybe he can help out in the playoffs, because that's when I'd really like to have him. I would thoroughly enjoy it.

He has been by far the best color man of anyone who I ever worked with, and that's no disrespect to some wonderful people. He has filled the void with his expertise on hockey and people know him and believe him. He's my ace in the hole, the best.

CHAPTER 33
ON THE ROAD AGAIN

One of the tougher parts of being with a minor league hockey team is killing time on the road, but over the years I've managed to have some fun.

We were set to leave the airport in Des Moines one, and it was under construction so they had these rickety old plywood corridors going. We got to this one area and we were stuck there for a while and until they were going to put us on the plane. We were just sitting around so I had a newspaper and I cupped it up like a megaphone and hid behind a couple of guys. I gave it the old P.A. sound, "Your attention please, your attention please, Mr. Reggie Primeau please report to the United counter, you have a phone call." Reggie lights up and all the guys were giving him the business and he's laughing. So he takes off down this long corridor, and I yell "Reggie, stop, stop. Reggie, that was me." I yell at him and he never stopped and went all the way out, and when he came back he was just embarrassed to all get out. I said, "Reggie, I tried to stop you, I really feel bad." Everybody laughed about it because Reggie really bit on the paging job and he took off like a shot.

Reggie is a full-blooded Indian and he has never been a sensitive person about his race. We had a young fellow in here named Harley Hodgson in here in 1962 and he was also a full-blooded Indian. He was a good-looking kid and the girls immediately struck some fascination with him. One night there's a big crowd outside the locker room door, and Harley knows there's going to be a couple cute little ladies out there he wants to talk to, so he gets his shower and puts on his tie and gets everything ready to go. He's there combing his hair in front of the mirror, and finally, he thinks he's got it done pretty well and he sees Reggie sitting there. He says, "Hey, Reggie is my part straight?" Reggie says, "Yes, your part is straight but you feather is on crooked." Harley didn't know what to say to that.

Reggie was always involved in so many things because he loved to have a good time. Once, Reggie decided he was going to learn to play the harmonica. He was Lionel's roommate at the time so he's driving Lionel nuts trying to learn to play this thing, and he's not doing very well. We were at practice one day and Reggie is tooting away when Lionel chirps in, "Reggie you're never going to learn to play that thing." I said to him, "Reggie, it's really not that hard. You just have to learn how to use your tongue on the grate so only one sound at a time comes out." So he's honking and tooting and I said, "Reggie, come here," so we go around the corner. Now everybody is getting dressed in one area, and so I'm talking to Reggie and I've got the harmonica so I played "The Old Gray Mare" and Lionel comes screaming around the corner. He looks and says, "Jeez, Reg, that was good." Needless to say, Reggie put it in his pocket and never played it again.

Another time we were out in Des Moines at the Oak Creek Ice Arena and they had Bob "Battleship" Kelly. As it turned out, Kelly and one of our big stalwarts had a super disagreement and they decided they'd duke it out, and they happened to be at center ice when they were doing it. As everybody knows, hockey players wear suspenders and garter belts in order to keep their socks and pants up. The two of them are really going at it, and Kelly is trying to get the jersey up over our guy's head and he's yanking and tugging and pulling, and finally off comes the jersey and at the same time, the suspenders broke. When his suspenders broke, our guy's pants fell down, and lo and behind, he was one of those guys who never wore underwear. All he wore was a supporter, cup and the rest of him was just the way he was born. Later on, I asked him, "What did you think when your pants came down?" "I just told Kelly, `Don't you dare stop fighting now!' "

On another trip in 1963, we're coming back from Minneapolis and we're leading the Millers 3-1 in the Turner Cup Finals and everybody is having a great time. It's a nice sunny day bouncing along the highway and we stop at this gas station out in the middle of nowhere. We get done and everybody gets back on the bus and we take off. All of a sudden about a half hour later somebody says where's Nellie? (Meaning Nellie Bullock.) "Oh, no, boys we must have left him at the gas station." Jack Loser who was driving the bus finds a spot and we turn around, and just then way up the road, you could see a great puff of smoke coming at us. As they get closer, the lights start to flash, and sure enough, Nellie had talked this guy at the gas station into trying to catch the bus. He has the old antiquated Mercury that used to be blue, but it was turning purple and it was burning more oil than gas. Nellie gets out of the car and crawls back on the bus.

We used to call Gerry Sillers "Hollywood" because he was a good-looking guy who loved the nightlife, and once again we're going to Des Moines. It's a long trip and the weather is terrible, just awful so we left at about 7 a.m. We didn't play that day but we wanted to make sure we got in there, and it turned out the trip was 14 hours to get there. The thing was, when Ken Ullyot said the bus leaves at 7 o'clock, come 7 o'clock the door is closing and we're leaving. He would say, "Close the door Jack, we're leaving." We're going down the bypass and we're about down to maybe to Lima Road when Jack says, "I don't know Kenny, did you forget something at home? Vi (Ullyot's wife) is right behind us, flashing her lights." "All right, stop." We stop and Vi stops behind us and who gets out of the car but Gerry Sillers. Ken gets out of the bus and goes back to talk to Vi, and here's Sillers wearing a pair of light pants and a T-shirt and a light jacket and it's like 20 degrees outside. He apparently had had a pretty good party the night before. Ken gets back on the bus and he is really upset. He said "Gerry, thanks so much for coming. I was just so afraid you weren't going to make it. We're so pleased you're here. You guys there in the back seat, would you please move over and come down the aisle. Mr. Sillers, I'm sure had a pretty tough night, and we're going to have to let him have a little rest, is that OK?" They vacated the place, Sillers went back and slept for about six hours. He never played in the series when we got there and when we got home he was gone in 48 hours. Ken just went back to talk to Vi at the car and said, "Violet don't you ever do anything like that again." She just felt sorry for him.

I remember the time we were going to Minneapolis in the days when we drove cars and I was riding with Kenny and Lloyd Maxfield who was driving. We left late at night because there would be less traffic, figuring we'd get there the next morning. So we're driving and what happens, Kenny's car starts to buck and snort and whistle and holler. Finally, the lights go out and we were in the middle of Wisconsin. There was a sign for Strum, Wisconsin so we pull into this little town with one stop light in the middle. We couldn't see anything so we stop at this bar and walk in to ask if there's anyplace to have somebody fix the car. The bartender says maybe and makes a phone call. He's got about two or three guys in the bar, and he says, "Hey guys, we're closing up here and going down to Shorty's." Everybody leaves the bar, he locks the door and we go down to this other bar. Shorty is there, but he's also the mayor of the town. By golly, he comes out from behind the bar, the guy who closed the other bar works the bar for him and Shorty leaves and fixes Ken's car. About an hour later we're off and flying again.

One time we were playing an exhibition game in Louisville in 1960. Back then we all drive in cars and sometimes we left and arrived at different times. It was no big deal as long as you got there at the right time for the game. That night one car left after the game and that was George Polinuk's car, and the rest of us all stayed over to leave the next morning. It turned out Polinuk was the smartest of anybody because he beat the massive snowstorm that came through and got home. The next morning we come out of Louisville, and and I mean to tell you it was a huge damp, wet snow and there's nothing there to clear the roads. We're just banging away trying to get through, and our car made it maybe 40 miles out of Louisville. There was no place to go so we decided to go into this farmhouse, and first of all, Ken had to talk his way in. The farmer and his wife were very, very reluctant to take us in. Ken had to pay up front before they'd let us in the house. We had breakfast and the whole thing, and by the time we got out of there, things were better and we could travel. The other two cars who were with us kept banging away and they got up maybe another 10 miles before they got mired down. The one car, again with Reggie involved, gets near a gas station/restaurant. When they got in there they guys were wet because they had to walk a ways so they got some extra blankets. The guys were covered up in the blankets sitting around. More people come in through the day and there's Reggie sitting in there on the floor in a blanket. One guy looks at him and starts to laugh, so somebody says, "What's so funny?" He says, "My God, that guy looks just like an Indian." Then the other car with Colin Lister, the team's business manager, gets stuck. He had Jim Baird and Con Madigan with him so they start to walk. Colin was not the strongest guy in the world and had to slog through this heavy stuff. All of a sudden Colin says, "Guys stop, I can't go any farther, I just can't go any farther." So Madigan says, "What do you mean you can't go any farther." "Con, I'm so tired, I just feel so weak, I can't go any father." So Connie says, "OK, look Lister. You sit here," and Connie has a hockey stick he's been using for a cane and he shoves it into a snowbank and says, "One thing, if you don't make it, as long as the stick is there we'll be able to find you when we come back." Colin walked the rest of the way, no trouble at all.

There are a lot of stories having to do with bad winter weather. Coming out of Merrillville one time we were just getting onto I-65 and Jack Loser is driving that day. We're pulling onto the on-ramp going north on 65 and this big semi comes flying by and he didn't give Jack any room at all and forced Jack almost to the edge of the bridge. Jack is pretty upset and the guys are screaming and hollering and calling the truck driver all kinds of names so one of the guys says, "Jack catch up with that son of a gun, we'll fix him." So Jack does catch up and as he goes to pass everybody on that side of the bus had their hind ends sticking out of the window and they mooned this drover. There had to be about 10 moons sitting there, and the driver's eyes were so big you could have driven a truck right through them.

In the old days with Indiana Motor Bus, Jack and Jim Loser did all the driving, and Jack did more long-distance driving than Jimmy did because Jimmy was in charge of bus maintenance, too. It seems like every story we tell functions around Des Moines because those were some of the biggest overnight trips we had. So this time we finish a game and we're coming back through a snowstorm. Ken decided if we got as far as Davenport we'd be OK and we could finish it off the next day. We got to this hotel in Davenport, and it wasn't the Ritz by any means, but they had rooms for us. The blizzard was so strong, I'm telling you the drapes must have stood out a foot from the wall with the wind coming under the windows. So we stacked towels and everything else up and kind of got it going, and there wasn't much heat in the building, either. So here I have this nice big bed, and next to it is another single bed. Jack conceded that since I was the biggest guy, I got the biggest bed. So then all of a sudden he realized it was one of those coin-operated vibrating beds so you could relax, and Jack said, "Would you mind trading beds. I'm so sore from driving through this storm and stuff, and we're only going to get three hours of sleep and I have to drive again, would you mind trading beds?" I said, "No, that's no problem," and I was so tired, I just went over to the next bed and flop I'm down. I wake up about 45 minutes later and I can hear Jack swearing. I got up and I look and Jack had put a quarter in the bed so it would vibrate him to sleep and the darn thing wouldn't turn off. It was still vibrating. It was buried in the wall, and he couldn't pull the plug out. I'll never forget that one as long as I live. He just had to grin and bear it. I think he might have had to sleep on the floor.

A Jack story that I'm alive to tell about was one of the most fantastic pieces of driving I have ever seen. We're coming back from Flint in the middle of the winter, and it's been snowing and the highways are icy as all get out. We were on 69 coming South, and all we had was two ruts and the rest of the road was icy. Now we're about 8 or 10 miles from the Indiana border. We were coming around a little curve and all of a sudden I hear a funny noise kind of going "Bing! Bing!" and I don't know what it is. The next thing I know, the bus jumps about three feet in the air. What had happened, the clincher rim that holds the left front wheel on had come loose and came off which meant the next thing to come off was the wheel itself. When it rolled over the wheel well, it jumped the bus way up in the air and down it came and here we got. We were running probably 60, 65 mph and we're going sideways on the way down I-69. Fortunately, I was sitting with my back to the front and I sort of leaned into the seat waiting for the crash. All of a sudden the bus started slowing down and it straightened back out, and Jack put it over on the side of the road and stopped it. How he did it, the Good Lord was at the wheel, I kid you not. Jack gets out and he goes around and looks and there's nothing in the left wheel well except the sprocket. All of a sudden Jack looks and his arm is hanging out. He dislocated his shoulder keeping the bus on the road. I don't know of anybody else who could have done it. As soon as we start getting out of the bus to take a look, a Michigan state trooper was going South and when he saw that he did a 180 on the road and came back against grain to make sure we were OK. So what we did was we waded through the snow because right across on the Northbound lane was the rest stop. There was a phone there and Jack called Jim who came up with another bus, loaded all the equipment. In the meantime, we walked in the woods, found that wheel up against a tree, and Jimmy put that wheel back on the bus and he and a mechanic drove that bus back to town, and we came back in the bus he brought up. If it hadn't been for the driving ability and the strength of Jack Loser, I couldn't tell you where we'd have been. It was unbelievable.

Of all the trips that we ever made, North, South, East and West, we never, ever hit a deer. One night we were coming back from Port Huron on I-69, and we're west of Flint. We're cruising along in pretty good shape, and all of a sudden, Jack does "Uh, oh!" He had just passed a car and he's in the left lane and the car is almost right alongside our door, and he's moving on by. He turned on the brights, and here's this great big buck. I'll never know how Jack missed the buck, but it never touched up and all Jack could say was "Oh, no!" The next thing there were no more lights alongside us. The guy in the car had positively crushed the deer. We pulled over to the side and the guy's grill was smashed to smithereens and the deer was deader than a doornail, but they weren't hurt. Fortunately, the guy had nowhere to go. If he had tried to veer, he would have rolled it over, but the deer came right out in front of the bus and he hit it right there. The whole sequence of events wrecked the car, but it saved his life. It was unbelievable.

Jack was the driver again one night when we were coming back on I-69 again, and man, it is so slippery you can't believe it. It's black ice. Once you get a bus going, as long as it doesn't break loose, it rolls along pretty good, but Jack was cautiously running about 50-55, and all of a sudden this guy pulls out in front of us quite a way down the road off one of the ramps. As he established himself on the road, he was running about 25 mph, which he should have been off the road to start with. So Jack is trying to let the engine drag us down rather than the breaks when all of a sudden the wheels lost traction, and now we are at the mercy of... that bus made the laziest, biggest 360 you ever saw. It was like slow motion, and as it came around, just as it was heading straight out, the truck is that far away and boink it hits the truck and it shoots off into the ditch. It didn't hurt the truck and we just kept right on going. Eventually when we stopped, we were heading the way we came so Jack couldn't go against the traffic, but he managed to get enough traction that he backed the bus up on the right lane about a quarter of a mile until we got to one of those crossovers and then he turned it around and we went on again. He knew not to fight it and to let it run. He said, "Here we go guys!" and we just made a huge turn.

We didn't fly too often to games, which was just fine with Norm Waslawski. He totally dreaded flying, and whenever that came along he would really get upset. He would become ill. We were going to Omaha once and we were heading into Chicago to change flights and the pilot comes on the intercom and says, "Ladies and gentleman we have an emergency light on in the cockpit. We have checked all our backup material and everything seems to be fine, but because of the type of emergency the light shows, we are going to put down." Now Waz is really sick. We use an alternate runway at this airport because they didn't want us on a main runway in case something happened which didn't please Waz. We come down and by the time we touch, what's alongside us but three fire tricks and a couple of ambulances. Waz was about to die right there. Then when we got it parked, Waz finds out that the light that was on indicated there was fire on the aircraft and they couldn't figure out where it was. We pert near had to pry Waz back onto the airplane to finish the rest of the trip.

CHAPTER 34
STAYING OUT OF TROUBLE AWAY FROM HOME

There was a story in Des Moines again. Ken and I had been out to dinner that night and we came back under the marquee of the hotel and here comes Lenny and Lionel down the street a ways so Ken says, "Let's wait for them and we'll go in and have a beer." They are about 10 feet from getting under the marquee, and all of a sudden this huge bag of water just misses Lionel and splatters all over the street. So Kenny jumps out real quick and he sees a window go down. He's counting floors, and he says, "You guys go into the bar, Bob and I'll be right back." We take the elevator up to 6, he tracks down the hall to where he thinks it is and knocks on the door. Not a sound. He knocks on the door again, and not a sound. Then he says, "All right, whoever is in there open the damn door right now." You hear all this hustle and bustle going on behind the door, and all of a sudden the door flies open, and who opens it but his son Ronnie who was one of the younger players on the team. Ken just looked at him and shook his head and says, "Oh, no, not my son the hockey player." The reason it took them so long to open the door was they had a pail of water set up over the door so when anybody walked in they were going to get doused.

We were in St. Paul in the playoffs one year and Ken was a bit of stickler on getting to bed the night before a big game. It was a cold night, and it always seemed in those days of the steam-heated hotels that Kenny always got the room where the steam pipes would be going kaboom all night long. He called trainer George Polinuk and asked him to help him move to a different room. This is 1 or 2 in the morning, and they are walking down the hall and all of a sudden Ken can hear this talking in a room. He says to Polinuk, "Who is that?" and George says, "I don't know, Ken." "You do know, who the hell is in there?" "I think Teddy Wright and Fergie and Thornson" so Ken knocks on the door and they open the door and he says, "Having a card game and didn't invite me, huh," and the guys knew they were in trouble. Bob Reed from the Journal Gazette was on the trip, and the next morning after practice Ken has a story and talks about fining four guys for violating curfew. He didn't say what it was, just violating curfew. Reed is saying, "Aw, Ken, that's awful, you shouldn't find those guys for something like that." Ken says, "Well, they're being fined, Bob. If you want to pay their fines, I'll take the money." It wasn't five minutes after the newspapers hit the streets the next day that the wives are calling and saying, "All right where were you guys last night?" It was so amazing because the minute the papers hit the street and the girls found out the guys had violated curfew all they could see was the guys in the bar or doing something like that. Fergie as big and tough as he was, that Joanie could wrap him right around her finger. He was scared to death.

We always stayed over in Des Moines a lot and the boys were having a poker game one night and the word got out that Ken was doing a room check so everybody scatters as quick as they can. Teddy was in the room so he wheels it down the hall and all of a sudden he can hear somebody coming. There's a long big drape on this window so Teddy jumps behind the curtain, and just stands still, but when he did, he backed into a radiator and burned his hind end like it wouldn't quit but he couldn't yell. Sure enough, Ken goes cruising by and Teddy thinks he gotten off OK. Now Teddy is going to dive into the room, but he realizes he left his keys in the other room where the poker game was going on.

We were golfing at the Elks one day and Lionel and I were partners and Art Stone and Lloyd Maxfield were the other pair. We had a $2 bet going and we lose the front nine by a stroke so we're down $2. We come to 18 and we either have to win 18 or we lose $4. What could we do but press. We could press and win the hole. Lionel was pretty nervous, and he was pretty nervous. He was the last guy to commit to the press. You are forcing the bet so it's winner take all. Even if we win the back 9 we're a wash. They're looking at winning $4, and we're looking at going away scot-free. Lionel just argued and argued, he didn't know what to do. We tee off and everybody hit a good shot. I hit a long drive coming in on 18 which was a par 5. I hit a three iron off the fairway and I'm on the green but I'm about 65 feet away from the hole. Art Stone, his second shot is on the green and he's about 25 feet from the whole. It ain't looking good. I'm the first one to putt and to make a long story short, I drop that sucker for an eagle. Lionel was all over me like we'd just won the sweepstakes, but Art still had to putt. Art missed his putt and had to settle for a birdie. Lionel has never forgotten that story.

CHAPTER 35
CHANCES AT THE APPLE

I was pretty well involved in hockey at the local level with WOWO and had never envisioned myself as being an NHLer. I began to get comments from a lot of people who listened to WOWO who thought I had a unique way of doing games. It still didn't start my interest in being an NHL announcer. Then one day I got a call.

The first chance I had to go to the NHL was with WBZ, the Westinghouse station in Boston when they carried the Bruins. That would have been around 1959 or 1960, and they were in the process of changing play-by-play men at the time. I'd had a chance to go to WBZ in another capacity before that as a morning drive man because of my jock background, but I turned that down. At this time they'd interviewed several people for the job and I was one of them and I was told by the GM that if I wanted the job, he was pretty sure he could get it for me. At that point, the Bruins had a lot to say at that time had a lot of say about what went on, and back then with only six teams, it was very political to get a play-by-play job. The GM told me the story and said, "If you come to work here, to do this job, don't worry about it because you're protected and we'll make sure nobody messes with you." I asked what happened to the guy before that, and this kind of thing happened all the time. Maybe a guy has been on the air for four or five years, and his big sponsor is Rosebud Coffee. All of a sudden Rosebud is gone and the next sponsor in is Bokar Coffee, and their representative says, "I don't want that guy. He's Rosebud Coffee, so I want a new voice." When that happened, you had to go with the flow. He said, "There will be some animosity, but we'll protect you." I said I if have to come out and take a job that I like with that hanging over my head, I don't want it.

After that, I had another chance when the Minnesota North Stars came in before they hired Wally Shavers' dad. Wally was the voice of the Saginaw Gears. I could have had the North Stars job ahead of Wally Shavers' dad, but I didn't want that because again it was a contract job. It had no affiliation to any station. I'd go in on a contract basis, and maybe they'd like me for a year or two, and maybe they wouldn't and after that, I'd be out in the cold. I didn't care for that kind of a deal.

Then in 1967, I had been elevated to marketing director at WOWO, and the first day I'm on the new job at about 10:30 the phone rings and it's the Detroit Red Wings. They want to know if I'm interested in coming to Detroit as the voice of the Wings which was my dream job. I turned it down because Westinghouse had been very good to me. I had just assumed a brand new position and had a lot of responsibility in their organization and I loved the people I worked with. As badly as it broke my heart, No. 1, I turned it down because of Bruce Martyn. Had it been anybody else maybe I would have taken it anyway, but I really struggled with this. I felt I owed a lot to Westinghouse because they did so much for me in terms of developing me. When I talked more about the job in Detroit, I said, "Where's Bruce Martyn?" They said Bruce had been let go because the Red Wings had been sponsored by Stroh's beer for years and years, and Bruce was the voice of the Red Wings and the voice of Stroh's beer. A new beer came to town and I think it was Pabst and they wanted nothing to do with Bruce because he was the Stroh's man so bingo he was out. That's when they asked me to come in. Had it been someone other than Bruce, maybe I would have overlooked even the Westinghouse stuff, but there was no way I was going to come in directly behind a good friend of mine. Eventually, Bruce got his job back because they hired some people who didn't do a very good job, and also they tried to cut Bud Lynch out and he was their broadcaster before Bruce. Bud came in and did the color for Bruce, and it was a pretty good combination. I don't think I would have had any trouble in there at all because I had known Lynch for a period of time, but with Bruce hanging in the background, I didn't want that job. I started doing hockey because of Bruce leaving WSOO and going to Detroit to become the voice the Red Wings. I had been doing hockey in Marquette at the same time Bruce was doing hockey in the Soo.

In 1968 they were having a problem in St. Louis because Jack Buck would do their games until the Cardinals opened training camp and then it was "See you later." Gus Kyle was an old hockey man and he'd fill in the rest of the year. He was also their ticket manager. KMOX had their night show on and they are talking about how come they have to play second fiddle with Jack Buck, and somebody calls in and says, "If you're looking for a hockey play-by-play man I've got the guy. All you have to do is listen to WOWO, 1190 in Fort Wayne." Sid Solomon III, who owned the club, called me and wondered if I'd be interested. He asked how soon I could come down and talk to them. I had three or four days and skipped down between games. They said they would get back to me and they did with several times to come down there when they needed me to do some games. I'd do a Tuesday-Wednesday-Thursday. They did a lot of back-to-back games. I went down and did five games with them. When it was over, Solomon said, "We have definitely decided we want you. You're our guy. So he takes me down and through the offices and he introduces me around, including to Gus Kyle, as the new voice of the St. Louis Blues. Then he took me to KMOX and they had an incredible nucleus of people at that time and Jack Buck was in the meeting. He's the lord and he gets up and he said, "Well Chase, I've heard you myself and I think you'll do a heck of a job for St. Louis. I'm really pleased that you're here. If there's anything you need in St. Louis, you just give me a call and I'll do anything to help." I said, "I really appreciate that." "But one word of caution, keep your blasted hands off the St. Louis Cardinals." Then he started laughing. "No, I'm only kidding." I said, "Kidding or not kidding, the only thing I'm interested in St. Louis are the Blues." In a matter of days, I had accepted the job but I told them I couldn't come immediately because I still had some commitments to fulfill in Fort Wayne. They said they could get by until I could get there. What killed it all is I'm leaving the station at 4:45 on a Friday to do the IHSAA championships in Indy on Saturday. They call and they want me in St. Louis on that Saturday and Sunday to do a weekend deal with Chicago and Detroit. I say there's no way I can possibly do that because I'm going to the state finals and this is an obligation I have for my station. That's what it took really to get Kyle and some of the guys working in the background to torpedo me. I hadn't talked to Mr. Solomon, so whatever they had said probably cooked my goose. So Monday I called to tell him how sorry I was, but I would be available ta, da, ta, da, da, da. All of a sudden, I can't talk to anybody because they are out and about and gone. I finally wrote a letter to Mr. Solomon because they owed me for two games I had done. I got a letter back saying, that they had made a decision. Scotty Bowman had brought a friend in from Ottawa, and they liked what they had heard and he was available immediately so they were going to hire him. The rest of that story was legendary because Dan Kelly was one of the greatest play-by-play men of all time. A couple of years after that when the all-star game was in St. Louis, I was there for the dinner the night before and after the dinner, I went up and said, "Dan, can I talk to you a little bit. I just wanted to meet you and congratulate you on the tremendous job you do. My name is Bob Chase and I'm from Fort Wayne." He says, "Oh, my gosh, you're kidding. Just a minute. Honey, honey, you'll never guess who this is." She says, "No, Dan, I won't." He says, "OK, when we were back Ottawa who did we listen to doing hockey games back in the states? Honey, this is Bob Chase." Dan Kelly listened to me religiously out of Ottawa. If I were going to lose a job to anybody I would feel honored to lose the job to Dan Kelly. He was an amazing broadcaster and his son does a great job now. He was perfect gentleman, very talented and a real good guy.

Scotty said a couple of times over the years, it's amazing that we could have worked together. At that time Scotty had come from the Ottawa 67s, and Dan Kelly was their play-by-play man.

The next chance I had was with the Washington Capitals. Lefty

McFadden who owned the Dayton franchise was hired by Mr. Abe Pollin to be one of his executives in Washington. When Lefty got there he called me and said, "Bob, I'd like to bring you to Washington and be part of our sports pool here with the organization." It was really strange thing because they had this talent pool of sports announcers. You weren't Mr. Hockey or Mr. Basketball or Mr. Football, but you were hired into the pool. It was very, very uncertain because this was just beginning. Whether I was going to be the big dog or not in hockey was still a question. If I was going to go, I wanted to be the voice of the Caps. Lefty was pretty sure it was going to happen, and if I could be patient he'd work it out. I told Lefty, "A bird in the hand is still worth two in the bush to me. I know I'm not making sensational money here, but I am more concerned with my state of mind and stability. I've got a wife and I've got kids, and I don't want to be out tramping around and lose an incredible job with this company. As badly as I want to do hockey, I think I have to think of my family and their security first. If I knew I was going to be the voice f the situation that would be one thing, but wow." He said, "I can't say anything more than that right now, Bob, because I'm new here myself. I'm trying to get you in."

A lot of people probably would have just jumped at the first thing that came along. I've never been much of a jumper. The only two jobs that broke my heart were the Red Wings job and the Blues job because they were jobs with the hockey club. The rest were all contract jobs. First, you have to have an agent, and I didn't want to get into it in that level.

I don't regret that I didn't get those jobs. I felt honored to think that somebody thought of me as being somebody who was capable of doing them, but I guess I'm not a gambler. In hindsight, my life couldn't get any better than it is. I'm not rich, but I'm happy.

I was talked to by KDKA at one time and they were the Westinghouse station in Pittsburgh and at that time they were bidding for the Penguins. They wanted to know if I would be available if they got the contract, and I said yes. The bid didn't come open at that time, and they eventually got the contract about two years later, but at that time I didn't care anymore.

The strange part of it is I never called any of them, they all called me which was amazing and I can thank WOWO for that. A lot of people that I never met for many years until I went to the NHL meetings in Montreal... I'd be in a group and somebody would say, by the way, have you ever met Bob Chase. The reaction would be, "Oh, my God, I've listened to you for years and I've never met you." It's amazing the hockey people in the NHL who listened to me as they traveled back and forth. I tried to be as complete as I could at the time and talk about the NHL scores and such. A lot of people listened to me.

CHAPTER 36
KOMETS WHO WERE CHARACTERS

Over the course of our history, we've always had some pretty good trainers and most of them have been backup goaltenders. One year we had Harold Ellis and he was a wannabe goaltender so one night we're in Muskegon, and Harold got his chance to play. Everything was going along fine and he was covering his angles and not getting into any trouble, but he was getting braver and braver. As his confidence built, he was getting a little more aggressive. At that time Muskegon had this big 6-5 defenseman named Gerry Glaude. He was an old Quebec Aces guy and played in some NHL games with Montreal and he had a shot like a cannon. Anybody who ever got in front of his shot realized, be careful. Well, Harold wasn't aware of this and all of a sudden Glaude winds up from the left point and it was going to go by the net clean and clear, and I think that's probably what inspired Harold to stick the glove out. When he stuck the glove out, you could hear it just like hearing a catcher's mitt go "Pow!" It was like somebody put a hypo in his arm because he just went completely relaxed on the left-hand side. His hand came out, the glove dropped off and his face looked like somebody had ripped his arm out of his socket. They had to hold up the game for about two minutes while he walked around shaking his hand. After the game, the guys were kidding him and he said then he wasn't sure if his hand was on or off. It totally numbed his hand and his arm. That's the last time he tried handling hot shots.

He was a very athletic, strong little guy, but he was very nervous. You go up behind him and go "Boo!" and he'd jump about a foot high. One night we're coming home from Toledo, and there are two seats sort of inverted and facing each other. Well, Harold had commandeered them and decided to go to sleep, so while he's sleeping the guys got this diabolical idea. When Harold went to sleep, he really went to sleep. So they get all this tape and tape Harold up. He never even knew they were doing it. They taped his legs together, his arms to his side, and they got him all taped up as hard as they could. It was all set up so that the minute they got him secure, we all sat down and Jimmy Loser hit the breaks on the bus and everybody yelled. Believe it or not, Harold jumped straight up on his feet in the aisle, broke every piece of tape that was wrapped around him. He was so strong, and his reaction was so quick that he burst all the tape on his feet, his arms and his legs and stood straight up. The guys were completely in awe of what he did, and he was petrified. He thought he had bought the farm. That was a fete of strength I didn't ever think I would see. He was a pretty tough little guy.

Years ago Ken brought in this goaltender named Muzz McPherson. We already had Glenn Ramsay, and I had known Rammer form a long time back. He came to us from a stint in Cincinnati. He came into camp and he was a little lackadaisical, and Ken liked to see effort, and this McPherson was stoning everything in sight. You couldn't have gotten a pea past him with a cannon. Well, we're getting close to the beginning of the season and you only kept one goaltender. The one day I talked to Ken and I say, "I can't believe this McPherson," and he says he was a heck of a little junior goaltender. As Ken's good judgment prevailed, he decided when the season started he was going to start with Rammer but he kept McPherson around a little bit. It just so happened Ken's best friend was Kenny Wilson who owned the Troy Bruins and his goaltender pulled up lame. Kenny said, "You won't believe this but I've got a kid here who I had to really think whether to keep he or Ramsay." "Good, send him down." So the two teams have a game the very next night and he gets stoned 17-1. I don't think Wilson talked to Ullyot for three months. He thought it was a set-up. Needless to say, Muzzy was packing the next day. It was so unbelievable because he had played so well. His one and only game in the IHL and he gets beat 17-1.

We once had a trainer named George way back in the early days who came to use from Cleveland where he had been an assistant trainer. He was a quiet little guy and a loner. No one knew very much about him. He was a good trainer and a backup goaltender of sorts. It was amazing because George must have had a million friends because we'd get on the bus he would write letters, and he would write letters and letters. It was obvious George had a lot of friends because he kept getting letter after letter after letter. Finally, it turned out George was almost a hermit. When he'd go on a bus trip he'd write letters to himself and then he'd get them when we got home. He was, unfortunately, a very lonely man, but nobody knew that. He sort of led the guys on that he had a lot of friends, and he was always writing to somebody. It turned out in the end that he was writing letters to himself. That's just a short bit about another type of character you meet in the game.

Edgar Blondin was a funny little guy. He was Mr. Hustle and he did anything he could to help win a hockey game. He wasn't a goal-scoring machine by any means, but he did his job. One day in practice he says to his center Art Stone, "Artie, some night in a game, how about giving me some of the passes. You're giving Eddie all the passes." So Art says no problem at all. First shift out he hits Edgar with a pass, and Edgar couldn't handle it so it goes into the corner. Pretty soon, here's Edgar and Artie gives him another pass, and bingo, he couldn't handle that one so it goes in the corner. Edgar comes up to Artie, "Look, don't pass the puck to me all the time, give it to somebody else!"

Edgar was kind of the Casey Stengel of the team. He came into practice one day and it was a slippery bad day and he was a little late. Somebody says, "Edgar, you're late, what happened?" "I was coming across the bridge down there and there's a bad wreck on the bridge and I got held up." So somebody says, "Did anybody get hurt?" and Edgar says, "I don't know if anybody got hurt, but you should have seen that car. It was folded up like a Concordian."

One of the funny guys was Puggy O'Brien, a big, rangy defenseman about 6-3. He had a shoulder that kept popping out. He used to go to sleep at night using a necktie for a sling so he could roll over without the shoulder popping out on him. One night he forgot to bring a necktie so he used skate laces to put it together. During the night apparently he rolled over and the skate laces got tangled up and he cut the circulation off in his hand. When he woke up his hand was just throbbing and he can't figure out why. When he went to move to get the string out, he popped the shoulder out.

Jokes on the bus aren't that prevalent anymore, but they used to happen all the time. Somebody would be sleeping, or maybe there'd be four or five guys in a card game and hotfoots were the big thing. They hurt. Sometimes you didn't realize somebody was getting it until you smelled burning leather. About that time the guy who was getting it would react. Nobody ever said much about it, but it always got back and they'd get even one way or another. Another thing that used to happen was the guys would be sleeping and they'd lean back in the sleep and there would always be one wag that had a can of shaving cream. He'd plaster your shoes with shaving cream so you'd get up to get off the bus and go into the building. If you weren't looking, all of a sudden there would be this gunk all over the front of your shoes..

Lionel was studying for his insurance exams later in his career and we'd go to different places for lunch. Lionel knew we didn't make a heck of a lot of meal money. So Lionel would say, "That's OK guys, I'll pay for it with a credit card and you guys can pay me at home." They'd get home and Lionel would say, "Hey, Lenny that was $4.50 for the meal." And Lenny would say, "Lionel, you didn't say we had to pay. You said you were treating us, right guys?" Lionel would about go into convulsions, but they would always pay him.

Being a Canadian, Lionel was a big fan of tangerines which were a big Christmas favorite in Canada. Lionel had a friend over in Chatham which was in the league at the time. So Lionel convinced his buddy to get him a crate of tangerines, and he paid for them at the rink before the game and then he put them behind the last seat in the bus to come home. So we're on the way home and we stop at the border. The customs guy gets on the bus, the same guy who saw us on the way up, and he said, "How'd you do guys, win or lose? Anybody buy anything." So he walks all the way down the aisle to the back of the bus, bends over to look and comes back to the front and we're all going, "Oh, no." Tangerines are totally illegal to bring into this country as foreign fruit. We're thinking, "Oh, brother, here it goes." He comes to the front and says, "Merry Christmas, guys," and gets off. Everybody breathes a big sigh of relief. So Lionel used to wear blinders so he could go to sleep at night on the bus because he might have appointments in the morning or whatever. He goes to sleep and all of a sudden I can smell orange peels. The guys are in the back of the bus, they got into the crate and they are taking the peels and throwing them on Lionel. Pretty soon Lionel can smell it and he wakes up and he's on the back of that bus like a raging bull. He is really, really mad. Well, the joke was on Lionel because the reason the customs guy let us go and Lionel didn't know it until he went back there was they were Florida Oranges. His buddy had taken him, telling him he had sold him tangerines. Here's Lionel trying to sell oranges by the bagful on the bus on the way home.

Lionel was very competitive financially, and he was a good guy. He was the only guy who could make money on $3.50 a day meal money.

This goes back into the mid-50s when Joe Kastelic was playing for the Komets against Cincinnati. We were short-handed and Joe was coming out of our end on right wing with the puck. As he comes to the blue line, there wasn't anything to do with it except to dump it, and he didn't want to jam it, he wanted to make it go so he kind of gave it a flip. He gave it a mighty flip. The shot went off the end of Joe's stick and way up in the air, in fact, it went over the scoreboard. It just kept right on going, and nobody knew where the puck went, including their goaltender Jacques Marcotte. All of a sudden the puck smacked down beside him and slid in. No. 1, Marcotte went nuts because he didn't know where it went. Nobody else knew where it went, including the referee Hal Jackson. Now it was on a Sunday afternoon and in those days because we had beer sponsors we weren't allowed to broadcast on Sundays because of the blue laws, so I would do the P.A. work on those days. Now Hal doesn't know what the heck to do with this one, so he made the biggest mistake he ever made in his life. He skated over to me and said, "Bob, did you see that puck all the way?" I said, "Hal, yes I did." And he says, "It's a goal." Marcotte broke his stick over the crossbar, threw it up in the crowd and he was just totally livid. They threw him out of the game, and George Polinuk came into finish the game and we scored 10 on him.

CHAPTER 37
INCIDENTS IN OTHER ARENAS

Toledo was always a riot, I don't care when you went in there. One night they had a big kid Chris Kotsopoulos who goes after Jumbo Goodwin and he really worked him over. Jumbo wasn't a fighter and at that point, I couldn't believe a guy with Kotsopoulos' size and skill was so gutless he had to pick on somebody like Jumbo. Well, apparently his parents were listening in Toronto. The press box was right over the nice and maybe 35 feet up. So the next time we go in there, it's a warm-up and some guy pokes me and says, "Some guy down there wants to talk to you." I look over and here's Kotsopoulos and he's calling me everything but a white man and said if he ever saw me where he could get a hold of me, he was really going to take care of me. Feeling in the spirit of the thing, I flipped him the bird, which didn't help. So all the time in warm-ups all the thing he could do was look up at me and shake his fist. I tell you, I screwed him up big time he had a terrible hockey game. It never got resolved, because I never saw him and he never saw me. You had to walk out the back door in Toledo right by the locker room of the Toledo team.

Another night we get in there and we're totally besieged. The fans are banging on the locker room door and they want us bad. Teddy Wright had played in Toledo before he had played for us so he gets up and says, "You ready guys?" so he darts out and grabs this guy and yanks him into the dressing room and shuts the door. He says, "OK, now you are going to pay." They threatened the guy, and they were going to make him run the gamete with hockey sticks. They scared the heck out of the guy. Teddy says, "Here's your alternative, get in the shower" They soaked him down completely, and Teddy brought him to the door and said, "Now you tell the rest of those guys if there's anybody else who wants to start screaming and hollering, it won't be just me, it will be four or five of us and we're going to drag him in here and it won't be as easy as you getting wet." They cleared out completely from around the dressing room. Even when we walked out of the building they stood about 15 feet away to scream.

The only place I've been swung at was in Toledo and that was on dime beer night. We'd come in early and this one concession stand would always open early and I'd get my coffee and talk to the ladies. One of them says, "I wish we wouldn't here tonight." I said, "What's the matter?" "It's time beer night and the regular people don't even come on dime beer nights. It's just a mess, we don't even like it." It just so happened that was one of the nights when the young guys got overly brave. A lot of people used to scream at me from five feet away, they'd spit on me and stuff like that, but they'd never get to close, and a lot of them were kids and you didn't dare touch a kid. In those days I had two great, big boxes to carry that were probably 35, 40 pounds each. I'm going around the corner and there are kids who are just hammered screaming and yelling and one guy comes up and takes a swing at me. He missed me and I dropped everything, and I grabbed him by the lapels and I jammed him up on the wall. All of a sudden here come two ushers, and they're backing me so the other kids stayed away. I told the kid, "You have two choices and none of them are good. You get out of here right now, or if you want to give me any crap, I'm going to nail you. " I let him down and he took off. He didn't realize I was very serious. He really tipped me. I don't normally get angry. I learned from the time I was young, you just don't lose your temper but I did that night because he took a swing at me. The two ushers backed me up and said, "Bob if there are any repercussions, we are your witnesses." They wrote their names down and gave them to me and we never heard a thing. That was the only time I've ever been physically accosted. I was just lucky that the other kids didn't grab my gear and run away with it. I think I surprised everybody, including myself.

We're coming out of Toledo another night and the stick boys are putting the bags on the bus and Ralph Keller comes out and walks around the other side and sees guys pulling the bags out the other side. He took off and a couple of players took off with him. The guys scattered in different directions and one guy made the mistake of running toward the river. Ralph caught him and threw him into the river. He said all of a sudden when he went splash he thought, "Oh, my God, I hope he can swim." Needless to say the kid could swim and he ran up to that parking lot looking like a drowned rat.

When we joined the UHL in 1999, the first time we went into Binghamton, the starting lineup is introduced on the ice, and lo and behold who was introduced with the starting lineup but me. We got back in the dressing room after the game and Kelly Hurd said to me, "Chaser, I've heard a lot of things in my life, good, bad and indifferent, but that's the first time in my life I can remember the play-by-play guy not only getting an introduction but getting a big hand as well." All through that area when we'd go out there, everybody kind of knew me if they were hockey people because our signal was so strong for years that they listened to me.

Probably my severest critic was always Murph, and she listened to the games at home and she always wanted me to do well, but one night we're in Toledo and at that time they had a player by the name of Billy Booth. This was in the early 1950s, and he was just a dog eat dog competitor. He wasn't a big guy, but he was a whirlwind. He'd fight at the drop of a hat, he'd do anything. He was a strange little guy. When you saw him off the ice, he was meek and mild and quiet and shy. He'd hardly look at you. The minute he pulled the gear on, he'd tilt, and this one night he was going bananas. The way I described him was just what I saw. I came home and Murph was really upset. She said, "What would happen if his wife or somebody heard what you said?" I said, "Yeah, you're right, but it was so amazing when it hit me I just described what I saw. He just tilted, that's all there was to it. His eyes were wide, he just went crazy." So the next time I go into Toledo, this lady comes up to me and she says, "Are you Bob Chase?" She said, "I'm Billy Booth's wife. We don't very often go to the games since we've got the kids at home and they are small, but you know the other night when you talked about Billy? We sat there and laughed and laughed. You hit it right on the head." I had to tell that to Murph when I got home.

We also once had a game that was delayed because of sunshine in Toledo. My broadcast partner Robbie Irons was the goaltender at the time and it was a beautiful Sunday afternoon. It was very, very warm outside so they opened a couple of skylights in the roof of the Toledo Sports Arena. Well, warm-ups were fine and dandy with no problems, but they came back out to start the game, and there about 15 feet in front of Robbie is this great big square of brilliant sunshine that had come through the open skylight. As it turned out nobody who was there at the time knew what to do. It was a Sunday afternoon, and the maintenance people who normally took care of that weren't around. There was a lot deliberating and Robbie said there's no way he going to play with that thing out there, and who could blame him. So they hemmed and hawed over the thing, and they postponed the game for a half hour. Lo and behold the sun moved enough after a half hour we dropped the puck and played the game. Once the sunspot got away from in front of Robbie, we were ready to go. That's one time in my life I ever heard of a hockey game being delayed by sunshine.

We've had a few games where fog was a problem. They weren't bad enough that I couldn't see to broadcast, but if the fog got too deep, they'd stop the game and all the players would skate around in figure eights to swirl up the fog. We'd drop the puck and go for another 10 minutes, and it would get so foggy you couldn't see the puck on the ice. As a broadcaster, you lied a little bit and hoped you got it right. One night a fog game took us four and a half hours to play. It was just awful. Toledo eventually got these big fans and put them in the corners so they could blow and get enough circulation.

They used to play in this old building in Grand Rapids that was just a terrible, terrible building. They used to call it the Owls' Nest. The roof leaked all over the place and especially when you'd get a big load of snow on it and it started to melt in the spring. There would be drips and leaks coming from all over the place. Even while the game was going on, the big drips that would hit the ice would build up little humps because it would still freeze there like little warts on the ice. You had to play with it while the period was going on, and then the Zamboni driver would shave them off at the end of the period. Usually by then, they'd be big brown spots on the ice because they'd pick up a lot of the dirt from the roof.

During one of those games in Grand Rapids, it was a warm day, and our press box wasn't the greatest place in the world, either. There were all kinds of leaks in the roof even in the press box. Moe Bartoli was the general manager there and he set me up -- you know those patio sets that have the table and chairs and the umbrella? -- he set me up with one of those chairs and an umbrella, and here I am sitting underneath there doing the game and there's water dripping all over the place.

There was also a Zamboni story in Grand Rapids. It was such a terrible building, the worst in the league and the worst the league has ever seen. Every piece of equipment in it was nothing but junk. It was out in the middle of a field where there was little grass, and if the snow melted or it rained, it would get all sloppy and muddy. Their Zamboni was so old, if it had a serial number on it, it would have been 2. It was just awful. One day the flooding the ice when all of a sudden the Zamboni breaks down, and they can't move it. There's water still coming out of the Zamboni. A guy who had a tow truck was at the game, and he had it parked outside. They opened this one end where they used to bring the Zamboni in and out so the tow truck could come in. He's got dual tires on the rear, and there's mud all over them, but he backs in and puts the hook on the Zamboni. He starts to drive off with it and he got about 30 feet when front bumper falls off the Zamboni. There it is sitting there on the ice. Rather than going back out on the ice, he finally went out farther and reeled it in with his tow hook. They had to hand scrap all that stuff off the ice before they could finish the game.

The coldest arena I have ever been in was in Des Moines. We were in there one night and the boilers had blown up and they had to repair them. It happened at the end of the building where they just happened to assign the visiting broadcaster. There was no wall at the end, just this huge tarpaulin hanging down because they had pulled the boiler out. Until they put another one in, they weren't going to finish the wall. There I am up in this corner looking down on the game, and it was probably 10, 15 degrees at best outside. Thank goodness I had a pullover and a nice warm long coat and gloves. As I broadcast my voice is freezing on the microphone and there's frost all over the microphone. I'm so cold I'm just shaking. I counted while the game was going on there were 114 people in the building. I counted them all. That's what I called a cold day in Hell.

The building in Chatham, Ontario, was a crazy place. They had no heat in the building except right over most of the seats. They had these long radiant heating rods which would throw enough heat down so the crowd wouldn't freeze up. They had this little press box they had was just big enough for their guy and a couple statisticians. It was like a Quonset hut from where the roof meets the seats up high. They had these two boards and the boards went out at an upward angle and were sort of clamped around one of the arches that came down. It was a walkway and beyond the arch on the end of the boards they had a little box about four feet square. It was like a box on a dunk tank. When you got out there the thing kept bobbing up and own. They had run a cord out there for electricity and then they forgot about putting the phone line in. Fortunately I had about 80 feet of phone line so we could make it work, but it got pretty precarious every time I would move. The game got to be pretty good and I 'm bouncing around like I always do. Man, that thing is going up and down and up and down, I thought for sure it was going to break and I was coming down. Was it cold up there, too!

The other place that was a terrible building was in Marion, Ohio. The building was like a Kraft cheese box, long and very narrow. They had no press box, so in order to do the games there, they had a grating overhead about 45 feet off the ice. Then were my table was sitting they had some planks, so here I am up over the game and when it passed underneath me I couldn't see it until it passed through to the other side. I'd lose them until they came to the other side. Once you got out there, you were stuck there until the game ended so you better hope you had brought everything with you that you were going to need.

What's amazing is that in all my years as a broadcaster, I have never ever been caught in a situation where I had to go the bathroom in the process of the play-by-play. That's one of the blessings of using tape between periods when you can. Usually my tapes are five to six minutes long so in most cases you could get back and forth in plenty of time. Usually at the end of each tape, I have a sign-off and they would play spots. I always used to tell them to keep playing spots until I come back. I know there was one time in Muskegon where you had to go a long way that they had run out of spots by the time I got back.

There was a year when Des Moines and Fort Wayne were in the Turner Cup Finals. When Des Moines came here, WHO would pick up my broadcasts, so I got to know the fans in part because we were sitting in the crowd. They were a great bunch and we had a lot of fun when they'd come up and talk to me before games. We were kind of sitting right in the crowd. This was game No. 6 on a Saturday night and we were leading the series 3-2. We did not get it put away. and they were leading 5 or 6 to 1, and the next game was going to be in Fort Wayne next afternoon. I'm sitting there with Bud Gallmeier from The News-Sentinel and Carl Wiegman from the Journal Gazette. Late in the game, the announced that if the Oak Leafs win this game, the fan busses leave at 4 a.m. for Game 7. After I heard the announcement, I said, "Oh, boy it looks like we're going to have a lot of Des Moines fans in Fort Wayne tomorrow afternoon to see that one." And this fan sitting behind me goes, "You're gosh darn we are!" Only he didn't say gosh darn. The minute he said that Carl Wiegman says, "J.C., don't you know he's on the air?" Now I've compounded it with Jesus getting involved at the other end. Now Carl is so embarrassed because he's a very religious sort of a guy, and it just blurted out. So 50,000 watts of prayer came out at one time.

The only arena I ever sat in the crowd was right here in Fort Wayne. We used to sit in section 25, row A with 1, 2, 3 and 4 for our seats. We had some pretty vociferous people sitting right behind us, including Pete Hagerman and his wife. They were just great. One night something happened and it was kind of crazy, and Pete was so excited about it, he pulled me by the shoulder because he wanted to talk to me about it, and he says, "Gosh darn it, they can't do that, can they?" Again, he didn't say gosh darn it. So it's right there on the air and what do I do. Poor Pete realizes what he's done and then he feels like 2 cents worth of dog bones. Another night Ray Perry, one of the owners, is on the P.A. system and Pete is up there again. Perry gets on the P.A. and he has a question for the referee, so he's saying "Referee, stop the game. Referee, stop the game. Get over here!" Pete says, "What the heck, he can't do that, can he? The crazy son of a gun." Again, he didn't say heck or son of a gun. All I said was, "Folks, I'm really sorry, but he can do that."

After that, I moved up into a crow's nest before they eventually built a press box.

CHAPTER 38
CHARACTERS OF THE IHL

The first time I ever went to a league meeting was in Toledo and we had all the owners sitting around this table in a restaurant. So conversation moved along and all of a sudden Muskegon owner Jerry DeLise asked Commissioner Andy Mulligan a couple of questions. So Andy says, "Jerry, you know we talked about this last week and I told you in essence as soon as I get an answer we'll get it solved so don't worry about it." Jerry says, "Well, I don't want to wait. I want to know right now!" So they get going, and Jerry says something, and finally Andy says, "Jerry if you don't quiet down I'm going to have to declare you out of order." There's a great big basket of hard rolls right in front of Jerry DeLise, and when Andy said that, Jerry said, "You son of a gun, you'll never get me..." and he starts winging rolls at Andy. Here are grown men in the middle of a business meeting and one of them is firing rolls at the other. Andy later apologized to me. "Bob, you must think this is a pretty, rowdy, raucous group." Then DeLise apologized, too, but by then I had found out he was a hot head. I'll never forget him winging rolls down the table at the commissioner.

When Muskegon came into the league, we happened to be the team they opened their history at L.C. Walker Arena. We went up a day in advance because they had a luncheon the day of the game and introduced both teams, plus it gave us a chance to skate there in advance. The luncheon was over and we went back to our hotel and I was staying with Ken when the phone rang and they wanted Bob Chase. It was Jerry DeLise who was the owner of the Muskegon Zephyrs at that time. He told me,

"I've been considering this thing all day long, and I'm not going to let you broadcast tonight." I'm going, "Wow, why? What's going on?" He said, "After the luncheon I talked to some of the press people and some of my friends, and they tell me they've been listening to you out of Fort Wayne for a long, long time." I said, "Well, they probably have." He said, "Well, I'll tell you this much, if you're broadcasting out of this building and I have Muskegon people listening to you in Fort Wayne, there's no way you're ever going to broadcast out of here." I said, "Whoa, this is outlandish. I can't believe you'd say this." He said, "You're not taking people out of my building." So I explained it to Ken and gave him the phone. So he talked to Jerry and they about got into a fight. Finally, I got back on the line and DeLise made me a proposal which we adhered to almost to the day he was gone from the place. He said that any time on a mid-week night that Muskegon played in Fort Wayne, I had to promote the fact that the Komets would be there on Friday night or that Muskegon would be home Friday or Saturday night playing whomever. He finally felt that was a pretty good idea and that's how we settled the conflict, but I'll tell you he and his wife Wynn would sit there on Wednesday nights when Muskegon was in our building listening to the broadcast. If I didn't promote or give him what he thought was appropriate, he'd be on the phone Thursday saying, "I don't think you did a very good job promoting that Friday night game," but it never cost him a thing. It stoned me right off the top because it was the only time I ever had that kind of a reaction.

They were two of the most different people I've ever met in the game. His wife was actually bigger in stature than he was, and she was a tough lady. Kenny Wilson was working with him one time and he was n the office. Jerry was at the ticket window talking to somebody and he had some comments he made to the fan across the glass that Wynn didn't like. She's standing back there out of sight, and she is just kicking him in the behind like a mule, and Kenny Wilson is just sitting there watching the whole thing. Jerry never turned around, he just kept talking, and boom, she kicked him again about four or five times. You never messed with Wynn. He was so strict about preserving the sanctity of his place. Jack Loser was the bus driver and he used to come up to the press box to keep stats for me. Jack always wore his Indiana Motor Bus shirt, and Jerry kicked Jack out of the press box with that shirt on because it was advertising for somebody other than an entity of his own choosing. When we'd go up there after that, they never questioned Jack as long as he didn't have an Indiana Motor Bus shirt on. Those are the crazy little things that you had to cope with. They were characters.

Jerry was a miser and was the original Scrooge when it came to money. One night there was a shot deflected and went up into the crowd and it ended up on a concrete level area just at the top of the first section of seating. This little kid picked it up, and Jerry ran over and ripped it out of the kid's hand, at which point the kid's dad came up and decked Jerry right on the spot. Everybody agreed that everyone was a little too short, and they kind of let it go right there. The kid got the puck and I don't think Jerry charged him for it.

He always was trying to impress people with his contacts with the Montreal Canadiens who gave him some players. Sam Pollock was running the Canadiens at the same, and Jerry was always talking about Sam this and Sam that. Something happened at a league meeting one day and I was at the meeting. Andy Mulligan says, "We need a ruling on this. Jerry, you're a good friend of Sam Pollock's aren't you? Why don't you call him and see if he can help us," and he hands Jerry the phone. Jerry gets on the phone and gets all the way through to Sam Pollock and says, "Sam this is Jerry. No, Jerry from

Muskegon." Apparently Sam didn't recognize him and he said, "Jerry DeLise the owner of Muskegon." Needless to say that humbled him to a degree and everybody was just rolling. You didn't hear a heck of a lot about Sam Pollock from Jerry after that.

I was always not harshly editorial but once in a while, I had comments on officiating maybe above and beyond a little bit. Those were the days when Bill Beagan was the commissioner of the league, and being a former official, he was very much oriented toward the officials. Unfortunately, here we are 50,000 watts that roared all over the Midwest, so Beagan would listen to see how things were going. One night I don't know what I said, but I was especially harsh on one of his officials, and the next day I get a call from Beagan. He's very upset about what I said, and he said, "I'm enclosing a letter to you and you will abide by my comments or as my letter will indicate, you will be in a major problem." He made the mistake of sending me a letter. I get the letter and it says, "Any more offensive comments about the officiating and I would automatically be restricted from every claiming myself as the voice of the IHL again. Plus, he would not allow me to broadcast out of any other building in the league." I took that letter into Carl Vandagrift who was the GM at WOWO. He read the letter and all of a sudden a big smile comes over his face. He said, "You're in a pretty bad spot now. Bob, the reason you are here is because you are the resident expert on hockey. You are the person who lends credibility to what goes on. Your knowledge allows you to comment on any facet of the game as you see fit as long as you don't overdo it or become overly vindictive. I've heard things you've said, and I've seen some games and I can understand what prompts you to say what you do, but now you are really n trouble." I say, "Like what?" He said, "If I ever hear you pull back from not making comments regarding the conditions of the game or the officiating, then you are in trouble with me. Don't worry about it because this guy just made the biggest mistake of his life by sending us this letter. The Westinghouse attorneys would eat this guy up without even using salt and pepper." Had it only been verbal, I would have had no evidence of any kind that he had threatened me. When the letter showed up, here it was in black and white with restrictions that are totally beyond any legal areas. Years later I think I told Bill about that. Bill never, ever did that again and we ended up as lifetime friends.

He was protecting his officials, being an old official himself. It was known in the league that officials could do no wrong and there was no sense calling Bill to complain about officials because nothing was going to happen.

When Andy Mulligan was the commissioner of the league, his entire life was hockey. He'd call you in the morning and say, "Bob, Andy here. I just wanted to see, what have you done for hockey today?" That was him. I'd say, "Nothing yet, Andy," and he'd say, "Just remember if you can do one little thing for hockey every day it's good for you and good for the game." He was never a threat in any way, although one of the things with Andy came when he was running Toledo. He had kind of commercialized Toledo and called them the Toledo Monroe-Matics Mercurys. Andy would call and he'd say, "Bob I was listening to your game last night and you're still not using the full name of my team." And I said, "Well, Andy, yes I am." "Well, Bob, I beg to disagree. They are the Monroe-Matics Mercurys." And I'd say, "Andy, quite frankly there's been a ruling on that here, and Monroe-Matics is a commercialization which we're not going to plug on the air. We'll do the Mercurys all night long, but Andy, at home, call them what you want, but they are not the Monroe-Matics Mercurys in Fort Wayne, Indiana, they are the Toledo Mercurys." And he said, "Well, I'm a little disappointed, but I'll abide by that." Andy was a wonderful man.

I never really got into any real trouble with any of the commissioners. I've never been vicious but there are times when your eye has to guide your comments. If you see it and it's rampant enough that in y our mind it is affecting the game or your emotions, you have to be careful, but you have to report what you see.

The officials have all treated me with respect. I can remember one time I was having my 25th-anniversary celebration and I had different gifts from different people. WOWO gave me a big plaque and a couple of sponsors gave me some things. The league gave me a plaque and lo and behold who shows up in the middle of it, but the officials who gave me a plague. It was a very nice plaque that I still have. We were playing Muskegon that night. After the presentation was over, I go back up to my old place to broadcast, and I hear this announcement. "Ladies and gentlemen, the remainder of tonight's game is being played under protest. Coach Lallo of the Muskegon Zephyrs has protested the game." I don't what this is all about, and I don't find out until after the next day when he goes to the league office. His thinking was, "How in the heck am I going to get fair treatment out of the officials in Fort Wayne when the head of the officials gives their broadcaster a special plaque in the middle of the game?" That was resolved as well.

I've always had a good relationship with the officials. I interviewed referee Hal Jackson many, many times. He was an old Red Wing and Blackhawks defenseman, and he was one tough set of nails. Jackson was a great, great referee, and he helped the guys on the ice. He was a rough and tumble guy, and he liked to let the game got, but if you got cheap, he let you have it in a hurry. He'd be skating along and he'd say things like "Artie, head up, here he comes." He didn't like to see guys get hurt, but he liked to see it stay rough. He was one of the first guys who initiated a tolerance level. If it looked like it was getting real chippy, he'd get the captains together, and say, "OK, I'm not going to change what I'm doing, but I'll tell you this much. If you get a fight, I want everybody to back away and let them fight. The first guy who gets in there to create any kind of a problem, you're gone." He had to prove it a few times, but all of a sudden the atmosphere changed. He liked fights, but he didn't want gang brawls. The guys realized what he meant by it. A lot of guys had big mouths and as long as it was a gang brawl, they were in the middle of it. All of a sudden when they realize everybody clears out and it's me and him, whoa baby, a whole different attitude went into the game.

When I first started doing the games in the IHL it was strictly a hockey league where hockey people formed and owned the teams and they did a pretty decent job for the time. They all had their own direction they wanted to go, and they were all so different. They were competitive among themselves because almost all of them at that time were Canadians.

Fred Huber who started the league was a hockey man all the way. I didn't see him that often because he always had so many things going on in and out of hockey. You could see him if you happened to be in Detroit. He has his own agenda to go with.

One of the more colorful guys who was a GM in the league was Lefty McFadden who was a legend in Dayton. He was a minor league pitcher, hence the name lefty. He played a lot of ball around the Dayton area and got involved in Dayton businesses. He was a confident guy who always had a smile. He was just a typical old Irishmen whom everybody loved, and when he got involved in the league he was different from the other people because Lefty was a promoter. He had promoted auto racing all over the Midwest, and that's how I originally met him. When he got into Hara Arena in Dayton, he had some pretty wild ideas. He knew how to promote a game without ruining it. This was back in the days where they felt, "Look, if you not interested in seeing hockey which is the great sport in the world, then forget it, we don't want you." But Lefty never saw that side of it, he just saw how to get fans in the seats and make a little bit of a circus out of it. He did some wild things, the kind of stuff that now has become almost passé in the league. Because of his abilities in promotion, he was hired by the Washington Capitals organization and went right in the middle of their group as one of their promotions people. He was just a great guy, very honest and he was always available. You never saw Lefty hide from anybody in his building.

In Indianapolis when I first came into the league they had a guy by the name of Mel Ross. His original claim to fame was running a travel agency, and he was kind of hooked on hockey and was the head man for a group as a director of hockey operations. He wasn't a hockey person. Ken Ullyot worked with him a lot and helped subsidize Indianapolis one year to keep them in the league to make sure they had enough teams to play with. Following that they had a disastrous explosion at the Fairgrounds Coliseum in Indianapolis during an ice show. They thought maybe it was propane gas tanks in the concessions stands under the bleachers, and it killed about 60 people. I went down to cover it and got there about 3 a.m., and they were using the ice surface as a morgue. It was a pretty sad thing. Mel Ross had also promoted the ice show, and that was a defining moment in the personality of Mr. Ross. They couldn't play hockey there because they had to get the building re-approved, and Mel left the game at that time and died a couple of years later. I'm sure the impact of what happened there shortened his life.

Teddy Garvin wore a lot of hats from general manager and coach in Toledo and GM in Port Huron as well. Teddy was kind of an early day, if I can use the comparison, Gregg Pilling, only Teddy resorted more to finding people who would do his bidding. He created mayhem on the ice so many times. He had people in Toledo especially. He had the one line, Murder Inc, and they quite frankly put fear in the whole league. When they all started on the same line, you know No. 1 it was going right now because the gloves hit the ice before the puck half the time. Teddy used a lot of intimidation.

His psychology got him in trouble a lot of times because he played to the crowds for sympathy and would get them so wound up he couldn't stop them. The crowds would go nuts. One night up there they knocked the glass down around the rink because he couldn't stop them. It was in the spring and it was playoff time. They had these fans around the kind to blow air so it wouldn't fog up, and they knocked the fans down and threw them on ice, they threw chairs on the ice and they threw chairs at Toledo policemen. Teddy would just get flat out of control. He did wild things like the night he showed up on the bench walking around with a Superman outfit on. That positively incited the crowd.

When he went into Port Huron he was a little bit more subdued, but he was the whole bit in Toledo and could do whatever he wanted. Once he got there he had Morris Snyder to contend with and Morris was more of an orthodox hockey person. Teddy was a good guy, and a great interview and was very knowledgeable about hockey, but he could go nuts sometimes.

I met Kenny Wilson on two fronts. When we first came into the league, he was the GM in Troy. I later knew him because he and Ken Ullyot were life-long friends. He ended up with Peoria Prancers and Danville Dancers, and then he ended up in Des Moines and Toledo, too. Kenny made the rounds. One of the few places he didn't get was Fort Wayne and he was responsible for the hiring of Ken Ullyot, and they had offered him the job first. He ended up doing a pretty good job in Des Moines.

Toledo is the only city I know of in the IHL that won a Turner Cup and folded the team. Ken Wilson was in Toledo for a while, but that whole Toledo psychology was kind of a lost cause. The last hockey job he had was working for Jerry DeLise in Muskegon.

The end result with of all these guys was they were dedicated hockey people and each one had their own take on how they were going to get the job done. The serious ones with good connections brought good hockey players into the league and produced some good teams, but it was in an era when they did not believe in spending good money to promote the team.

CHAPTER 39
GOING HEAD-TO-HEAD WITH TED

Strangely enough my career has been without any major controversy. I don't know why. I always tried to be mature about what I did, and I was knowledgeable enough about the game I think people respected me. I think was discreet enough and respectful enough not to get myself into those situations where I could create any kind of controversy. I just tried to be fair.

I got multitudes of letters over the years that I wish I had saved. A lot of them were from players' parents and relatives. I tried to most of the time be complementary to the guys who played. I knew enough about the game to know it wasn't an easy game to play. You have to have a lot of respect for those guys who go over the boards and play. I've always said there are no cowards in hockey. None. You can't be a coward and go over the boards and compete because it's a tough sport with no place to hide. I tried to treat everybody as fairly as I could.

I got a little controversy going one time with Dayton and Ted Lebioda. We're in Dayton one night and something happened out of frustration and they get a little melee going and up comes Lebioda and sucker-punches Johnny Goodwin. He drops him right in his tracks. The moment it happened, my reaction was and out it came, "That's the most gutless act I've seen in my life. He wants to call himself as man and he would do that to a player with the talent and ability of Johnny Goodwin." I just said I thought it was a disgrace to the league to have a guy with that kind of morals playing. I let him have it, but he was a bum.

I get a call from Lefty McFadden, and he told me that I was going to have a problem when I came back to Dayton. He wasn't threatening me, he was warning. I wanted to know what the problem was, and he said, "Apparently it spawns from some remarks you made about Lebioda and the fight he had with Goodwin." I said, "Yeah, I remember it and I'll never forget it, Lefty." I think I'm as fair as anybody, but I had never seen such a cowardly act in my life. He's got a defenseless guy who he knew couldn't fight and he comes up and unloads on him. I said to Lefty, "I'm sure you've been a broadcaster for many years, and I'm sure you could have controlled it better than me, but I was at the end of my line because there was no defense for what I was going to say." He said, "I understand, but the problem is Mrs. Lebioda is really after your butt. Here's the story." Apparently people in Dayton had heard the broadcast when I called him gutless and their kids in school were telling his son that his old man was gutless and it was creating an incredibly emotional thing for the child. And Mrs. Lebioda was having problem as well as some things Dayton fans commented to her about what I had said. I knew I had to face it, so I go down there, and I told Lefty, "When I get set up in the press box, if Mrs. Lebioda and her son want to come in, let's handle it right there and we'll talk about it."

I really apologized for what I had said only from the reason I had never ever intended this to be an emotional scar on anyone, especially a young kid who just adores his father and the guy's wife who has tremendous pride in her husband. I said, "It was a case of you've seen your husband, you've seen what he's done and you've seen how he's acted. Maybe you've been able to resolve all this and accept it all. I couldn't handle it because of the kid he went is after one of the nicest men you'll ever meet. I really profusely and profoundly apologize from the bottom of my heart. Son, believe me, I know what a father's love for his son is. I have sons and I was a son to my father, and I feel really, really badly about this and I hope you'll accept my apology." They kind of said they would and then she came back after he was gone and said, "But I'll never ever, in my own mind forgive you." I said, "If that's the way you feel about it, I can't do anything about it. At the same time, it's something that I had not said, but as long as you want to be that forthright with me, I'll be that forthright with you. I appreciate you and I respect your husband because he is a hockey player, but forever and ever he will remain gutless in my eyes."

Did I watch my back a few times going in there. Pembroke and Purinton watched my back a few times when we went into Dayton. I'd walk in the door and Levioda is just leaning against the door looking at me. I was ready for him. I thought if he's coming, boy, I better get the first one in. If he'd have given me any crap, I'd have just unloaded on him right and then taken the beating. Pembroke and Purinton were really good, God Bless them. Pember said, "Chaser, you don't even ever have to raise a hand in anger. If that son of a gun gets within five feet of you, don't even worry about it. You're right he is a gosh darn coward." They didn't like him either.

That was the end of that story. I never had a problem with him again, and he cycled out of the league. That was probably the most spontaneous or outspoken I ever was with anybody.

CHAPTER 40
THE TRUE HIGHLIGHTS OF MY LIFE

All of the kids were their own persons. There were no two alike.

Probably it worked out so easily because of Murph. She was the world's greatest mother to my mind. Really I wasn't around the house that much and in the wintertime I was always gone. On the weekends once football started, I'd be gone for football and then hockey and basketball and my winters were a blur. I tried as best I could to be part of the kids' lives. They understood it. We were around them and we had a pretty family and a pretty good home. We weren't as much mom and dad and the kids as we were a family. Everybody was all a part of it. I think it helped the kids grow and be more responsible and also be more interactive with us. We never really worried about our kids. They all confided in Murph because sometimes I wasn't available and they all trusted Murph, probably more than me because occasionally I would lose sight of what they were really telling me. As we grew up, we were always part of our kids' activities. Our vacations were always spent together. We didn't go many places because we basically went back up to the upper peninsula and did a few other things like going to see baseball games in Detroit.

My eldest son Mike probably set the standards for the rest of the children, and he set the bar pretty high. The other kids as they grew up, while Mike was still there, he had a profound effect on them not only in their scholastic abilities but in their respect and their goals and who they were. They always looked up to him because he was always doing good things. He was a heck of an athlete in high school. The kids were very impressionable at the time. He was all-city in football and he was excellent in track, and scholastically Michael was always aware of where he was. Failure was not in his vocabulary.

Mike set the bar for achievement, and the other kids picked it up. He would have been first in his class, except in his senior year at North Side in 1960 he was taking Spanish and he was excellent at it. He had to write a thesis in Spanish and he wrote about Cuba and Castro and how Castro was a communist. His Spanish teacher would spend his summers working in Havana at a hotel, and got so upset at Mike he gave him a bad grade. That's the only time we had to go to bat for Mike for any reason. Unfortunately, the grades had already been recorded and the records or done or otherwise he would have been the valedictorian. He had Castro completely booked at that time.

Mike wanted to go to med school, and he got the full ride at Michigan. Then he was going to go to IU med school when an unfortunate turn of events happened. In the interim IU med school and the federal government and a lot of other people had brought a whole bunch of foreign medical students into IU. They had filled up their quota and Mike was considered an out of state matriculation because he went to Michigan. I never figured that one out. By one day he missed the chance to register, and he'd already been accepted, but they changed the rules. The one day that he missed he went from 1S to 1A in terms of his designation for the draft. He was going to be drafted. We decided we better look at the options and the best one we could see was the Army at the time.

He went to officer candidate school and got his commission, graduating as a second lieutenant. Right out of all his training, bingo, he was overseas because the Viet Nam war was escalating tremendously. He ended up as a company commander, but five weeks before he was to come home he was critically wounded. He triggered a bobby-trapped howitzer shell. Had he not been combat wise, he wouldn't be here because the moment he heard it click he froze. In the explosion he lost his leg and pretty much the whole side of his body. It was 17 months to recuperate in army hospitals.

He kind of gave up the quest for a medical education because of what he had gone through so he decided to go to law school. He applied to seven law schools and was accepted by all seven, including Harvard. He said, "My choice is automatic, I'm going to Michigan." He graduated Cum Laude and practiced law for a couple of years. He got to the point where he just couldn't morally continue in the work he was in.

He was involved in a law group in Detroit originally and then he moved to California. He could never really bring himself to accept that he helping defend a guy who was blatantly guilty, and they had to somehow find a way to circumvent the law. He called me one day and said, "Dad, I'll be home in about a week or two, and I want to go apartment hunting." I said, "What, have you got a job in Fort Wayne?" He said, "No Dad, I've done my last as an attorney. I can't in all conscience continue to do what I'm doing."

Mike was fortunate because he was told by a surgeon in Japan while they were trying to put him back together that as soon as he was ready to go back he would come to an Army hospital in this country and they would immediately say, "Captain, don't worry about it, in another couple of weeks we'll have you in a V.A. Hospital back home." This doctor said, "You tell them, no way. They can muster you out of the army until you are satisfied that you that you have been rehabbed. Too many people are emotionally bound and kids want to get home and they'll do anything to get there and they lose all their benefits at that point." He calls from Fort Dix when they fly him in and Murph and I jumped into a car and were there the next day. We didn't know what to expect, and he's sitting there on this bed. Here's a kid who weighed 185 pounds and was a great athlete, and here he is 115 pounds, just skin and bones, minus a leg. It was so tragic, but thank God he was alive and we still had him. We hadn't been in there more than 15 minutes and this big, old fat nurse came in and said, "Well captain, this is Mom and Dad, huh? Well, Mom and Dad, don't you worry, we'll have your son pretty close to you soon. He'll be in Chicago or Indianapolis in a V.A. Hospital in a week or two." Mike says, "Like hell you will." She says, "What do you mean?" and he says, "That's not going to happen." She said, "Don't you want to be near your Mom and Dad?" and he said, "When I'm ready." She just didn't know what to say next. They did let us take him out that night and we had a nice steak dinner and a couple of drinks. He hadn't had alcohol in so long he felt them right off the bat.

When he came home from California, he retired. He's a very intelligent, smart man and he knew what to do with his money. He took care of himself. Mike could be a host on a radio or TV talk show and would blow you away. There isn't anything he doesn't know about sports. He knows anything you want to know right now about the NFL, the NBA, the NHL. He hasn't been overcome by it, but he's absorbed all this knowledge about sports. He's amazing. When he starts to spout sports,

I just throw in a couple things and he's gone. It's unbelievable how he loves sports.

Kurt was more directly influenced by Michael than the other kids because he was old enough before Mike went away to absorb a lot of what Mike was and he just worshipped Mike. Nobody was more devastated than Kurt that Mike got hit. Kurt emulated him in so many ways, and scholastically as well.

Kurt is a very intelligent kid. He never achieved the academic excellence that Mike did but he was pretty darn close. He was very industrious. You didn't have to supply stuff for Kurt. He got very good grades in high school, and before you knew it he had checked out all these possibilities for college scholarships so he could assure himself of going to IU which he wanted to do. By the time he was ready, he had two or three different scholarships, plus what we gave him and he had his career pretty well launched. He was involved in journalism and was on the photography staff with the newspaper and covered most of the sports events. He had a camera which was a Nikon that Mike had gotten on R&R and Taipei. I would say if he had to buy the camera at that time it would have been worth about $3,500. Kurt would be down there taking pictures, and the professional photographers would be checking out his camera saying, "Where did you get that? I've never seen one of those."

We were down there one day for a football game, and Kurt had these red overall with white vertical stripes, and you couldn't miss him on the sidelines. There he was right in the middle of it all and he was so intent on what was going on, but here comes student body right. As the whole defense goes over to try to collapse the Indiana rush, Kurt never saw it coming and just disappeared under a whole ton of football players. He gets up and shakes himself off. We thought he had gotten killed.

He did very well at Indiana. At that time his childhood sweetheart was going there, too, and they were bound and determined to get married. Nothing we could do was going to deter them, so they got married and went back to campus and we helped them out. And they got along pretty well down there, but neither one of them ever graduated. Then Terry got pregnant and she was working at that time and Kurt was looking for work. She worked at Allen County Motors for Mr. Boland. She and Mr. Boland's daughter were very, very good friends so they hired her in the accounting department. Here was Kurt and he was driving courtesy cars at the time. Mr. Boland was a very dear friend of Hilliard Gates.

After talking to Kurt he goes to Hilliard and says I have a heck of a kid here you can use. After Kurt interviewed, he got hired as a TV technician. He continued to progress in that organization until he became a producer-director, and over the latter years of Hilliard's lifetime, Kurt was Hilliard's personal sports producer.

He became an incredible authority on the newest trends in television, and when digital came along there was nobody there to teach anything, but Kurt is just a hands-oner. He just has that native ability to touch something and make it work. They were changing their equipment at WKJG and they brought this new digital board in. They had to wait for it to be installed, but it could run and Kurt would take extra time when he was done and fiddle around with this board. They get the thing put in finally and now the guy is running a seminar to teach all the people who to use this. He's showing them how to transfer images from point A to Point B. He's going along and all of a sudden Kurt says, "Wait a minute, what you just did, you don't need to do that. There's a simpler way to do it." So by the time they are done, Kurt had done four or five different things that this guy who had built the board didn't know it could do. Right away the company wanted to hire him, but he and Terry had a couple of kids and didn't want to move.

Eventually he and Terry had a falling out and they had three boys at the time. Then when he realized WKJG was gone, two years before it happened, he started looking and was hired an NBC owned and operated in Birmingham, Alabama. This was an incredible opportunity for him, which he took, plus he was getting to use all the newest technology before it went anywhere. When he got there, he knew more about it than most of the technical people because he's just a genius with that kind of stuff.

We were never curious to find out in advance whether our children were going to be boys or girls. It was kind of like Christmas and why spoil a miracle? The Lord had already put the plumbing together and you got whatever He prepared for you. We were totally overjoyed to have a girl. Now we've got our family.

Karin was a good-sized girl right from the beginning and was always bouncy and very chubby when she was young and she leaned out as she got older. It was obvious with her personality that she would never know an enemy. From the time she was a little kid she always smiled and was very happy, very loving, very trusting and a just a complete joy as a little girl. We found out fairly early in life that she had a pretty good talent for sports. She also had a talent for music and was going to get involved in orchestra and things like that in junior high school. So when she gets there, lo and behold, because he's bigger than everybody else, what do they give her but a cello. She doesn't want to sit there with some big goofy thing between her legs. She just decided right there she had lost her interest in orchestra and devoted more time to things like basketball, track and volleyball.

She began to develop those particular talents. She was always bigger than all the rest of the kids almost all the way through school. She becomes a natural at basketball and volleyball, and surprisingly enough turned out to be an excellent track athlete. Volleyball turned out to be her A sport. She was good enough at al sports to become the first girl to ever win an N blanket at Northrop. Then she went to Indiana but she didn't get a scholarship there but she played volleyball her whole career. When she was a junior she got a scholarship in volleyball. Then she was also the scholar-athlete of the volleyball group. A plaque with her name on it is still up at Assembly Hall.

Then she came here. I had talked to Bob Armstrong who was the AD at Snider at that time. He hired her as his volleyball coach because Tom Beerman had retired. Well, he forgot that he had also hired somebody else so he ends up with two volleyball coaches. Karin was a teacher at Lakeside Junior High, and she's coaching basketball, track and a variety of other things. Before the year was over she got a call from IU who wanted her to come back as a grad assistant in volleyball so she said yes and went back. Everybody in the athletic department knew her and loved her. Then when she got her grad year out of the way she was hired as assistant coach at Penn State under Russ Rose. How much more fortunate could you get than to be tutored by one of the greatest coaches of all time in women's volleyball? She did her three years there.

The job came open at the University of San Francisco, and Karin's name came up very quickly. She started a five-year run as a coach out there. Her problems were they were such as a cerebral school, you had to have at least a 3.0 or better average or they wouldn't accept you on scholarship. They were very strict about it and it was a very expensive school to start with. She had a terrible time recruiting. Karin had five full scholarships and one partial, and here she is playing against all these big schools who have 12 scholarships. Lo and behold the second year she was there they walk into Pepperdine and beat Pepperdine. She rose to be the shining star at San Francisco, but eventually she just couldn't hold it because she couldn't come up with winners because they didn't give her enough resources.

So after her stint at USF Karin was hired by a private middle school in San Francisco to be their AD and teach some classes. It was strictly a girls school. When she got there, she was immediately asked to become involved in the AAU programs and the club programs. The first year it was an afterthought by the time she said she would, and all they had was a handful of scrubs. My God, you should have seen that group. They looked like the United Nations, just an assortment you couldn't have put together if you tried.

Karin took one look at them and they were all small so she knew for sure she didn't have any kind of an offensive team so she began to develop a defensive unit. These little kids bought into Karin like you wouldn't' believe. They had no fear of anything. They'd dive and roll and dig and get all skinned up and go right back at it. Karin would go and play in these tournaments and other coaches would come watch their games and wonder how she got her kids to play like that. They did it out of desperation. They wanted to play so badly, they would do anything so they could play. She went to Junior Olympics for five straight years with those kids and never won it, but usually ended up in the semifinals and occasionally the finals. This one team had so much success he parents go together and made Karen an offer to follow these kids all the way through.
When she and Vic were married they moved to Los Angeles and she was approached by Santa Ana Mater Dei to take over their

volleyball program which she did for three years. Then Karin took on a whole new challenge. She left the coaching field and became involved in special education academy in Williston, Vermont, specializing in dyslexia. She accepted the position as dean of women at the school and at the present time that's basically her responsibility. She teaches and is beginning to develop a variety of athletic programs at the school.

David was a surprise child, the only unplanned one, but he turned out in his own way to be the most amazing kid in the whole family. David is the guy who educated both Murph and me on bringing up children. Fortunately discipline was never a problem with the first three, and David seemed to have the ability to know how to challenge us at every curve. Not in any malicious way. If there was some trouble somebody could get into, poor little David could find it.

David was a good athlete, too, right from the time he was a teeny tiny kid. He showed an athletic gift at a very early age. When I think he was five, they formed the Allen County Hockey League, and they started putting travel teams out. One day they said, "What about David?" and I said when he's old enough. They played at the coliseum, and I bought him a pair of skates. The first time out, he's flopping around holding onto the boards, and then he got a chair and started pushing it around. By the end of the first week, he's got a hockey stick and he's skating around all over the place. He was just a natural.

In a matter of weeks after he first got a pair of skates he was proficient enough to go on a travel team. He played park board hockey as well. As he came up the line, he and Brian Thornson came up together so Lenny was very active in coaching at the time which is probably the greatest thing that ever happened to David. David wasn't a great big strapping kid who could shoot a puck through a stone wall, and they were always kidding him about how he couldn't shoot it hard enough to crack an egg. Lenny told him it only had to cross the goal line, and David really picked up on that and began to get these skills. Lenny would go out there and play with him and stick handle and David would come back at Lenny, just the two of them because Brian wasn't interested because that was just his dad. The things that Lenny taught David were positively unbelievable about how to play the game. He just kept going and going and getting better and better.

When Pete Crawford was here, he sent David up to where he lived and his dad coached a Tier Two team up there. It gave David a chance to try to expand his hockey skills. He went to an open camp for about 80 kids, and after about two days, David called one night and said, "Dad, it's really tough here. I never knew how much they hated Americans. I've been called names that I didn't even know existed. It doesn't bother me, and I'm going to stay." Two days later he calls and says, "Mr. Crawford told me to get my stuff and move it into the other dressing room and then come and see him. He wants me to sign a contract." He signed the contract. The first time around the league David said he never had such as long three weeks in his life because in every building the program would say, David Wallenstein, Fort Wayne, Indiana. He said, "Dad, even the grownups were yelling at me. It was unbelievable." Finally after a couple of times through the league, they finally got used to the fact that they weren't going to scare me and they let me play."

He had a pretty good time there, except his senior year in junior he wasn't going to be drafted, so they let him go. Then there's Ivan Prediger in Des Moines who had told me to send him out to him earlier. David calls me that day when he got cut. I asked him what his next step was and he said, "That's why I called. Rather than go home I talked to Ivan in Des Moines. He wants me out there for a game Friday night." He drove straight through to Des Moines, had one practice and played or Ivan the next night.

He played out there and had a good year, scoring 27 goals, but most of the people were looking for at least 30 goal or better scorers. He got a couple of opportunities to look at college and was accepted to Notre Dame. Then in the summer, he got a letter from Lefty Smith who was coaching at the time telling him they were going to de-emphasize the program and go to a club program. Then David picked up the phone and called the University of Alabama-Huntsville. They weren't sure if they wanted him or not so I talked to coach Doug Ross and he said well, send him down. Ross never played freshmen, but he had three kids that year David, a kid by the name of Mike Finn and a little Italian kid I can't remember now, a little kid from Detroit and they were a freshman line. They might get on the ice three times a night, and I'll be danged every time they got on something happened. One night we're down there and they are leading 3-1 and it's in the last five or six minutes of the game and they get two penalties. He'd been running his lines to the point where the only people he had left to put on the ice to kill this penalty were these three kids, and they paid the price like you wouldn't believe it. They were diving and blocking shots, and the team didn't score so they won the game. David was one of the stars of the game.

Starting in his sophomore year the local television station had a sports program every Tuesday called the Wizard Watch. They called him Wally the Wizard, and when they had home games they did footage on him. He had moves that you couldn't believe, and he used them when he had to and they were amazing. They always had Wally the Wizard highlights. He turned out to be the only two-year captain of any sport at UAH and had a number of scoring records.

Right after he graduated, David went to work for another former UAH grad who had been one of the early coaches when they were a club team. He was in the steel fabricating business, and he really liked David. In the meantime David met Debbie, and her mom was fairly prominent in the community and had strong ties to the newspaper editor. The editor knew who David was because he was also a UAH supporter. David interviewed for a job there and was told he would eventually advance to a high level of responsibility but he first had to learn the business from the ground up. He threw newspapers all over northeast Alabama, and whatever there was to learn about the business, he learned it. He eventually became involved in circulation and now is the circulation manager for the Huntsville Times.

He has continued to play hockey to this day. Shortly after graduation, there were a number of UAH alumni who stayed in Huntsville. They formed a senior team and went to tournaments all over the county and won the majority they entered. David is also a hockey official for recreational leagues in the city of Huntsville.

During his senior year, David came up to try out for the Komets when I was the general manager. He had an outstanding camp and in the course of the camp and the preseason games had the highest plus-minus ranking of anybody and also tied for the scoring lead. We were working with the Washington Capitals at the time and right toward the end of camp, they sent in five players, two of which were centers and we already had Colin Chin on the team at that time. Robbie Laird made the decision that he had to cut somebody, and David was one of the people he cut. Robbie said to me, "Do you want to tell him?" and I said, "No, Robbie, you are the coach. You should tell him." He called

David in and they had a long conversation. After that, Robbie came into my office and said, "Man, what a guy. You have a hell of a guy there."

Jimmy Burton was playing with us at the time, and he came and sat in my office and said, "Chaser, we should have kept him." I told him, "I really appreciate what you are saying Jimmy. This was a real tough thing for me to cope with and I wanted to stay hands-off." If it had been somebody other than a relative of mine, I'd have been in on the decision, but not this one. Then Chinner came up, and he and David had grown up playing together, and he said the same thing.

When they sent the five people in, somebody had to move and David was a center and we already had two at the time and here come two more. He was the rookie in the crowd so he was the one who was the odd man out. Robbie said to me, "I don't know how to tell you this, but I'm going to have to cut somebody. David might be the odd man out, and I don't know what to do." I just told him, "Robbie you are the coach, you're the one who has to make the call."

David had a chance to go with John Tortorella into the ECHL, and Phil Wittliff offered him a chance to play in Milwaukee. David only wanted to play in Fort Wayne and I think he was pretty broken up with it, but he never showed it. He knew he could play here, and so did I. If I had intervened in some way, which I could have, it wouldn't have been fair to David. I really wrestled with that for a long time. I could have imposed my will and Robbie would have had to take him, but I couldn't do that to either one of them.

So he went with Tortorella for training camp and he gets down there and they have an exhibition game. About seven, eight minutes into the game, here we go and the benches erupt and Tortorella is yelling, "Get out there and get somebody." So David goes over the boards and the first person he grabs he asks what he wants to do and the guy goes, "Do I know you from somewhere? You play college hockey? You played for Huntsville, right? I played for Ohio State, We played against each other." So they stood around and talked the whole time. Then the next game they had another brawl, and David said he knew that wasn't what he wanted to do.

Three days later he was gone back to Huntsville. Then he got married and he just felt he'd given it a shot. Like he said, "If I do it again, maybe I don't make it again, and once is enough." The only place he wanted to play was in Fort Wayne. He knew in his own heart he could play.

He still plays in a senior league once or twice a week and officiates most of the recreational hockey in Huntsville.

He always was a good golfer and he turned a lot more of his energy to that. He worked his game down to where he was a 1.5 handicap, and two years ago he won the Huntsville city championship. I said to him, "The way you hit the ball and the way you move it around, you ought to practice and who knows what you could do?" He said, "Dad, the minute I start to practice, then I'm apt to get serious about it and then all the fun of it goes out the window and I become a slave to golf. I love golf so much I don't want it to ever be that way."

He and his wife Tonya have two boys and a daughter, Daniel, Cory and Maggie.

CHAPTER 41
BRAGGING ON THE GRANDKIDS

My parents were always very strong on lineage and also on perpetuating the family. When Kurt was born, I called home and Mom answered the phone and I said, "Congratulations, Grandma," and I told her it was a boy, and she said, "Oh, my God, I have to go tell your father" so she had to run right over and tell my dad he had a grandson. The second one to come along was Karin, who was greeted with great glee. The third one to come along was David and he was born in September and the next June we go into the Upper Peninsula and when David was a little boy his hair was white. He was the blondest kid you ever saw in your life. Dad walked out of the house and when David got out of the car, I guess because of our Scandinavian background, Dad looked at him and said, "Oh, my God, Erik." I said, "No, it's David," and he said, "I know, bucko, but he looks like an Erik." Kurt was 8 or 9 years older than that and for some reason or other that struck him, and his first son was named Erik because of Grandpa.

Erik was our first grandchild and has done our family very well. He and his wife Misty, in turn, have produced two sons, Chase and Hunter.

Kurt's second boy's name was Kyle. He was going to Ferris State and was studying nuclear pharmacy, but he left halfway through. He'd come to an impasse in his personal life and he showed up here one day to say, "Well, Grandpa I came to say goodbye. I'm enlisting in the Army," and my heart just about fell through my shoes. This would have been in the mid-90s when things were really bad. He was quite pleased with what he had done, and I gave him all the support I could. When he got through his basic training, he volunteered for the 82nd Airborne and was accepted. His career turned out to be a pretty dramatic one because the 82nd was one of the units who were in the forefront of the second Iraq War. He served 14 months over there before coming home, getting to the rank of sergeant. He and Dawn were married after he got back from Iraq, and they, too, presented me with a great-grandson whose name is Max.

Kurt's third boy is named Chad and he was born deaf. He showed a real resiliency to cope with his problem. He got through high school with very few problems. His junior and senior years he went to Gallaudet University in Washington D.C. When he graduated, he had a chance to go to college there as well, but he didn't go because he said the college was way too liberal for him. He enrolled at Rochester Polytechnic Institute and he's doing computer-aided design and graduated in the spring of 2008.

In all, there's six grandchildren and three great-grandchildren. Maggie is the only girl. Karin is Maggie's life. Karin is her angel, her inspiration and her everything. They are two peas in a pod. Maggie is just turning 13 and was born on Murph's birthday, by the way. She and Karin are joined at the mind, and Maggie was the flower girl in Karin's wedding. She's also a soccer player and she's pretty good at all the positions.

Murph and I both are soft touches. The grandkids were God's gift to start with and then to be doubly-blessed to have great-grandchildren is even better. That's something I never thought I'd live to see, and if it hadn't been for heart surgery and my successful health, I'd never have lived to see them.

CHAPTER 42
TAKING OVER THE TEAM

When David Welker bought the team in 1989, he was looking for a general manager. It was always a dream of mine to be involved in hockey at a full-time level. I didn't really want to leave WOWO, but this opportunity came along and I thought, "Wow, I have to do this." It was one of those situations of a lifetime that when it presents itself you can't say no. Plus it kept me here. I just knew I could do the job.

Robbie Laird was already there as much coach and I had a tremendous alliance with Robbie. The league had mandated to David that if he was going to buy the club, he had to have Robbie Laird as his coach. They wanted some stability there right away. Robbie and I had always gotten along well. We had a long conversation with the three of us about what was going to happen. I told David, Robbie had done a good job, is well-liked and knows a lot of people. Robbie has to be the ultimate authority for who plays hockey with the Fort Wayne Komets. We ran with that agreement, and it worked out pretty well.

Then David kept kind of getting more and more involved because David is the kind of guy who whatever he did he had to have his hands on. He wasn't the kind of guy who sat around and said, "That's nice, go ahead." He just kept kind of getting into it more and more. Probably one of the straws that really brought him in tight was the hiring with Al Sims. When he met Al, he wanted that association. Probably had it been somebody non-descriptive it wouldn't have been a big deal, but suddenly here are almost 500 NHL games, he played with Bobby Orr and all that, and David was attracted to the luster. That's why he hired Denny McLain a little later. He got more and more involved when we hired Al to the point where he began to take over. At which point we had a conversation about "If you want to be the general manager, then be the general manager. He said, "No, I hired you to be the GM," but I'm getting more and more fed up. It wasn't because I didn't love my job, but because I couldn't do my job.

IHL Commissioner Jack Riley told me when I took the job that I shouldn't be doing play-by-play. I said, "Jack, this may be a temporary job." And I explained it to him. I was still on the station at that time and it began to change direction and then the station was sold, a guy named Price bought us and hired a guy named Joe Buys to run the station. Joe was trying to get back together all the people who made the station click, and he was after me a number of times to come back. As the burden got heavier and more frustration set in with the Komets, I was totally disillusioned with what was going on. Whenever things would get tough, David would say, "You know what I could do, I could fire you." It was either that or "It's my money, and I'm going to spend it any damn way I like." So those were the two threats he made all the time. Those were his two standard answers to anything.

It became very easy to go back to WOWO because we were in the process of crusading to get the station back got where it belonged. I also realized then I was never going to be successful working for David because there were too many limitations. God bless him, it was his money and his way and he could do no wrong, so why should I stand in his way? The only guy who survived was Robbie because he'd have been completely at sea without Robbie because he knew nothing about hockey.

Then Al came along. The day that we brought Al in to introduce him at Heritage House, David didn't know Al Sims from a hole in the ground until he looked at the record book. I walk in the building and there are three seats at the head table, Robbie, Al and David. There had been four seats when we set it up. He was trying to embarrass me but at that point, he hadn't been around long enough and people figured it out.

He used to tell me, "It's a funny thing when I talk to people around hockey, and I tell them that I hired Robbie Laird as my coach and you as my general manager, cripes they are most excited about you being the general manager than they are about Robbie as coach." I think that may have part of the situation.

We were working with Washington and the Olympics were going in Calgary so David went to the Olympics and chased Capitals General Manager David Poile all over Calgary for days on end. Jack Button shows up one day in Milwaukee and he's going to ride the bus back to Fort Wayne with us. Jack didn't just show up like that much, but he was there. We get on the bus and he sits with me and he says, "Bob, the reason I'm here isn't just a pleasure shot. I'm here to talk to you and Robbie because we're here to sever our relationship. By the time David Poile put up with Welker for like 10 days... Every time he looked around, Welker was there, and he just right then and there knew was never going to be."

I got a few things accomplished in the two years I was there. One day the phone rings and Flossie says, "Bob, I just got off the phone with a guy who wants to know if we need an assistant coach and could help run the power play. He just got back from Europe and wants to eventually be a coach." I said I don't know we'll have to talk to Robbie about it. Robbie ran the hockey operation and I wanted to make sure he was in control. She gave me the slip and I didn't pay much attention to it, and

Robbie comes back after practice at McMillen and says he's going to lunch and he'll see me about 2 p.m. "Before you go, we have to look at something. We got a call from this guy who wants to know if we want to hire him as an assistant coach. His name is Al Sims." Robbie says, "Al Sims, the Al Sims?" So within a matter of an hour, we consummated the deal and it took him a few days to get in. Then we told David about it. Al came in and did a good job working with Robbie and he did run the power play and coached the D. Then when Robbie left it was a natural progression for Al to become the coach.

I also started the Hall of Fame when I was general manager, and when I left it kind of fell by the wayside. I had tried to start one for a long time but I could never get it off the ground until I could get my hands on it. I feel very good about that because there were so many great guys in this town who had played for the Komets. When they are contracted to say, "You are being inducted," they are completely thrilled. This means a lot to those guys. It really does.

That lasted until it blew up at a meeting in Montreal. We were sitting in an IHL meeting, and Robbie and I were there and David came in to sit with us. There were probably six or seven teams at least that had NHL scouts who they were working with to bring players in. I had been working with Phil Esposito and the Rangers and had a really good relationship with Phil. He was really hot on the idea because he knew the building. We were going to get together during these meetings to talk about a working agreement. The day before, we're sitting in this meeting and David gets up and says, "If we're going to be successful is we can't let anybody tell us how to run this league which means the one thing we don't need is any interference from the National Hockey League. We don't want anything to do with them." Here's Billy Inglis sitting across from us and I thought he was going to come right across the table. He had a guy from Detroit sitting there. Within a matter of an hour, that swept throughout the entire meetings. I never ever heard from Esposito, not even to cancel the dinner or anything. He never returned my calls, not one.

It gave us one of the biggest, juiciest black eyes in the NHL that you ever saw. About three weeks later I finally got a call from Esposito and he apologized. It's pretty obvious now that we can not enter into a working agreement. That was the end of that.

I never got to achieve what I thought I could do as the general manager, but it was a highlight of my life to have been a part of hockey at that level. I could pick up the phone and talk to almost anybody in hockey and even though I'd never met them, they knew who I was. That blew my mind. It's amazing how many people had listened to me over the years. I could talk to a lot of people and if I left a message they'd always call me back. I felt very special about that.

The whole thing worked out because WOWO gave me a hell of a job to come back to the station.

CHAPTER 43
THE YEAR IN EXILE

In 1985-86 we switched the broadcasts from WOWO to WBTU, because Bob Britt had run up quite a debt to the station and they couldn't get their money. It was a very frustrating year because I knew our audience was gone. WBTU was not our sports, hockey audience. It was a country redneck audience and they could have cared less about a hockey game and I got the mail to prove it. I used to get some pretty crazy mail from those people. It was obvious we were in the wrong place but here wasn't anything we could do about it because the decision had been made. That was a year from hell. You realize there's nobody listening. That's in the days when AM radio was still pretty strong and a lot of people didn't have AM-FM radios, they had AM radios. It was a lost year. We suffered through it, but before that year was over they got it straightened out and we went back to WOWO.

It was embarrassing, very difficult. WOWO knew at the same time nobody was listening. They were good enough to allow me to do it. They had not lost interest in it, they were just trying to collect their money. The next year we were right back where we belonged again.

The station was besieged with calls wanting to know what happened to the hockey. The reaction to the hockey at the time we left there was much more dramatic than when we pulled the plug on Indiana University a year ago. We might have gotten 25, 30 calls for that, but the hockey, holy caramba, letters and phone calls were coming in from all over the place. We couldn't really say any more than what we did because you can't really go on and say, "Well, the guy didn't pay his bills." Once it got straightened out and we were re-wed it worked out fine. In some respects the agreement we have now with the two stations, people have become accustomed to it and the internet has been very good to us so people can listen from all over the world.

CHAPTER 44
YOU GOTTA HAVE HEART

Health has never been a problem with me, and that's been part of my family situation. A couple of years before I let up to my heart surgery, occasionally when I'd overexert myself, I'd get kind of a little pain in my chest, and I kept thinking maybe it's angina, but I didn't want to surrender to the feeling. It didn't get any more intense, and I was able to kind of cast it aside until one day in March of 1998. It was a beautiful day and I was out washing the truck in the driveway. All of a sudden, I just started getting tired and I got this incredible fever and then this awful pain in my left arm. I was just perspiring profusely. I went and sat down on the porch. Murph came out, and said "What's wrong," and I told her. She ran in and got the thermometer and I had a temp of about 102 or 103. She said, "Bob, there's something wrong here. You know what I think we're doing. C'mon, get in the car, we're going to down to Parkview Emergency."

We get in there and explain my situation so they put a nitro plaster on me and calm me down. We really, really didn't get a heck of a lot decided. I had heart palpitations and stuff, so they treated me for that and sent me home. Then the next time it happened, about four or five days later, we went out to my doctor and in the process of the examination, I had been lying down in the table and when I sat up I passed out. The nurse was taking my blood pressure and all of a sudden she said, "No pulse, no pulse." Murph just let fly and said, "Get EMS right away." I kind of fainted I guess. When I sat back up, I'm looking at six EMTS. Two ambulances had taken the call. When they saw me, a lot of the guys knew who I was so in the ambulance I go and back to Parkview. I made them promise, please don't use the sirens. Let's not make a big deal out of this.

So I get in and this time they treated me a lot more seriously and I was hurting bad. That was late on a Wednesday afternoon. They got a cardiologist for me and began to take a variety of tests. On Thursday they did an angioplasty. They did it as I was lying on the table, and I could watch the monitor and see these little things crawling around in me. The technician would say, "Oh, oh Bob, look at that one. Boy, you're blocked all the way there." Then he'd say, "Bob look at this one here." I was so fascinated with it. They come up with four and then they go around, and oops there's another one. It took a while for them to restore me and get me out of it, and in the meanwhile, one of the doctors went out and talked to Murph. He was explaining that I needed a quad bypass and they were scheduling it for the next day.

The nice thing is it gave me no time to worry about it. I didn't panic, but I got a little apprehensive right off the top as anybody would. We let the kids know. David was up here from Huntsville in a matter of hours. All the kids were home except Karen who could not leave her job in San Francisco at that time. She was beside herself. The next morning I get on the gurney and we head in and this little Oriental guy comes bouncing down the hallway, and says "Murph, what are you doing here?" It was a doctor she had worked with when she was with Fort Wayne Medical. He was an anesthesiologist. The told me, "This kid is unreal." Now I feel great because I know I have the best heart surgeon in town, and then I get this guy so I can't do any better.

I had this total serenity about me that I just could not understand myself. I was completely, totally at ease and laid back. I think working on a philosophy I had gotten from my brother-in-law who had undergone the same surgery about a year and a half previously. Art would say, "You know, there's really nothing to worry about because under you go. If it's successful you wake up and if not, what the heck, you don't know what's happened." I figured, not a bad logic.

I came out of it in excellent condition and then Karin called that same day and wanted to know if her dad was OK. This was the day of the surgery, late in the afternoon. They got up on the floor with the call, and the nurse said, "Yeah, do you want to talk to him?" Karin was just flabbergasted that she could talk to me. She just cried when she heard me.

What had happened because she couldn't be there, Karin has one of the greatest networks of friends all over the world. You can't believe the network that this lady has. She sent out a special email that went out to at least hundreds of people, maybe thousands, saying her dad was having this surgery and if they had a moment, could they please pray for my safety. I tell you when I heard that I knew why I was so serene and calm and was just so completely relaxed and accepting when I was sitting on that gurney. Prayer was working for me. I could feel it. It was an amazing feeling. I've never had a feeling like that before or again in my life. It was just unreal. I was at peace with the world completely.

I've not been the fella who is the first guy on the church step every Sunday morning. I have been an off and on church-goer, as have Murph and our kids, but I have never ever doubted my faith nor have I not remembered it every day of my life. Going to church is something that is very, very worthy of your time. If you don't go to church every week it still doesn't mean you aren't as good a Christian as long as you have the morals and the ideals that you believe. If you don't believe it, you're not going to be a Christian. I have always been a Christian and so has Murph and our kids were raised in a Christian atmosphere and morality. They have selected their own churches and they have grown older and married.

The physical side of this surgery, I had seen people come out of this with tubes and hoses. I'm thinking, I hope that never, ever happens to me. Well, it did. The only thing I could think of when I woke up was, "Oh, brother." I knew I was still pretty well sedated, and I kept thinking, "Where is it going to hurt?" Where it hurt was, immediately after I got myself up they gave me the cough test. All the fluids that your lungs have collected while you have been under anesthetic are sitting down there and are bubbling and they have to get it out. Here come these two nurses with great big pillows that they put on my chest, and this technician comes in and they have this tube going down my throat. He squirts something down my throat at which point I gagged and coughed. These girls were just pressing for all they had on my chest to make sure it wouldn't hurt as much. I couldn't imagine how much that would have hurt if they had not been there because it was just like sticking your finger in 50,000 watts. Wow! But it was over just like that and I got rid of all the junk they wanted me to. That was the only real pain I ever had from it.

Then on the other side of it, I still think that what helped me recover so quickly was faith again. I never had any thought in my mind at any point and time that I wasn't coming back again and I wasn't going to be OK. It was going to work out perfectly because I knew all the people who were my doctors. I had total faith in my doctor and faith in God and that was what did it.

CHAPTER 45
GOODBYE TO THE I

The beginning of the end of the International Hockey League came when the Central league folded. Salt Lake and Indianapolis came into the IHL in 1984 and then Phoenix in 1989 as the league began to make moves that foreshadowed its demise. No. 1, their geography began to span the country. They began to add teams from Orlando to Atlanta, to San Antonio to San Francisco to San Diego and the geography and the cost of operation just began to go out of sight. The fact that it was a union league didn't help any because players were getting automatic 10 percent raises, and it raised the operational costs of some teams who could marginally afford it and others that couldn't afford it at all. They began to fold like a house of cards.

The Komets were probably an island of stability in the whole thing because they were able to maintain their market position by being smart enough not to overprice themselves. There were a couple of high profile players who came in, but they were under NHL contracts and didn't cost Fort Wayne a lot of money. At that time the Komets also began to sign Russian players who were cheaper.

I saw a lot of people coming into hockey at that time who had no regard for the longevity of the game or the league. These were often people with enough money to use their teams as toys. It destroyed the partnerships that kept the league going over the years, and it was pretty obvious that the slide was not going to stop. It drove the likes of Ken Ullyot, Bill Inglis and hockey people like that out of the business. The minute there was no more stabilizing influence of hockey people, the league just blew up. After the work these people put in for many years, they were ignored.

Several people got immensely rich over it, because of the expansion fees, but at the expense of putting the hockey league down. Many teams were using the expansion money to stay alive, and the minute that the franchises dried up so did the league.

I was heartbroken when the Komets left the IHL. I was concerned that it signaled the beginning of the end because at that time the Colonial Hockey League was almost a rogue league. They had very little image, sort of a magnified "Slap Shot."

It really took quite a while for me to be comfortable. I'm not worried about the Colonial Hockey League, I'm worried about the Fort Wayne Komets. At that time I was wondering if I could sugar coat the pill enough to have people realize Thank God we've got Hockey and really tout the Frankes for what they were, heartfelt and sincere people who lived and died hockey. My mission to maintain the image the Frankes wanted. Fort Wayne hockey fans got their money worth, and that's was what counted to me, the quality of Fort Wayne Komet hockey. There were a lot of people around the edge of it who were willing to bury it at any moment if they could.

I still consider that Fort Wayne deserves a league with more prestige that they have now, but you have to give it a chance. There will never be a day in my thoughts that Fort Wayne will not have hockey. If it got to a point where the IHL could not function, the Frankes I don't believe would ever lead us into the AHL. I think they would sell the team, fall back and consolidate their forces and say thank you, Fort Wayne.

The new people, if they didn't understand what Fort Wayne meant in the marketplace, they'd have trouble. An AHL team would be merely an instrument to develop players, and I don't know how well that would wash here. The expense goes up, the ticket prices go up and it's a whole new concept. Fort Wayne fans like their stability.

I don't think Fort Wayne fans will pay for it. That's been my thought all along. Look, if we can't make the AHL, then who can, but how would you feel at $25 bucks a ticket? See what it costs to run a team. Whoever the local investor is in the AHL, he's there to pay the rent, pay the expenses and let the players go. His chances of making money at this by the time you pay for a franchise is little or none. I would hope I'm wrong, but I would fear for the future of the game here at that point.

CHAPTER 46
THE CLASS OF 65

Eddie was an assistant coach really with Kenny and he was always back there. He kind of turned the reins over to Eddie. His presence was obvious all the way. Eddie was a little volatile as a coach as he was as a player. He couldn't stand less than perfection. The thing is he had a great bunch of guys and they all understood Eddie. Quite frankly, no discredit to Eddie or anybody, that club could just about have run itself. You had so much leadership with Eddie and Thornson there was always somebody to take the bull by the horns and lift them. It was so amazing in a game when we'd go flat or just not be up to it, someone would find a way to get a goal. Maybe Thornson would walk through the whole team by himself. If he really had to he could put the team on this back and go for it. Eddie was that way, too. He would die to win.

CHAPTER 47
U.P. WITH THE HALL OF FAME

In August 2008 I was in Lutheran Hospital recovering from my right knee replacement when Murph brought in a letter with a postmark from Escanaba, Michigan. It said, "With great pleasure, I inform you of your selection to the Upper Peninsula Sports Hall of Fame. The selection was made by the U.P. Sports Hall of Fame's executive council. The public announcement will be August 16. The induction ceremony will be April 25, 2009."

I was completely floored. I'm amazed. I looked at it and I put it down because there were a lot of people around in the room. I must have read it four times in an hour just to make sure I was reading it right.

Some of the names in the sports hall go back to George Gipp. Two of the more famous people who are in the hall of fame who are still active are Tom Izzo and Steve Mariucci. They were old buddies from Iron Mountain who played football and basketball at Northern Michigan.

I've known about his place for years. In fact, one of the people who put this together, C.V. Money, was the athletic director and coach of every sports team at Northern Michigan University. He was a transplant to the Upper Peninsula, but he felt there were so many great athletes and great stories up there that no one had ever tried to honor that he was one of the linchpins to try to put this whole thing together.

I told the Komets, I don't care what day it is, I'm going to be at it. This is a little bit above and beyond what has happened to me. This is one I'm not going to miss because it's a once in a lifetime thing.

On the notification, he said I'll have an opportunity to make a brief speech. Please try to keep it at about three minutes. When I started to think about that, I've never really been at a loss for words, but I'm at the shrine. I'll think of something or I'll have Murph do it for me.

My mother would just faint, and my dad probably wouldn't crack a smile but he'd shake my hand and he'd be very thrilled. That's the only thing sometimes when you do have accomplishments and honors – the people you really wish could see or know are

LIVE FROM RADIO RINKSIDE

our parents and they are gone. So you do it for the present, and the kids are thrilled about this.

CHAPTER 48
RETIRED NUMBERS

Eddie Long: If you are going to make a selection to be your leader, to be your first retired number, the whole history of Eddie says he's your man. He wouldn't have had to establish all the scoring records he did, but his longevity alone and his reputation around the city would have been enough to qualify him. With Eddie, the older he got the better he got because he got smarter. He had all the skills and all the tools just to be a good solid hockey player. He wasn't going to be the Gordie Howe of the league, but he was always going to be up among the leaders. You could always count on Eddie to be there every night and give you everything he had.

He came into this league in the early days where there was nowhere to go. In today's way of thinking, Eddie probably never would have seen the IHL. He'd have been in the AHL and then have gone from there. What you saw was what you got from Eddie, He was 100 percent hard work and dedication.

Len Thornson: He was the kind of guy you could watch him play for a month at a time and you'd win a few and lose a few and you didn't' realize until after you started to analyze who did this or that, geeze, Lenny was a part of everything that happened. He was a catalyst for so many things and all good things came to him because he shared his talents with people. He was the most unselfish player I think I've ever seen. Lenny didn't care if he had 50 goals or 5 goals. He was proud of his scoring accomplishments, but I think the assists meant more to him than the goals. He was such a brilliant playmaker. He was a quiet leader. I can never remember any emotional uproar that he was involved in, and that included some of the cheap shots he's taken in his lifetime. People grew to respect him gave him his space. There were a few guys who took a few runs at Lenny, but he'd put their name in his back pocket. All of a sudden here comes the guy in the corner to take a run at him, and the next thing you know the guy is flat on his back and Lenny was skating way. I don't think I ever saw Lenny get knocked down, but he was fair. He had the respect of all his peers in the league. He was just as nice on the ice as he was off the ice.

Lenny's skills were all part of his psyche. You didn't realize how skillful he was because it was the things he did naturally. He had such a native ability to play the game that he reacted to the game in whatever circumstances were presented. He didn't have any set patterns. He just took whatever came and made the most of it. He could pass the puck with such pinpoint accuracy which is a real art because he had a variety of wingers. He had some guys who could fly, and other guys who were very meticulous. Once he got going with those people, he just knew how to treat them.

Lionel Repka: Lionel is probably one of the premier defensemen who ever played for Fort Wayne. Probably there were fewer opportunities for a defenseman in the NHL than any other position. Those guys inherited positions and stayed there. Lionel played with and against some of the great defensemen of his era in this league and the western league. He was a strong, strong guy and had a lot of respect because of his toughness. He wasn't a duker, but if you wanted to mess with him he would knock you flat in nothing flat. He could move the puck. In your own end, he knew how to move you. Probably the guy who played a lot like him was Troy Neumeier. He never let you cut inside, but once he got you into the corner he'd punish you on the boards. In a scrum behind the net, you couldn't take the puck away from him. In his way, he was a great team leader as well. Everybody was more of an equal back in those days. Everyone respected everyone else's skill and there was such an incredible skill level on the whole team that to excel was pretty darn good. Lionel was the first Fort Wayne defenseman ever honored for the Defenseman of the Year.

Personally, Lionel was totally community-involved. He was very extroverted and he just made friends so easily. He was a fun guy to be around, and Helen was kind of his count-ego. They made a lot of very good friends, and as Lionel grew in the business community, he really got into the community and did a lot of things. He chaired a lot of functions around the city and chaired a lot of committees and really gave of himself to the community. I think it shows today in the respect he and his family have from so many areas of the business community. Just look at the Ron Repka golf tournament and the people who come to that because Lionel and his family made some very lasting impressions on the city.

Reggie Primeau: He was the kind of hockey player that any coach would want because not only what he so completely coach-able, but he was such a complete package as a player that you didn't have to coach him. He was fun-loving kid who kept practices loose as can be. He was a funny guy off the ice and he always had fun on the ice. Most of the time when you saw Reggie playing, you saw him smiling. He had all kind of crazy moves and was a great passer. He wasn't a huge high scorer and was just a great team man. He never lost that lust for life and fun and being a member of the team.

Reggie could play any position on the ice because he had that fundamental ability and that skill level. Center was his big spot, but wherever you needed somebody, you could put Reggie over the boards and he knew what to do. He was a joy to be around and to watch. He was always a lighthearted guy. You never saw Reggie in a heavy moment. You still don't, which is an incredible credit to his endurance, personality and faith with the things he's been through.

Robbie Irons: As a player, he was one of the more superstitious guys that I ever watched play the game, and goalies are crazy anyway. Everything had to be laid out in the right position and it had to be just so. Trainers used to go crazy with him. That's the way he used to build himself up for games. He was really quiet when he was getting ready for things and never bothered anybody else. He became ill every night before games, and if he didn't, you had to wonder, `Gee, what's wrong with Robbie tonight?" Once he got on the ice, look out, he was a tiger.

He was an outstanding player in juniors, good enough to be drafted by the Rangers and once we got him set up here, they traded him to St. Louis and what happens is he's backing up the two greatest goaltenders in the history of hockey night after night. What he didn't know, he learned, and he also had to learn to control frustration. Finally, when he came back here, he was ready to stay and had some incredible years. Rarely was he not in every game that he played in. He started right at the beginning of the mask era. We used to always tell him, "Robbie, that's the most ugly facemask I've ever seen. Why don't you paint it up and brighten it up?" He said, "Yeah, sure, I'm not making myself a target." He had that pale old blue thing.

Terry Pembroke: In his own way he is an institution. You have to say he's one of a kind. I've never met anybody quite like him as an athlete who loved what he did with a passion, was pretty good at it, and in fact, sometimes I think he was overlooked at the wrong time or he would have been an NHLer. He had the swagger, the ability and the toughness, but again here's a defenseman and in those days defensemen spent a lot of time looking for work. Everything meshed well for him here, and he did a lot of good things personally around town. He had a lot of adventures around the city and made a lot of friends but always maintained his integrity. Pemmer was confident about himself and he didn't mind if you knew it. He was one of those guys if you wanted to try him, there he was and he backed it up.

I know he and Cal went to Omaha for a while, and I think he realized he wanted to be here. He came back and got his things going here. He had some highs and lows going in his lifetime, and he played the game for all it was worth.

Robbie Laird: Robbie Laird was probably one of the most dynamic rookies we ever had. He was not a gifted athlete by any means. He had to play the game with everything he had at his command to make room for himself. It was recognized in pro hockey who he was and that's why he got the respect to get the opportunities play elsewhere. He had some real good numbers. Pound for pound he still might be one of the toughest kids I ever saw play in this city. He didn't care who you were or where you came from, if it was time to go, it was time to go. He was consistent, well-disciplined and put up some pretty good offensive numbers. He was a good defensive team player, too. He was always a little introverted when he played and when he coached. I thought when he got to the coaching end of it, he had one of the toughest situations in that he had to coach some of the guys he had played with. I thought he did a heck of a job with it and immediately was able to rise above friendships and assert professional relationships.

Steve Fletcher: If there was anybody who was controversial

when it came to having a number retired, it was Steve. All the other requirements that the others had met, he just didn't meet them, and a lot of people felt it was a bit of a PR move. Then all of a sudden if it's Steve, how come it wasn't this or that guy? Again, you had to be around Fletch. If you didn't understand him, everybody loved him because he was such a free-spirited guy. When it came to being a team man, he was right there for everybody and anybody at any time on and off the ice.

He took on every heavyweight who showed up and he beat every one of them. I remember one night when Peoria brings in Tony Twist and he goes after Pokey. Fletch goes over and says, "Hey, you keep messing with my goaltender, and we're going." A couple of other things happened. Twist runs Pokey another time, and Fletch goes, "It's now," and did they have a brawl. Fletch really roughed him up. He really put the hammer on him. I think everybody was enjoying it, including the officials because here were two of the toughest cats wearing blades in those days.

Colin Chin: At least to this moment, never was there a hockey player born in Fort Wayne who came close to his skill levels. He played at a time in the IHL when I don't think it got any better than those years. All the skill players who weren't in the NHL, as many of them played in the IHL as anywhere else and Colin still stood out among those people. He had an unusual personality. He was a feisty, yappy bugger, but he was a courageous kid who stuck his nose in and got the job done. His skill levels were unbelievably good, and he had the respect of his teammates and of the league.

It was fun to watch him skate on the ice when he was 4 years old. You knew the way the little rascal was dangling around you were going to see him somewhere, but he never grew up. When he was playing on the travel teams, and my son David

LIVE FROM RADIO RINKSIDE

played on a lot of those teams, as the word got out about this little guy from Fort Wayne, we'd go to Hamilton, Ontario or Sault Ste. Marie or wherever and people would come over and say, "Where's this Chinese kid you guys got playing for you?" His reputation was out there, and he didn't disappoint anyone. I never saw a game when they dropped the puck that Chinner didn't come to play.

CHAPTER 49
THE MEN BEHIND THE BENCH

Alex Wood: I didn't get to know Alex well because he was just here for the one year and then he made his home in New Haven. He had coached for Andy Mulligan in Toledo before coming to Fort Wayne. Then there were a couple of players Andy gave him to start out with. There wasn't much discipline at that point and time, and there wasn't a lot of discipline through the first several years of coaching. There was much less structure than I thought there would be. He was always interested in the team and was a booster of the Komets. He was a nice guy to have around.

Doug McKaig: He was the first guy to coach here with an NHL background. He played for Detroit and Chicago, and he brought a different perspective to it because he played as well as coached. He wasn't professionally the technical coach like you see today but people played for him out of respect. He was the best insurance policy you could ever find because he was major league tough. He was well beyond his prime and had leg problems but he played defense. He never hurt hockey in Fort Wayne ever. He was a good ambassador, but management got to the point where they had to have serious winning hockey and Dougie turned out to not be their guy.

Eddie Olson: When they let Doug go, Ernie Berg came to me

and said, "You're going to like our next selection because he's an old friend of yours." Eddie came in, here again, he was having problems at that time trying to find players, and there weren't many people who would cooperate with an American coach. It was classic discrimination. He worked hard and played as well. He had relative success, but again he didn't have what they needed and they realized what they had to do was find a hockey man who could not only sit there and blow the whistle but who also had some basic idea of organization and the front office.

Ken Ullyot: They offered the job originally to Kenny Wilson who was in Troy, but he didn't want to leave there and the natural move was to recommend his friend Ken Ullyot come in. He told Harold Van Orman and Ernie Berg there was somebody he knew of who could get the franchise headed in the right direction. When Ken looked at the job, he wasn't sure he wanted it, but that was a turnaround point in the history of Fort Wayne hockey. He didn't realize the problems he was going to have until he got here because he never had a chance to look at the books. There was a time I think when Ken was ready to pack it up and get out of here. They had to give him a lot of responsibility because he had to fight off the IRS and every bill collector in North America to be able to keep enough back to run the team. I have called him the savior of Komet hockey, and he was exactly that. He was the first complete coach-manager person we ever had who really knew about hockey.

He started to bring in good players and immediately had competitive teams. The fans were pretty discouraged at that time and I think had there been one more bust year, I don't think hockey would have survived in Fort Wayne. In spite of the fact that the Pistons were out of town and we were the only sport left, there were a lot of people knocking on the door to do other things. But Ken saved it all, by the way, he came in, the adversity he faced and the way he addressed the problems to make hockey viable for years to come.

Marc Boileau: We ran through the gamut of coaches for a while when Ken decided to vacate the bench, but nobody really grabbed it. We were in kind of crisis mode again so they bring in Marc. He came in basically as a player-assistant, and Kenny ran the team until that night he went after somebody on the ice and took a swing at them and got kicked out. I think Ken was really looking for an opportunity to let Marc have his head so he could run with it. Marc had done a lot as an assistant and he was ready. Marc had a few connections, and Ken was part of that with Jack Riley in Pittsburgh. That was magic where Pittsburgh sent in the players, Marc stirred them up and we won a very dramatic championship. That led to Marc getting a head coaching job in Pittsburgh.

Gregg Pilling: Pilling is a coach who left his mark here in Fort Wayne in many, many ways. He had innovation that wouldn't quit. When Ken hired him, he knew Gregg was a little bit of a loose cannon, but he also knew he had been successful. Pill had some pretty good struggles with Ken on the way to do things. At home, Pilling would play it according to the rules, and on the road, we played Pilling hockey. God, did they have fun. He had a bunch of free-spirited people and a lot of good talent and they put it all together and made it work. Everybody loved Pill. He knew how to measure certain guys. D'Arcy Keating was one. He was a great competitor if you fired him up. Maybe we'd be on our way to Muskegon playing hearts, and Pilling would be playing with us. He'd just defiantly wait until the right spot and unload the Queen every time on D'Arcy, and D'Arcy would get redder, and redder and redder. Here we come again, we're within 30 miles of Muskegon, and we're about to break up the card game, and bang, Pilling lays it on him again. D'Arcy was so mad there was fire coming out of his eyes, and Pill said, "You know what, don't cool down. Keep that attitude because I'm putting you on the power play tonight." D'Arcy gets a goal. One night we go up to Muskegon again and Moose Lallo was totally a formula guy who stuck to match-ups. We're on the bus and we're sitting back at the card game, and Pill was talking with Pembroke. "Pemmer, I got a hell of an idea tonight. Just to start we'll start all five defensemen so we mess Moose up." Moose is looking at this thing and Bryan McLay was the captain and he goes, "All right, Moose, what the hell do you want to do now?" It totally destroyed Moose. He changed things back to normal 20 seconds in, but Moose could never catch up to it. We beat them 5- or 6-1. These are the things Pilling did. He made the game so much fun. The guys never knew what to expect when they got off the bus. He did a lot of things like that, like the night in Saginaw where he flip-flopped the goalies. Who would have ever thought of that? He was very innovative, and I thought he had a real place in the business, but it never worked out. He was his own man.

Moose Lallo: He was one of the funniest guys I was ever around. He was a complete gentleman, but hockey was his world, and there's no possible way you could get him away from it. He was completely dedicated to his superstitions. There was something for every move, and everything had an omen. If there wasn't one, you could put one in Moose's head in two seconds. One day we're loading the bus, and I come back into the building after bringing some stuff out, and I stop and rather than going through the open door, I went over and opened another door and came back in. I noticed Moose was watching so I went back with another load and I stopped and went back through the other door again. We get on the bus and Moose asks what in the world I was doing. "Moose didn't you ever hear, when you are loading the bus, you never go in and out the same door. That's bad luck. The rest of his time Moose never went in an out the same door. He was that superstitious. He was unbelievable. He was strictly a bread and butter coach and all he understood was effort. He wasn't very articulate, but he got his point across. The thing he couldn't handle was those people who didn't have Hockey 101 in their repertoire when they came to camp. He used to bemoan the fact that every year they were getting dumber and dumber. He was from a different era.

Ron Ullyot: It was obvious then that the next coaching coming in was going to be Ronnie, Ken's son. Ron was a damn good student of the game. As a player, he was never the big flashy hockey player. He went out and did his job and did it pretty well. He came out and you knew what to expect from him. When he got to coaching, it was kind of like that, too. He had some good ideas when it came to coaching, but his place in coaching was not where he was. Unfortunately, I think Ronnie would have been the consummate college coach. He had all the wisdom of the game. Some of the guys felt they were at a disadvantage because he was the owner's son and they had a few clashes. The biggest splash was when they let Terry McDougall go. That was just a sad scene. Ron was very fundamental and coached well. They played well for him.

Rob Laird: Robbie had probably one of the toughest jobs of anybody who ever came in as coach. At the time when Robbie got the job, he did a hell of a job considering the conditions under which he was hired. He had a tough transition job because all of a sudden here he was coaching the same guys he played with on and off the ice. Wally Schreiber and he had been friends since they were little kids. All due credit to Robbie, he realized that with a broken heart, some of the very people he counted on to be his lead men weren't doing the job and they were taking a ride because their buddy was the coach. He coped with it. I saw him have a couple of huge run-ins with some of those people, but he reigned supreme to be the guy calling the shots. I think they finally got some respect for him.

Al Sims: Al was a bit of a surprise in respect to the year that he should have won it all, he never got the job done in 1992. You could see it slipping away. The minute we blew the league championship, everybody was saying, "Aw, who remembers who won the league championship? We'll blow their doors off in the playoffs." I didn't like that attitude and it ended up costing us. We had some soft spots, but by 1992-93 his leaders had all learned their lessons as well and were lucky enough to get a second crack at it. It's amazing to see how they matured, and so did Al. It was a miracle moment for Pokey Reddick. All of that chemistry all fell together at the right time, and it was a beautiful year. Once they got it together and got into that final run, it was pretty obvious they were destined to do something. I thought the emotion of all that was a real close-knit thing with Al and the players.

Bruce Boudreau: What an irony with Bruce coming in here. Here again was a case of a guy stepping in to coach a bunch of buddies he had played with and they never took him seriously. He just had to get out of town to establish himself as who he wanted to be. His whole image here was not Bruce Boudreau the coach, it was Gabby. It was obvious down the line that the guy had talent, but that was a step in the learning process and he must have learned his lesson well.

Dave Farrish: I had a great amount of respect for and I still think he was one of the best teachers Fort Wayne ever had as a coach. He was a good hockey mind to start with, and he really had a lot of innovative things he did as a coach. I think he had a couple of bad missions to perform to start with. I'm not sure how much leeway he had because he kept a lot of things to himself. He was not a very communicative guy when things were not going well. In fact, it took me half a season to get to know him, and he was a very nice guy, a real gentleman. I always respected him, and I see he's still doing well in the NHL. This was just another mind-stretcher on his way to somewhere else.

John Torchetti: John was the ultimate guy who whenever he did anything, I don't care if he was coaching a hockey team or a drinking a beer, he came to win. He wasn't the most polished guy in the world at expressing himself or going through the philosophy of hockey, but you knew if you came to play for him, you damn well better play. He told me "These guys don't know it now, but they're going to get me 100 points or they're going to be dead along the way." And he got it. The minute the season was over, some pretty good players quit on him, and it really broke my heart, almost literally. I was having my heart surgery then. I was four days out of surgery and I was home so Murph took me over there to visit with the guys as they got on the bus for Cleveland. I told her that I was really glad I wasn't making that trip because most of the guys had already quit. One of the people I was really disappointed in was Lee Davidson because I always had respect for him. I thought he played well during the year, but I think he got to a certain point and just cashed it in. We had one of the best lines in hockey in the Russian line, who if they were playing to their capacity should have given us a chance against almost anybody, and they didn't perform worth a darn. Basically, it was a pathetic collapse. Torchetti was not an easy guy to play for unless you wanted to play hard.

Dave Allison: Davey Allison was one of the most refreshing breaths of coaching that I had seen in my entire career. When he was on the ice, he was all hockey, but he always had a smile on his face and he loved what he was doing and wanted everyone else to enjoy it, too. He knew where hockey belonged and where it didn't belong. He didn't take it with him 24 hours a day all over the world. When it came time to go out and relax, he was Dave Allison and he was the most wonderful guy. His whole career was backward. He started at the top and worked his way down the ladder rather than up. Murph and I got to know he and Marion socially as well. He always had time for you and never blew you off. He was just a darn good coach and a great pro. He taught kids there were more values than going to the rink or going to the bar. I remember once in Knoxville we were playing and when we were going back to the hotel, he told the guys we were getting on the bus at 8 a.m. the next day. They were all moaning because they all wanted to go out, and he didn't say don't go out. The next morning they stumble on the bus in all kinds of shape. We ended up going to Gatlinburg and these kids had never heard of Gatlinburg, and it was a beautiful day. They were just moaning that they could have been sleeping or whatever. We get there and the place is just jumping. There were chicks on spring break all over the town. Davey told them the bus leaves at 5 p.m. By the time it was time to go, we had to wait on half of the guys and they all thanked him for it.

Greg Puhalski: He is a very scholarly guy who was very deep. He knew the game inside and out. He was a good minor pro player and he just had high expectations, and probably if anything, was impatient with people who could not do the minor fundamental things. He got wrapped up in systems because of the limitations of players so he could count on them as a cog. He was the consummate taskmaster. He demanded discipline from you. He was very quiet, and there were days I never talked to him. When Chief didn't want to talk, he didn't want to talk. He'd get so heavily engrossed in what he was doing. The one thing he did which really amazed me, we got on the bus one night and we had lost and everything was as quiet as can be. About a half hour later, he stands up and all of a sudden here comes this voice like a banshee wail." It was octaves above what it should have been. The paint pert near peeled off the ceiling. He just positively took pedigrees by the number. Oh, my God, did he go after them. Then he turns around and sits down. And it's not 30 seconds and gets up and lets them have one other great big whack. Now he sits down and I don't know what to do. Do I say anything, or do I say nothing to him? I proceeded to say nothing to him. We get home and I'm putting my gear in his office and he's in there calling his fiancé, and he says, "Sorry if I caught you off guard. They deserved it and they know right now they are going to pay for it." They had practice that same night. He got a lot of results out of his guys in his own way. He was a systems guy and people either played for him or wouldn't play for him. If they didn't like him, they might as well get out because he wasn't going to change. He had one of the best hockey minds I'd ever seen around.

Pat Bingham: He was a one-year experience. A nice guy, honest to God. Nobody could have been any more dedicated to the sport than Pat. He was the consummate computer. I think he changed chips in his head for every game. Without the computer, I'm not sure Coach could have done the job. He'd analyze every piece of the game. All the way up to a game he'd be watching games and then all the way home, day in and day out. He'd get in the locker room before the game, and he'd be watching game video. I told him about halfway through the year he had to find some way to let up. He was going to kill himself. He wanted to win and keep his name up top, and he was struggling with where he was, thinking it was a little beneath his stature. In a way, he was lucky he had Bruce Richardson with him. It was a strange, strange year. He left his mark.

Al Sims, tour two: He did all the right things. He had the utmost respect of his players, and now he's in the right place. All these kids who are coming out of juniors or college if they had any historical knowledge of hockey, they look around and see what Al did in the NHL as a player, starting with Bobby Orr. Al is always patient with the guys, and I admire him the way he talks with people. I also admire him for drawing the line. He makes no emotional decisions. Some guys walk out of his office and you know they are ticked because they don't think this should ever happen to them, but by the time they sit and think about it for a while they know Al has done the right thing. He doesn't let things fester because he has the courage to do things when they need to be done.

CHAPTER 50
KOMET CATEGORIES
Rankings in no particular order

Best shooters
Merv Dubchak
Joe Kastelic
Ron Leef
Barry Scully
Norm Waslawski

Most-lethal slap shots
Jim Burton
Scott Gruhl
Mario Larocque
Brian McKee
Jim Pearson

Best breakaway/penalty shot/shootout scorers
Merv Dubchak
Mitch Messier
Barry Scully
Konstantin Shafranov
Len Thornson

Best garbage goal scorers
John Goodwin
Ron Leef
Eddie Long
Barry Scully
Konstantin Shafranov

Most unpredictable shooters

Wayne Bishop
Kelly Hurd
Kory Kocur
Lonnie Loach
Roger Maisonneuve
Rob Motz

Craftiest passers

Viacheslav Butsayev
Colin Chin
Terry McDougall
Reggie Primeau
Lenny Thornson

Best defensive forwards

Ian Boyce
Colin Chaulk
John Goodwin
Peter Hankinson
David Hukalo
Bob McCusker

Best defensive defensemen

Guy Dupuis
Carey Lucyk
Troy Neumeier
Terry Pembroke
Duane Rupp
Terry Thomson

Best offensive defensemen

Jim Burton

Jimmy Pearson
Kelly Perrault
Lionel Repka
Jean-Marc Richard

Best goalies to win one game

Chuck Adamson
Robbie Irons
Bruce Racine
Glenn Ramsay
Kevin St. Pierre

Best Fighters

Shawn Cronin
John Ferguson
Steve Fletcher
Con Madigan
Cal Purinton

Toughest little guys

Dale Baldwin
Chick Balon
Andy Bezeau
Robbie Laird
Eric Sutcliffe

Best talkers

Dave Allison
Robin Bawa
Eric Boguniecki
Frederic Bouchard
Bruce Boudreau
Mike Butters

Ed Campbell
Keli Corpse
Jonathan Goodwin
Rob Guinn
Kelly Hurd
Eddie Long
Mike McKay
Mitch Messier
Dave Smith
Danny Stewart
Doug Teskey

Meanest on the ice, nicest off
Robin Bawa
John Ferguson
Steve Fletcher
Kevin Kaminski
Kevin MacDonald
Michel Massie
Dave Norris
Terry Pembroke
Cal Purinton
Bruce Ramsay
Andre Roy
Mitch Woods

Favorite opponents to talk to
Jock Callander
Kory Karlander
Bob Plager
Kevin Schermerhorn
Don Waddell

Best referees
Fred Blackburn
Bill Doyle
George Harrison
Hal Jackson
Sam Sisco
Mark Wilkins

Best places to watch a game
Memorial Coliseum, Fort Wayne
Wings Stadium, Kalamazoo
Pepsi Coliseum, Indianapolis
Bradley Center, Milwaukee
Peoria Civic Center, Peoria
Orena, Orlando
Gund Arena, Cleveland
Delta Center, Salt Lake
McNichols Arena, Denver

Worst places to watch a game
Cow Palace, San Francisco
Freeman Coliseum, San Antonio
Asheville Civic Center
Columbus Fairgrounds Coliseum
Omni, Atlanta
Stadium Arena, Grand Rapids
Fraser, Michigan
Hobart Arena, Troy
Veterans Memorial Coliseum,

Marion, Ohio
Oak Creek Ice Arena, Des
Moines

Funniest guys
Edgar Blondin
Keli Corpse
John Hilworth
Moose Lallo
Lloyd Maxfield

Fastest skaters
Andrei Bashkirov
Jason Goulet
Bob Lakso
Ron Leef
Art Stone

Most creative skaters
Colin Chin
Terry McDougall
Reggie Primeau
Bobby Rivard
Vladimir Tsyplakov
Terry Wright

Best Russian players
Andrei Bashkirov
Viacheslav Butsayev
Igor Chibirev
Konstantin Shafranov
Vladimir Tsyplakov

Top five Komets rivalries
Toledo 1960-1980s
Indianapolis 1990s
Kalamazoo 1980s
Muskegon 1980s
Rockford 2000s

Best one-year Komets
John Anderson
Murray Bannerman
Dan Bonar
Jim Boyd
Ray Brunel
Igor Chibirev
Pat Elynuik
John Ferguson
Randy Gilhen
Kevin Kaminski
Chris McRae
Tom McVie
Stu Ostland
Glenn Ramsay
Al Sims
Sid Veysey

Best forward lines
Bobby Rivard, Merv Dubchak,
    John Goodwin
Len Thornson, Merv Dubchak,
    John Goodwin
Terry McDougall, Robbie
    Laird, Al Dumba
Viacheslav Butsayev, Andrei
    Bashkirov, Konstantin

Shafranov
Bruce Boudreau, John
Anderson, Lonnie Loach

Best defensive pairings
Terry Pembroke, Cal Purinton

Duane Rupp, Lionel Repka
Carey Lucyk, Jean-Marc
Richard
Jimmy Pearson, Terry
Thomson
Guy Dupuis, Mario Laroque

CHAPTER 51
SPECIAL TEAMS: SOME OF BOB'S FAVORITE SEASONS

1959-60: I always considered that to be one of the best teams we ever had. They had talent that wouldn't quit at a time when the league had some great teams. Minneapolis and St. Paul were loaded, and the IHL was a great league at the time. That was the one I thought for sure we'd win our first cup with because I just felt it coming together as the year went along. We were the class of the league, and we figured we had it going. The likes of Ronson and Thornson, McCusker were great. Fergie was a tough guy with Connie and there was Duane Rupp and Lionel. They just had the ingredients that you felt we were going to win with, but then we had the heartbreak until 2 a.m. That's a team that I will always think was one of the best teams we ever had.

1962-63: It was a pretty good team, but they didn't compare to the 59-60 team in overall talent and balance. We just weren't as deep and skilled, and maybe the fact that we weren't helped us. They were steady but nobody was really star quality, and they just ground it out all the time and played their games. Chuck Adamson was the glue that held the team together completely. He played 70 games. That's a lot of games. The biggest thing was coming back to beat Muskegon in Game 6. We had Gary

Sharp who came in late from Greensboro, and he got the first goal of the game for us but then it was 6-1 near the end of the second period. Ken Ullyot was just going to pack it in and rest some guys, play it out and get ready for the next night. Then Lenny started making some plays, and all of a sudden we were right back in the game and Muskegon was on its heels. Then in the third period, Eddie Long made the damndest save you've ever seen and that was kind of the last piece of momentum that kept us going. Then Reggie, Rog and Waz took over.

1964-65: We were a good road team that year, and we had a heck of a battle in Minneapolis with them. We had beaten them and we're up 3-1, and all I can hear Johnny Goodwin saying all the way home, "Guys, can you believe it, we're leading this thing 3-1 now." That was another year that had a lot of ups and downs. Chuck was having some problems along the way stopping the puck, and we brought this kid in named Bob Gray. He was a blood and guts guy, tougher than hell, and not a bad goaltender. He wasn't here long and was sort of a temporary fix. He did pretty well and wanted to stay here, but he was going back to New York. After his final game in Des Moines, he gave the guys a pep talk like you couldn't believe. He called their numbers from A to Z, saying that what had happened to Chuck wasn't his fault and you guys had quit on him and got lazy. He let them have it, and it kind of turned us around in terms of the success we had the rest of the year. He only played nine games for us, but one night in Dayton we were playing Chuck and they were trying to intimidate us when Gray finally convinced Eddie to let him play up. He couldn't catch anybody, but he scared the daylights out of everybody on the ice. Whenever he came on the ice, the tempo of the game changed because everybody was looking to see where Gray was. He challenged everything he could catch, and some he couldn't but nobody laughed at him. He left on a high note that helped to spur us to that championship.

1972-73: There were some characters on that team. We had a tough team that year, too, and some of those guys were crazy. Wayne Ego was a funny guy, Dean Sherematta was a loose cannon. Bobby Miller was a strange kid who could play hockey. Chick Balon was one of the toughest little guys you ever saw. Bob Fitchner was definitely the boss. They were tougher than nails. The story of that year was the goaltending in the playoffs. Don Atchison, they were almost afraid to let him practice, and Robbie was the man, but then he got involved in that goofy fight. Atch had played some games, but when it came to the playoffs, nobody thought Atch could endure, but he was just totally stellar. That was a great combination of toughness, Marc Boileau's will, and a tremendous leader in Bob Fitchner. I know when we went into Flint during the playoffs, Len Hoyes put out this big article in the Flint Journal saying that if the Flint Generals intend to win the Turner Cup Doug Kerslake had to take Fitchner out. The game hardly started and Kerslake took a two-hander at Fitch, but luckily he missed him. Fitch put the gloves and the helmet down, backpedaled to center ice because he was right in front of the Flint bench. Kerslake came right at him, and when he reached back to throw a punch, Fitchner reached out with his left hand, pulled Kerslake in and hit him with a right and Kerslake went right down to the ice in a growing pool of blood. We never saw him again, and that broke their back. Then Ted Garvin tried to play us tough with Port Huron, but there weren't many people who wanted to go after Fitch. There was a guy named Dave Haley for Port Huron, and Garvin just told him to take Fitchner out. So Haley goes after Fitch from behind, and Fitch turtles on the glass and Haley is throwing at him and all the time he's saying, "Fitch, look, I didn't want to do this, Garvin made me do this." Needless to say, it didn't have much of an effect on Fitch. He took the beating and we won the game anyway. We had quite a ride back from Port Huron as we stopped many different times to refresh our lunch buckets. We were just on the southwest side of Lansing when Fitchner came to Marc and said, "Is it OK if we stop and get a couple more cases of beer?" Marc says OK, but he tells Fitch he can take two guys in and that's it, and they better just come back with only beer. They go in to get the beer and get talking and all of a sudden they aren't coming out, so somebody else had to go in and get him. To make a long story short, by the time they had gotten in there, Fitch had made friends with everybody and he was half in the bag dancing on top of the bar. We finally get everybody back on the bus and we came home. Ego is sitting in his seat with the Turner Cup in his lap and he won't let it go.

1977-78: That was one of the most enjoyable years I ever spent because of Gregg Pilling's antics and the way that he coached. We had two of the best goaltenders in minor hockey in Bannerman and Irons, but unfortunately, we had some injuries at the wrong times that negated our ability to win in the end. You're looking at guys like Danny Bonar, Al Dumba, Mike Penasse, Dave Norris, D'Arcy Keating, Mike Boland, Bobby McNeice.... The antics never became a distraction. These were the kind of things that made him different because the players would get into it and really get fired up. The guys were having the best time you ever saw. It was just a compilation of all those things that made him the most unusual coach that I ever saw around. I wasn't really surprised when Gregg didn't come back the next year because I don't know how long his run could have continued because of his unique way of coaching, but it was fun while it lasted. Nobody ever forgot it.

1985-86: We had a hell of a club that year with guys like Jimmy Burton, Wally Schreiber, Randy Gilhen, Steve Salvucci, Doug Rigler, Dale Baldwin, Craig Channel... but we lost in the finals to

Muskegon 4-0. That was Robbie Laird's first year, and that was a year I felt for sure again we were going to win it. We went up there and they positively, totally dominated us. Muskegon had a good team, but I thought with Robbie driving the boat we were going to win it. It was a high-scoring team, with a lot of goal production coming from all over, but for some reason when we hit the playoffs we just flat collapsed. People thought the series with Muskegon might be a toss-up, but nobody ever dreamt we'd go out in four straight.

1990-91: That opened a different era of hockey. That had to be one of our most powerful teams that we ever put together in terms of scoring, and maybe pound-for-pound the toughest team we ever had. They could score and fight with anyone, and they really took care of each other. It was "Don't mess with my friend." It was probably about the most spontaneously tough team that we've ever seen. There were a lot of fights that never happened because when it came time to go, nobody, wanted to make it happen against us. They weren't a bunch of goons, but they answered every challenge, and half the time they didn't have to worry about anything unless somebody got stupid.

92-93: That was sweet revenge for what we didn't get done in 1991-92. It was a somewhat similar cast except for the addition of Igor Chibirev. Lee Davidson had a pretty good year, Peter Hankinson, what a defensive gem he was; Bobby Jay put a lot of heart into it, as did Grant Richison and Dave Smith. There were some great names on that team. During the playoffs, I got to the point where I kept figuring we were good enough to win, but who in the heck was going to beat San Diego? They were a major minor pro team, and you always held out hope, but I never expected the sweeps. You had to take your hat off to Pokey Reddick because he gave as good an overall display of goaltending as I've seen. In the San Diego series, they tried everything they could to mess with his head, but he never let them. It was just an unbelievable experience.

97-98: The MiG line was as good as they wanted to be any night they went onto the ice. Viacheslav Butsayev, the game was so easy for him I don't think he ever broke a sweat. He was the kind of a guy who had the credentials if he wanted to play, he could play any place, including the National Hockey League. I think that line was as good as it was because of Andrei Bashkirov. I thought he drove those guys. He was so enthusiastic and gave so much every time he was on the ice, that all three of them had to work their hind ends off to keep it going. That was a team that didn't have a lot of toughness, and what they did have got hurt near the end of the season. The chemistry was not good, but John Torchetti overcame some of it. Bruce Racine was unbelievable, an island of calm and he never got embroiled in the other stuff going on. He was sort of like the father figure, but he was one of those few goalies who was a leader, too. Kevin Weekes proved he had a lot of potential and was a gentleman through and through. I don't think he could have profited as much anywhere else because Racer was such a giving person. Despite all that, that team turned out to me to be one of the biggest disappointments that I was ever around because of what happened at the end.

02-03: That was another one of those years where we had some incredible talent and this was truly a team. There weren't any cliques on the team and they played as a unit pretty well. They made some key additions in Chad Cabana and Marc Barlow. That team provided me with one of the most lasting memories I'll ever have which was "1-0 Joe." After watching Joe Franke grow up as a little kid hustling sticks for the guys, become dedicated to his job and then to see him get that chance and just come up just unbelievably huge ranks in my hockey memories with Pilling flip-flopping the goaltenders. That night, I couldn't stop chuckling. When the shootout came, I almost could hardly finish the broadcast. I could not stop laughing. He takes one of the guys on the other club and stones him in the shootout to preserve the win. Again, you were looking at a team who really had it all going, but it was a tough coaching job. Hardly anybody was on the same page as Greg Puhalski. He was different when it came to how he handled players. His concept of the game was system, system, system, and his margin for error was pretty small. He had a lot of guys with a lot of talent who responded and were leaders, and at times overcame some of the little nuances that he threw in. I thought Sean Venedam was a heck of a team leader. We had some kids there like Kevin Schmidt, who was a very quiet little guy. One of the most remarkable little guys was Marc Barlow, and by the time the playoffs came I thought he was the second-best point man we had next to Kelly Perrault. There was a lot of character on the team, a lot of different personalities.

07-08: Considering the league and our position in it – not according to the talent we've had over the years, but in the moment – the best hockey club we ever had. They all came together and played as a team, and all played for the end result. They worked for each other and got along on and off the ice. There were no groups, everybody was part of the whole. Give credit to Al Sims, and he had an incredible assist from David Franke who did one of his most effective jobs as general manager by helping Al procure some people and giving him the reigns. The entire organization was really in sync. Everybody responded in games. They expected to win and they won with dignity. They were unbelievable in one-goal games, and the amazing thing was how many times on the road they found a way to win. You could not intimidate them and there were some teams that tried. They were always hanging around and somebody would do something to light the fire, and here we'd come. Everybody played their role and they played as a team. We had some very versatile players on that club that you could plug into two or three spots like Brandon Warner and Jake Pence.

CHAPTER 52
SIGNING OFF

Along the way, with every bump in the road, there were always people to encourage me. I never had any negative vibes about what I was doing. So many people were around to help me as it went along, and the people who helped me the most were my family because of the crazy life I led. Being gone 40 to 50 nights a winter traipsing all over the world takes a pretty special wife to start with. The people that I worked for at WOWO could have at any time given me limitations, but they allowed me to do my thing. I always got encouragement from them. The hockey people like the league commissioners who I helped with, coped with and became friends with were all contributing factors not only to the success of the league but to my success because they were always cooperative.

I don't think I ever made any enemies. I made some temporary enemies with some fans from some areas, but in the long run, those are the same people who came back years later and said, "Bob remember when…. I really feel bad about what I did." Then they apologize for how badly they behaved. They have all come back and been friendly with me. I need to thanks all the coaches and players, too. I couldn't be successful either without the cooperation of all the players and coaches over the years, the way they welcomed me into the dressing room and the insights they gave me. I hope that when I'm finished with all those people in their careers that we remain friends.

I always tried to treat everybody with respect. Some people I characterized, hopefully not in a negative manner, but reacted to their demeanor on the ice and my descriptions sometimes projected that. All my memories are pleasant, even in some of the worst situations. You can look back now and smile and be thankful. It's a life where I wouldn't change a thing.

I can never in my own mind live up to the respect I've gotten from fans all over. It has always kept me humble and I guess I'd have to say from the expressions I get and the respect I get, all I can say is thank God I was given the opportunity to do what I had to to have a positive effect and enhance people's lives and give them enjoyment through sport.

The final thing I can say is thank you, Murph, thank you kids and Thank God.

CHAPTER 53
TESTIMONIALS FROM FANS

Back in the old days.......before the internet.......it was nice to be able to pick up chaser on WOWO when i would vacation in south Florida, the volume had to be all the way up on my little radio and i had to sit outside on the screened in porch to get the signal, it was nice to go back home for a couple of hours listening to the Komet game. I think the last time i did that was '93 or '94. – Mike Burgess

I have spent my entire professional life working in minor league sports in Fort Wayne. Throughout that time, I have had opportunities to leave but have to this point always chosen to stay because I love Fort Wayne and I've always loved the climate of minor league sports in Fort Wayne. I'm not sure I ever really understood the WHY behind that feeling… until I had the pleasure and opportunity to begin working with Bob Chase. Bob is perhaps the best example of being "comfortable in your own skin" and being happy with who and where you are personally and professionally that I have ever seen. He has obviously had countless opportunities to leave, but has always chosen to stay because he loved Fort Wayne... loved Fort Wayne Komet Hockey... and loved the absolutely irreplaceable role that he played in making it special to oh so many people over the last 55+ years. There are certainly others who have made greater impacts on their cities, their communities, and their professions. People who have led governments, cured diseases, and shaped the very infrastructures of our country. In the grand scheme of things, all Bob has done has been "that voice" that you've heard over the radio, television, and internet for so many years. But "that voice" has had as great an impact on the ears that have heard it... the people who have loved it... and the lives that it has touched. His impact on the game of hockey, the city of Fort Wayne, and the history of the Fort Wayne Komets will never be matched. He is a link to a time when decisions in our society were simpler, when "the little things" mattered more, and to when "that voice" on the radio could speak volumes to people about who they were and why they loved the team that they followed and the city that that team played in. There will never be another Bob Chase. Truthfully, there SHOULD never be another Bob Chase. The world has changed far too much for there ever to be another Bob Chase. As the history of our world is written, Bob will only be a very small entry in the global view. But to those of us who have had the pleasure to "know him", whether in person or simply in the comfort and joy that we gained by listening to "that voice"... Bob will be a very large entry in OUR view of history. Perhaps that will be Bob's greatest legacy. He will forever remain a very large entry in the memories of every fan who has ever followed minor league hockey in Fort Wayne and beyond. He will forever be "that voice". He will forever be "that voice" in the silent monologues in our heads of memories of games played, lives lived, and days gone by. I am proud to have had the opportunity to be Bob's colleague and prouder still to have been Bob's friend. Bob will forever be the voice that I hear when I think about Komet Hockey and will forever be the example that I use when my sons ask me what it means to be truly happy in life. As we all struggle with the challenges of our own lives and attempt endlessly to answer that question for ourselves... I ask you: Could there ever be any greater legacy? To me, Bob Chase will FOREVER be "Live from Radio Rinkside" – as long as they play hockey in Fort Wayne, long after he is gone, and long after I am gone. "That Voice" will live forever in the hearts and minds of everyone who has ever heard it and to everyone to whom Bob's story is told. So perhaps we should all allow this phrase to be the answer to the question of what it means to be happy... "On WOWO... Komet Hockey". – Scott A. Sproat, Executive Vice President, Fort Wayne Komet Hockey (2001 – present)

I have been listening to Bob Chase since I was a very young teenager. I remember that in my high school speech class we had to do a radio presentation of some sort and I decided to do "Bob Chase calling a Komet hockey game". I recorded one of the games on an old tape player and then tried to memorize it along with all the emotion that Bob put into it and then recreate it for the class. They somehow piped it into the classroom from a room I was in across the hall. Needless to say, I could not do justice to what Bob does day in and day out, but it was fun to try to step into his shoes for just a few moments. Bob Chase has been a Komet hockey staple in my life and it will never be the same when he finally hangs it up. Thanks for all the memories, Bob! – Teresa Beck

Most people listened to radio in the "Good old days." There

were three stations we listened to mainly in our parents' house (before FM). WGL... Len Davis and crew did mostly the high school sports (football and basketball); WLYV came along as a rock and roll/pop music station (with Jay Walker as a DJ); or I'd lay in my folks' car in the summer to listen to Jack Buck and Mike Shannon on 1090 KMOX out of St. Louis.

And then there was WOWO. In the mornings you would get up and listen to The Little Red Barn to get the forecast in the winter to get ready and deliver papers, or just get ready for school. But during the hockey season, WOWO radio meant Bob Chase and the Fort Wayne Komets. For years evenings were spent listening to Bob do the games, if we were not at the game..
For me, in the last of the 70s, I left Fort Wayne and was working out East. 1977 was the first year I was gone, and I was driving one night on the Pennsylvania Turnpike, and I came across WOWO radio. I thought, holy crap... it's the Komets! And Bob was raving about a kid named Jamie Galimore. So I tried to catch as many games at night as I could.

When I did come to Fort Wayne, I would go to the games while I was in town. Then in 1980, I moved out West and my brother and folks would send newspaper clippings of the games. My brother started sending me cassette tapes of the games. It was great to hear Bob Chase and listen to the Komet games. Living in Denver, we had the Denver University Pioneer college hockey, Colorado Rockies NHL hockey and the Colorado Flames CHL hockey. They were fun to watch and go to, but not the same. Everywhere I've been and gone to see hockey games, everyone knows of WOWO and Bob Chase. That was always pretty cool. Coming back to Fort Wayne in the late 1980s, I went to a lot of games, but it dawned on me, from my brother sending me those cassette tapes that I should start recording Komet hockey games, among other things. a couple of things come to mind.

During the 1990-91 season, there was a game in December, I believe, that the Komets went to Peoria. Now the Rivermen were tearing up the league. The Komets were short-handed and played the Rivermen tough.They might not have won, but I remember that at one point Bob went for 15 minutes plus without a break in the action, and I thought to myself.... dang, he can't even get a drink of water. (LOL).

But mainly I remember sitting in a hot steaming tub, drinking a cold beer, with all my equipment running (real smart), and Lonnie Loach scoring in sudden death overtime to beat Indianapolis in the first round of the playoffs. I'm surprised I didn't get electrocuted, but it was great to listen to Bob, how he handled it so professionally on the air, because I know I would be a terrible announcer being the "home" that I am.
You could hear the dejection after the first-round loss to Kalamazoo the next year, then to hear his joy of winning the cup in 1993. He and Robes do a great job together in the booth. But I think for people who are not able to get out to the games, or like Gert, who Bob was her eyes for so many years, that is what Bob Chase was to so many people. Not just a hockey announcer but a tour guide taking them places they themselves would never get to go.

"Bucko, give the score more often..."

This Bud's for Bob. – Dave Longsworth

My buddy Ryan Ash and I decided to go to St.Louis to see the Komets play in the playoffs against the River Otters at the Savis Center. The first game, as I am sure you remember we smoked the otters 8-1 or 8-3. My buddy and I were so excited after the win, and we just happen to find out that the team was staying at the hotel across from the Savis Center. So we decided to go over and check out the hotel bar to see if any of the guys came down and we would buy them a beer. Well, we did meet some of the guys and talked to them for a while, but the one guy who talked to us the most, and longest was Bob Chase. Bob talked to us for over an hour, about the game, hockey in general, to history, and the best games he remembers seeing. It was just such a nice time, and he treated us like he knew us forever. It was a night that I know Ryan and I will never forget, Bob was just a down to earth type of guy, very warm, and willing to talk to two young hockey nuts for a while over some beers. It really was such a great night. The bartender made last call, and Bob said that it was time to go to bed, but he thanked us for talking to him and wished us the best of luck in the future, and on our trip home. It really was a great time, I learned so much from him that night.

I don't know if this will help at all, but I thought that I would share, take care and GO KOMETS!! – Charlie Crawford

This isn't necessarily a memory I have, but whenever we go out and leave, my 7-year-old son announces the games just like he hears from Mr. Bob Chase, I think since my son has his disability, that listening to Chase on the radio is a thrill for him. There isn't one road game that I don't listen to Bob Chase with my son Jonathan. I think that that is the biggest memory that I will have. It's those times that I sat by the radio or the computer and listened to Chase because my 7-year-old son loves listening to him. – Mark and Jonathan Shepler

Mr. Bob Chase is the absolute perfect hockey broadcaster. He played the game. He knows the game. He knows the players that play the game. He has been a GM. He is the voice that when a was in the Army and stationed in Missouri made me feel like I was at home. When I vacation now I make sure I can get the internet. I have sat next to him and listened to that "Great" voice and closed my eyes. I was in whatever building in whatever city, I was at that game as seen through his eyes. Someday there will be someone to take his place NO ONE will ever replace Mr. Bob Chase. I am very proud to know him and even more proud to call him my friend. He is the last surviving WOWO ACE! Fort Wayne will never see his likes again. – Dennis Schebig

I've been a hockey nut ever since a babysitter took me to a Komet game when I was real young, and she saved my life by blocking a puck with her popcorn box. Later, I discovered and loved Bob Chase's broadcasts, and my respect for Bob's talents grew when my older brother Mark, who does not like hockey, said; "I don't have any idea what he's talking about, but it sure sounds like he does a good job". Many nights I want to bed with a cheap AM radio listening to Bob on WOWO.

After college, I moved to Charlotte, NC for about five years. This, of course, was before internet and B2 games, and I could not get WOWO on any of the radios in the house. In my car, however, WOWO reception was pretty strong in most parts of Charlotte. So, when my wife needed something from the store, or if I had errands, I would save them until gametime and then I would drive around listening to Bob and the Komets. I'd try to time my runs into the stores for commercial breaks to miss as little as possible. And sometimes I'd listen until the end of the game in parking lots, just driving around, or when I got back to my driveway. It was especially fun for me when Colin Chin played because I had played on a team with him in high school. My wife thought I was nuts, but she put up with it and still does. Bob always does such a great job. I always visualized what he was describing. Like a lot of Komet fans I'm sure, I've caught myself arguing calls; "he never tripped that guy!" Just this week

I told my son I was going to listen to a game on WOWO instead getting B2 because the picture in my head is clearer than the B2 feed.

Cheers to Bob! He's a big piece of the Komet experience and legacy. – Matt Ueber

Mr. Bob Chase really had a way to make you love the Komets and the game of hockey. Mr. Chase really knew how to draw people into the Komet passion. I grew up in the 70s going to one or two games a year and I listened to the rest of the games being broadcasted by Mr. Chase. Mr. Chase always made it feel like you were there. My first radio that I built was tuned into Mr. Chase's broadcast of a Komet game. However, my fondest memory is taking shots on goal as a young child in my childhood home's garage in southern Ft. Wayne while I imagined that I was Robbie Laird or Al Dumba scoring the game-winning goal while listening to Mr. Chase's broadcasts of the Komets. I credit Mr. Chase in making me a Komet fan today. I'm a Komet fan that hasn't lived in Fort Wayne in over 20 years but I still bleed orange thanks to Mr. Chase. Thanks, Mr. Chase for the childhood memories and thanks for the adult memories on the net. Every time I hear Mr. Chase on the internet it brings back that little child inside of me. Now, where is that nearest sports store so I can buy a net and some sticks to teach my two-year-old the thrill of Komets hockey? – Dean Schmitz

I first heard "He walks in… looks, shoots, SCORES!" when I was a young teenager in the early 60's. I had been a baseball-loving kid in Flushing, Queens when my mom died a month before my 13th birthday. My sister and I went to live with our aunt and uncle on Long Island where I fell in with a sports gang whose favorite game was hockey – ice hockey, street hockey, pencil hockey, you name it. My after-school hours were spent in pickup games on the pond or in the street, and my after-dinner hours were spent trying to pick up games from all around the eastern half of the United States and Canada on the little a.m. radio in my bedroom. Looking back, I now realize that I was using my radio to escape from the grief I was still harboring. Besides Win Elliott in New York, I found Foster Hewitt in Toronto, Danny Gallivan in Montreal and Budd Lynch in Detroit, but my favorite find was in the small city in Indiana with the big, big radio station. The voice with the most picturesque play-by-play of them all belonged to your own Bob Chase; and so, Fort Wayne became my hockey Never-Neverland, and "Chaser," my Peter Pan.

On Saturday nights from the Allen County War Memorial Coliseum and Sundays from places like Muskegon, Toledo, Port Huron, Omaha, Des Moines and Minnesota's Twin Cities, I would "watch" the players I'd grow to idolize through Bob's eyes and with his words. There was the Komets' Irish terrier captain, Eddie Long, who refused to back down to anyone; Len Thornson, the Jean Beliveau of the IHL, as regal as Eddie was scrappy; the tough, versatile Teddy Wright; Reg Primeau, perseverance personified; the cat-like goalie Chuck Adamson; and my favorite player, the backbone of the great Komet teams of the era, Lionel "Choo Choo" Repka. (I'd even tried to imitate what I thought was Lionel's skating style based on Bob's play-by-play descriptions.) That these images of the players on the Komets of almost 50 years ago are still so vividly imprinted in my mind today is the most meaningful testimonial I can give to the announcing artistry of Bob Chase.

Bob forged a style that could best be described as "American" while Canadian announcers of the day like Hewitt and Gallivan would, for the sake of detail, occasionally fall behind the action and catch up by announcing from past to present tense, Bob's play-by-play never seemed to lag. He described the action as it happened – he never missed a beat – and yet, he was still able to provide the detail he needed to paint for us a complete mental picture of the game. Whether by coincidence or intent, I noticed his deep baritone style in the work of Bob Wilson in Boston, and his verbal mannerisms were effectively copied by his one-time protégé, Mike "Doc" Emrick, during Emrick's early years in New Jersey and Philadelphia.

Within the past few years, I've been fortunate enough (through the generosity of Lionel Repka) to have been in Bob's company on several occasions, and I've been able to thank him face-to-face for all that he and the Komets meant to me in the time after my mom's passing, and beyond. I know of no one in the industry more deserving of the accolades he's received over the years than Bob Chase. You are Radio Rinkside, Big Guy. Long may you run! – Randy Dannenfelser

BOOK 2
INTRODUCTION

When we finished writing Bob's biography in the summer of 2008, it was the culmination of a long year of meeting two or three times a week along with always talking before games. We knew it was time to stop because Bob started to try repeating some of the stories.

"But it's better this time!" he'd say emphatically.

Yeah... I'd say slowly, I'm not repeating the four or five hours of work I did six months ago on the same blasted story!

And then we'd laugh — until a few weeks later when he tried to tell the same story for the third time. So we kind of knew we were finished.

But the story wasn't.

Bob lived almost eight more years and accomplished some amazing things during that time, like calling his 500th Komets playoff game in 2015. As much as I've researched, I can't find any other announcer who ever called 500 playoff games, let alone all for one team! The box scores aren't even available for all 500 games!

It was almost like Bob's first 83 years of life was the set-up for those next years which saw him finally achieve some national respect and recognition for his incredible career. Those were some of the most exciting, fulfilling times of his life.

And all the while, I was thinking, "Who would want to get on that blasted bus every weekend?" Bob did. Sleeper buses made a huge difference for Bob and the Komets.

The greatest thing about Bob's life is that he never stopped living, and new experiences always seemed to find him, leading to some wonderful stories. So we're going to tell the rest of Bob's story with this addition to the second edition. Because I couldn't think of a better way to tell these stories, they are as they appeared previously in The News-Sentinel, used with permission.

Blake Sebring
Jan. 15, 2018

Many of these stories appeared originally in The News-Sentinel and are used with permission.

CHAPTER 54
WOWO'S BOB CHASE TO RETIRE AFTER 56 YEARS
May 22, 2009

Bob Chase's black Labrador Duke needs to learn to sleep in. Most weekday mornings, Chase sets his alarm for 3 a.m. so he can drive to Fort Wayne's southeast side by 4 a.m. to begin his day as WOWO's sports director.

"I'm worried about him because he has an internal clock," Chase said. "About a minute before 3, I always get a cold nose on the cheek."

Chase, 83, and Federated Media announced his retirement as WOWO's sports director during this morning's show. Though his last day on the air will be June 5 because of an upcoming vacation, his last day of employment will be June 30 — 56 years since he came to Fort Wayne from WDMJ in Marquette, Mich., on July 1, 1953.

"As it continues to get closer, I get more excited because of the fact when we do leave, the rearview mirror doesn't mean a thing," Chase said. "It's what's ahead."

Chase and his wife, Murph, who celebrated their 59th anniversary on April 6, may travel a little more this summer. Or they may not, because, he said, there are no more deadlines except making sure he's back by October to begin his 57th season calling the Fort Wayne Komets.

During his career, Chase has done everything at WOWO, serving as sports director, general on-air voice and afternoon show host during the 1960s.

Among his individual highlights are interviewing Elvis Presley in 1957, watching the development of protege Mike Emrick, now the NHL's premier broadcaster, and covering President Kennedy's assassination. Other celebrities he has interviewed include Vice President Dan Quayle, Bob Hope, Nat King Cole, Frank Sinatra, Wayne Gretzky and countless others. He also called his seventh Komets playoff championship earlier this month.

He has received many honors, including being named to the Indiana Broadcast Association Pioneers Hall of Fame in 2000, being named a Sagamore of the Wabash in 2001, and being inducted into the Indiana Sportswriters and Sports Broadcasters Hall of Fame in 2004. The Komets retired No. 40 for him to celebrate his 40th season with the team in 1993.

"With Bob's retirement, we say goodbye to the last link to WOWO's illustrious past," Federated Media General Manager Mark DePrez said. "Yet, he never lived in the past, which is how he remained relevant to contemporary listeners. I remember the first time our out-of-town programming consultant heard Bob, and he couldn't believe Chase was a man of his age.

"Bob Chase, the on-air personality, is synonymous with the WOWO brand. He is a broadcasting icon, a living legend. He has meant everything to WOWO, and there will never be another Bob Chase. He is one of a kind."

DePrez said WOWO hopes Chase will continue to make periodic guest appearances, provide occasional commentaries and serve as the voice for commercials. Chase will also continue to be heard on WOWO as the voice of the Komets.

"That's real important, and I appreciate their commitment to me," Chase said. "I always had the intention when I hung it up at WOWO that I would still have the Komets for at least some time. For how much time, who knows? I haven't figured that out yet, but it will come."

Komets Vice President Scott Sproat said as long as there's a hockey game to call, Chase can be behind the mike as long as he likes.

"We're thrilled for Bob to be able to have had the distinguished career he's had not only with WOWO, but with the Komets, and to be able to choose his own exit strategy," Sproat said. "We should all be so lucky. We're thrilled for Bob to continue as the voice of the Fort Wayne Komets, and for he and Murph to start enjoying their free time."

Chase requested to be honored quietly and with little fanfare, but DePrez said WOWO is planning an on-air tribute to him on June 5 with a private reception held afterward.

Though he's always seemed larger than life, Chase always said it was the job that actually was. He said Westinghouse, WOWO's previous owners, always encouraged the on-air talent to be honest with the listeners and be themselves.

"I've always said I'm thankful for the listeners because had they not turned the radio on and invited me into their home, whether it be as a disc jockey, commentator, sports reporter or play-by-play man, none of this would have happened," Chase said. "If they turned on WOWO, I came into their homes at their invitation. I've always tried to remember that and maintain humility.

"That's why I'm so humble, and I can't believe all the things that are happening to me," he said. "What have I done to deserve all this? I'm not that good a guy."

When asked what his last day will be like, Chase said, "It will be a pretty mixed day when I walk out of there. I'm not going to look back on that day. I may go back and look around some other day, but not that day."

Duke will be waiting at home for a walk.

CHAPTER 55
CHASE IS RARE BROADCASTER TO EARN NHL HONOR
Sept. 12, 2012

It took cooperation from the National Hockey League and USA

Hockey to keep Bob Chase quiet for two weeks.

On Aug. 28, while driving his pickup and towing a massive fifth-wheel RV, the Komets broadcaster was dodging the traffic flying by on I-65 in Tennessee. Chase and his wife, Murph, were riding home from visiting family in Huntsville, Ala., when the cellphone rang at 10 a.m.

"Bob, it's somebody for you," Murph said, handing him the phone.

"Is this Bob Chase?" the voice on the other end said. "Thank goodness I finally found you. I've been trying for over a week the get in touch with you. This is Gary Bettman."

Instantly, Chase, 86, started wondering why the NHL commissioner would want to talk to him.

"I wanted to be the first to let you know and congratulate you," Bettman said. "You have been chosen to receive the Lester Patrick Award for 2012."

Starting in 1966, the Lester Patrick Award has been presented by the NHL and USA Hockey as a lifetime achievement award for service to the sport in the United States. Past winners include Wayne Gretzky, Gordie Howe, Bobby Orr, Phil Esposito, former NHL commissioners and Olympic gold medal-winning teams - basically a Who's Who of the Hockey Hall of Fame.

This would be comparable to an actor receiving a lifetime achievement award at the Oscars.

"While we're talking, everybody is going 70 miles per hour and I'm trying to keep the truck on the road with tears streaming down my face," Chase said. "I just kept driving because there was no way to get off the road."

One thing most of the winners have in common is they have been interviewed by Chase — whose real name is Wallenstein — during his 59 seasons calling Komets games, which is the longest run with any professional hockey team, breaking Foster Hewitt's run with the Toronto Maple Leafs from 1927 to 1963.

Because the NHL waited until today to make the announcement, the Chases have told only a few people, which has been a blessing because every five minutes or so, Bob just says "Wow" and shakes his head as if he's a boxer who recently caught one on the chin.

It was definitely an uppercut.

"I've said `Wow' so many times, thank God there is that word," he said, laughing with joy. "When you look at who's won that award and the significance they had on hockey, they are all National Leaguers! It's almost kind of scary that they considered me. I'm still processing because I can't believe it. I'm still trying to assimilate what has happened to me.

"I have a hard time placing me on that list. In terms of prestige, I have to be the most minor person on that list."

Two weeks later, he's still shocked. Maybe it won't fully hit him until he's in Dallas to accept the award Oct. 15 at the 2012 U.S. Hockey Hall of Fame Induction Ceremony and Dinner. He'll share the award with Washington Capitals president Dick Patrick, grandson of Lester Patrick. This year's Hall of Fame class is Lou Lamoriello, Mike Modano and Eddie Olczyk. Only four media members have previously been honored with the Patrick Award: broadcaster Dan Kelly, writer Stan Fischler, broadcaster John Davidson and Chase protege Mike Emrick.

"This almost validates his entire career," Komets General Manager David Franke said. "It doesn't get any bigger than this."

The Chases already have one major banquet to attend, Sept. 22 at Northern Michigan University, where Chase has been named the school's distinguished alumnus for 2012. He figured that was the crown jewel of his year, though his 60th season with the Komets starts Oct. 12 and the team plans to top it with a few surprises.

"You can't believe the stuff that has filtered through my mind since I heard this," Chase said. "Ever since he told me, I've been overwhelmed. It is hard to comprehend. It's humbling. I don't have the words."

He'd better figure out what to say before Oct. 15.

CHAPTER 56
CHASE WINS NHL'S AWARD FOR SERVICE
Sept. 12, 2012

Across North America today, younger fans are hearing Bob Chase won the Lester Patrick Award for service to hockey in the United States and are wondering, "Who's Bob Chase and what did he do to deserve this?"

Chase is having a debate in his mind to figure out how he fits on the list of past winners. He figures the only way he deserves to be near such prestigious company is to interview them, which he's done with most of them before.

Here's why he deserves to be on the roll call: No one has ever introduced more people to hockey and maybe no one has caused more people to love it.

Sounds crazy, right? Except it's still probably true.

Before 1995, WOWO's 50,000-watt signal could reach as far as the Canadian Maritimes, the U.S. East and Southeast coasts, and pretty far into the western sections of the country. About the only area WOWO didn't reach was a stretch between Portland, Ore., and Orange County, Calif., back to Fort Wayne because of the signal's direction and competition with other high-powered stations.

Chase has even received letters from servicemen in Europe as far as the Mediterranean Sea and from U.S. embassies in South America where they were picking up the signal.

Players said a perk of signing with Fort Wayne was their parents could listen to all the games in their living rooms.

Throughout the 1950s and much of the 1960s, WOWO and Chase was the only broadcast throughout the International Hockey League and the only hockey broadcast throughout much of the rest of the country. During the era of six NHL teams, the game he saw was the only one to visualize for many young fans who'd fall asleep listening to their transistor radios hidden under the covers.

Just like the St. Louis Cardinals introduced baseball to much of the South and West before the sport migrated to Los Angeles and San Francisco, Chase and the Komets much did the same thing.

There are hundreds of stories about Komets fans driving around Florida or Alabama or even as far west as Texas late at night so they could tune in the final moments of a playoff game. Former Komet Terry Pembroke used to call about once a year to say he was listening while sitting on a horse somewhere in south Texas.

My favorite comes from New York native Randy Dannenfelser, who grew up listening to Chase in the 1960s before losing track of the Komets. He was driving through the night three decades later when just for fun he flipped the dial to WOWO and found a Komets game.

"Man, this guy sure sounds just like his dad," Dannenfelser thought.

Just last week, Komets legend Len Thornson got a call from a Montreal radio personality who could talk all about former IHL players because he used to listen to Chase. He also knew everything about Thornson — who retired in 1969.

Now 40-some years later, Komets broadcasts are seeing a resurgence thanks to the Internet where anyone can listen from anywhere, and Chase is still there describing the action, spreading his infectious energy and love for the game.

He's always been there. Of the 4,490 regular-season games the Komets have played, Chase has likely called more than 4,000. When he missed a game on April 2, 1992, because of food poisoning, it was the first time illness had knocked him off a broadcast since 1958 when he had pneumonia. Until he suffered heart problems in 1998, Chase had broadcast all 351 playoff games the Komets had played. He missed the final 10 regular-season and four playoff games but came back the next season after quadruple bypass surgery to call 70 games.

He also missed two playoff games in 2009 to be inducted into the Upper Peninsula Sports Hall of Fame but has called the next 43 in a row for 491 of the 496 Komets' all-time postseason games. He wouldn't mind calling No. 500 sometime next spring. It's unlikely more than a handful of announcers have called 500 playoff games in any sport, let alone with one team.

During all that time, entailing all those thousands of miles riding on a bus or in a caravan of cars, Chase has influenced millions. Any potential fans he missed, his protege Mike Emrick has enraptured, and he gives Chase credit in helping develop his Hall of Fame career. Without Bob Chase, there would have been no one to inspire a baseball-loving boy from LaFontaine who later became the greatest hockey announcer ever. Chase deserves this award and every hockey fan's thanks just for that.

Today there are millions of hockey fans because Bob Chase introduced their fathers, grandfathers and maybe even great-grandfathers to the game. Then throw in the mothers, grandmothers and great-grandmothers.

That's who Bob Chase is, and why he's winning the Lester Patrick Award.

CHAPTER 57
HOCKEY WORLD HONORS CHASE
Oct. 16, 2012

Bob Chase's night at the USA Hockey Hall of Fame banquet was even better than his friends hoped for.

The 86-year-old Komets broadcaster received the Lester Patrick Trophy for service to hockey in the United States on Monday night in Dallas.

"It had to be one of the most memorable moments in my life," Chase said. "You don't move to those heights very often when you spend your life in a sport like this. I'm glad I'll have pictures to help me remember it all. This was top-of-the-mountain stuff."

The award ceremony was the culmination of an exhausting few days for Chase, who started his 60th season with the Komets on Friday night, called the team's win in Evansville on Saturday and then flew to Dallas early Sunday morning.

Along with his wife, Murph, Chase was joined by his daughter, Karin, and her husband, Vic; his son, David; former Komet Terry Pembroke and his daughter Tara; protege and NBC broadcaster Mike Emrick; and Komets owner Stephen Franke and team president Michael Franke.

"What a night!" Michael Franke said. "We've been doing this for 23 years now, and for me, this was probably the most unbelievable night ever. It was a tremendously humbling experience for Bob because of the gratitude so many people expressed to him. It was greater than I ever thought it would be to see the emotion expressed from everyone."

Chase shared the honor with Washington Capitals president Richard Patrick, the grandson of the man the award is named for. The Hall of Fame inductees were former Dallas Stars center Mike Modano; longtime player, coach and now broadcaster Eddie Olczyk; and New Jersey Devils General Manager Lou Lamoriello.

"Lou Lamoriello started his speech by saying, `Bob Chase, I met you and your family last night,' " Michael Franke quoted. " `Your enthusiasm and energy are unbelievable. I need some of that right now.' "

Chase and Patrick were interviewed by ESPN's Steve Levy during an early portion of the dinner for 15 minutes. Chase choked up a few times, thanking his wife and mentioning a few friends from the past, but he made it through.

"What's that like where there are so many hockey fans in the country that are lovers of the sport because of the joy you brought to them?" Levy asked.

Part of Chase's answer included, "I thought very, very seriously about the custodial responsibility I had, not only for the station but also for the sport I was broadcasting. I made many friends with hockey players, moms, dads, you name them, who used to sit and listen to me because their kids were playing in Fort Wayne."

Levy later said, "You young kids out there who want to be hockey broadcasters, my advice to you is whenever Bob decides to hang it up, don't be the guy who follows him! You never want to be the man following the man, you want to be the man following the man who followed the man."

All of Chase's family and friends were stunned by the respect he received from all the dignitaries.

"It was a class act," Pembroke said. "They treated Chase royally, and probably 40 percent of the crowd was all professional NHL people. The number of people who came by and said they listened to Bob Chase when they were growing up was almost overwhelming."

Chase said he was a little surprised by the number of people who came up to talk, thank him and get their picture taken with him.

"It was just the most enjoyable night," he said. "The pomp and ceremony were pretty unrivaled. Having my name on the lips of a lot of pretty important people made me feel good. That was once-in-a-lifetime night, and I'm glad it happened to me."

CHAPTER 58
RADIO CALL A PERFECT MEMORY
Nov. 10, 2012

About a minute after signing off his post-game show, Komets announcer Bob Chase's daughter Karin called from Colorado.

"Dad, Vic and I were going out to eat, but we couldn't leave until it was over because you guys were having so much fun," she said. "Was that ever something!"

"I got her approval," Chase said with a more energetic grin than an 86-year-old should have at 11 p.m. after a long day.

Anyone who listened to Friday's 5-2 Fort Wayne win over Evansville approved as Chase shared the booth with regular color man Robbie Irons and America's voice of hockey Mike Emrick from NBC. Though Chase has been defining hockey radio broadcasts for 60 years and Emrick on the television side for 40, this was the first game they described together.

When the Lafontaine-native Emrick started his career as a teenager, he'd sit in a Memorial Coliseum corner talking into a tape recorder. A few years later he shared some of his recordings with Chase at WOWO, and that relationship grew into a gift for the sport they love. Emrick has taken Chase's passion and dedication to the world's stage and then refined it to his own level of grace and precision.

No mentor could be more approving, no student more respectful. Putting them together for one game, they exceeded even a perfectionist's expectations. The trio had fun calling the game, and that helped make sure everyone listening did, too, even a good part of the 7,707 Memorial Coliseum fans who had radios or smartphones.

"That was the objective," Emrick said. "Sometimes when you have the idea, 'We're just going to have fun,' then all of a sudden something happens and you all of a sudden forget that. Fortunately, I don't think that happened tonight. We're pleased if people had a good time."

How could they help it? That was guaranteed by the preparation Emrick and Chase built for 2 1/2 hours at the morning skate. As Emrick quizzed every stick boy and player, they all looked like they were 10 years old and meeting Santa Claus.

"It was a big thrill for a lot of guys," Komets coach Al Sims said. "Even some of the guys from the American League had to come to Fort Wayne to meet Mike Emrick. It was a pretty neat thing."

And though forgetting about the broadcasters as soon as the opening faceoff fell to the ice, the Komets were determined to win maybe a little more than usual. It's the only time they'll ever have the world's best announcer call a game they were playing in, after all. Emrick has called Olympics, National Hockey League All-Star Games, World Cups, Stanley Cup Finals and now a Komets game. To the players, this time the broadcaster added to the prestige of the event and raised their level.

"Any time Mike Emrick is broadcasting your game, you want to make a good impression," forward Kaleigh Schrock said. "He knew more about me than I knew about myself. To have him with Chaser, that was a real honor to play in that game."

The broadcast itself wasn't perfect. It was better than that. Squeezing into the small home radio booth that was built for two people, the trio eventually forgot they were trying to fit in and around each other and just called the game. Without realizing it, they did what they do better than anyone. The laughs flowed with the game.

At one point, Emrick remarked that it has been at least 10 years since he called a game on radio, which is much different than describing the action on television.

"You have a lot of right-wing boards and left boards and near corner and far corner that you don't say on television," he said. "If you get paid by the word, and I hope Bob does, you earn double the money in radio."

There were also some classic Emrick calls. Any rust from the NHL lockout was scraped away like a goaltender scratching up his crease before the national anthem or a first-period facewash in the corner.

"Some discouraging words there from Henley in the face of Aaron Gens."

A late second-period post-whistle group shoving match was described, "A little extra from Rizk and a crowd will gather at the horn!"

Adding Emrick's descriptions to Chase's enthusiasm and Irons' explanations was about as perfect as a minor league game could hope to be called. The less they tried, the better the game became to anyone listening, and it was a pretty good game to see anyway as the Komets won their fifth in row.

"It's another highlight for the year 2012," said Chase, who recently received the Lester Patrick Award for service to hockey in the United States. "I don't know what goes on next. I hope like hell Santa Claus remembers me. Like I said in my wrap, in my fondest dreams I never realized this could happen. I never even dreamt of it happening until now."

Best of all? It sounded like a dream, too, one that every listener will always remember.

CHAPTER 59
CHASE RECEIVES "KEY TO THE FORT"
May 10, 2013

As 60-year Komets broadcaster Bob Chase said, this has been his year for awards.

Chase, 87, was honored by Fort Wayne Mayor Tom Henry with a "Key to the Fort," which goes to individuals who have made an extraordinary commitment to the community through a lifetime of stewardship and involvement.

Already this year, Chase has received the Lester Patrick Award from the National Hockey League and USA Hockey for his contributions to the sport in this country, and he was inducted into the Northern Michigan University Hall of Fame.

"The honor is incredible, and I'm kind of used to getting honored, but they just get bigger and better and more dear and more meaningful," Chase said Thursday morning in the mayor's office.

"The ones you come home to are the big ones. You people are the big people in my life, and Fort Wayne is."

Chase is just the third Fort Wayne resident to receive a "Key to the Fort" from Henry. The other recipients were the late Charles Redd, a former city council member and community activist, and Jane Avery of Community Harvest Food Bank of Northeast Indiana.

"It is my privilege to recognize Bob Chase for all that he has done for our great city," said Henry. "Bob's professionalism, character, humility and his love for his family and the Komets are all attributes that make him a unique and special man in our community."

Along with Chase's wife, Murph, more than 30 members of the media, friends, and former Komets and members of Komets management were present.

"You never know what's next," Chase said. "You think about things that have happened over the years, what is next. I didn't know what this was going to be until just this very moment."

Chase will begin his 61st season covering the Komets in October. It's the longest continuous tenure covering home and road games for a broadcaster with one team in all of professional sports.

"I can hardly wait now; I've got the key to it all," Chase joked. "I'm looking forward to it. I don't know what it's going to be, but it's going to be great because that's the way they are. When they change things around, look out, here we come, big-time and all excitement no doubt about it."

CHAPTER 60
CHASE PREPARES FOR EMOTIONAL DAY
May 28, 2014

Through the first 88 years of his life, Bob Chase has not been intimidated by many things, but today he's a little apprehensive.

The longtime WOWO and Komets broadcaster and about 80 of his fellow World War II veterans flew out of Fort Wayne International Airport at 8 a.m. on an Honor Flight Northeast Indiana trip to Washington, D.C. They'll visit the monuments and Arlington National Cemetery and return between 9 and 10 p.m.

"I don't think you can preset yourself," he said. "You have to be thrilled to think you are given the opportunity to go, but you just don't know what you are going to see. You have an idea, but what's it going to mean to you and what's the emotional impact? It's almost like going to war in a way. When you go, you go. You don't ask any questions because there are no answers until you lay it on the line and see what is next."

A native of Marquette in Michigan's Upper Peninsula, Chase enlisted in the Navy at age 17 in 1943 after he graduated high school.

"If you were drafted you went into whatever service they told you to, and I wanted to be in the Navy," Chase said. "My mom and dad had to sign for me, but I grew up as a Sea Scout (on Lake Superior). I was a water boy."

He began training as pilot, but his 6-foot-6 height meant he was too tall to fit into most airplanes. He accepted a position as part of a code-monitoring team at an underground radio station in

Oahu, Hawaii, as a liaison officer in cryptographic security. His group monitored all encrypted Navy traffic in the Pacific.

"Probably the most solemn thing that ever happened to me, including getting married, happened when I took the oath to defend my country," he recalled. "You don't realize what those words mean until you say them."

Because he had enlisted, Chase was not released from the service until December 1946.

As for today's trip, Chase was invited by WOWO afternoon personality Pat Miller. Chase said he's particularly looking forward to seeing the Vietnam Veterans Memorial in honor of son Mike, who was severely injured in 1966 when he stepped on a booby-trapped shell. He was hospitalized for 18 months.

Chase said he'll also look up some of his buddies on the World War II Memorial. He lost three of his childhood friends who were drafted after he enlisted.

"I think I'm prepared, because I'm looking forward to seeing it, but I don't know how I will respond until I'm in the moment," he said. "I'm excited about it, and I'm sure I will be emotional, but that's OK because I will be there with my peers. We'll support each other."

CHAPTER 61
KOMETS, SPECIAL FAN TO CELEBRATE CHASE'S BIRTHDAY
Jan. 15, 2016

Sometimes it's too easy to take Bob Chase's quality and 63-year tenure as the Komets' broadcaster for granted. The team will celebrate the legend's 90th birthday during pregame ceremonies Sunday, and Betty Bueker will be listening from her Auburn home.

Bueker will turn 98 on April 5, but maybe more importantly to this story, she lost her eyesight to macular degeneration more than 15 years ago. She listens to the radio all the time because it provides her entertainment and access to the world. About seven years ago, someone suggested she start listening to Komets games. Though a life-long northeast Indiana resident and a 1936 South Side graduate, she had never been to a Komets game and had watched only a couple of NHL games on TV.

Imagine becoming a hockey fan at age 90.

"I just enjoyed it, mostly due to Bob Chase because I could visualize what was going on because he was so good," she said. "He makes it interesting, and he actually tells what's going on so you can visualize the game. I still understand the game as he tells it."

For 40 years, Bueker and her husband, the late Frank Bueker, played in the Fort Wayne Philharmonic, meaning they practiced many weekday evenings and performed most weekends. Along with raising two children and then serving as the manager of the DeKalb Hospital gift shop, she did not have a lot of time for sports.

Now Bueker has become a devoted sports fan.

"I was never good at sports, but I like to listen to them, especially the Pacers," she said. "I tried to listen to basketball on TV, and there were two men, and they talked more about what they did when they were playing, and they didn't talk much about the actual playing of the game."

But the Komets, and Chase, in particular, are her favorites, though sometimes it's a struggle to pick up WOWO's signal.

"I think Bob is a unique person because I just think he understands people, everyday people, from what he says," she said. "I really get a kick out of some of his phrases. He has a unique way of expressing himself. He tells it like it is."

Chase's 90th birthday isn't until Jan. 22, but Sunday is the closest Komets home game to the date.

CHAPTER 62
NBC TO FEATURE CHASE DURING SUNDAY'S GAMES
Feb. 18, 2016

What's the greatest "Thank you" a protege has ever been able to deliver for a mentor? Mike "Doc" Emrick may have scored the game-winning goal.

When NBC Sports was looking for feature ideas to highlight Sunday's "Hockey Day in America" promotion, unequaled Hall of Fame announcer Emrick suggested a look at Fort Wayne's Bob Chase might be interesting. Chase is continuing his 63rd season announcing Fort Wayne Komets games, and though he just turned 90, he's still got the same passion, most of the energy and all of the knowledge that makes his call of games special.

So NBC is going to air a short feature on Chase called "The Doctor's Inspiration" sometime during the Buffalo at Pittsburgh game, which begins at 12:30 p.m. It will likely be broadcast during the first intermission, which would be great for Fort Wayne fans because the Komets have a home game starting at 5 p.m., and they plan to show the clip over the scoreboard.

"He is one of the greatest people in my life," said Emrick, a LaFontaine native who got hooked on the sport while watching a 1960Komets game. "I am proud to call him my friend. I hope the piece reflects how all of us feel about him."

The spot will feature footage NBC taped Jan. 2 during a Komets trip to Toledo and Jan. 17 when Emrick showed up at Memorial Coliseum to celebrate Chase's birthday.

"Everything that Doc told me about Bob is true," said NBC Feature Producer David Picker. "He's a towering figure both physically and where he fits in the game. He calls a game like you'll not believe. He calls a goal just the perfect way, and he signed off in just the perfect way. What Doc told me was spot on. No one knows Bob better than Doc, and for me to look back on both shoots and say, 'Wow, I saw everything that Doc was talking about,' was very cool."

The segment may be as short as two minutes, but Picker and the NBC crew spent about 20 hours with Chase, and more features are possible. The crew first interviewed Chase at the coliseum for four hours Jan. 2 before riding the bus with him to Toledo (picking up the team's bill at Tim Horton's along the way).

"My favorite part was one of two things, the bus ride from Fort Wayne to Toledo because it was just the team and Bob and everyone else was focused on the game," Picker said, "but it was an intimate moment when we could see his interaction with the team and the coach and how Bob approaches the pregame mentality. To get a glimpse of that was very special.

"The second part was once we got to the arena, just to see the preparation Bob takes once he gets into the arena. He insisted on taking the stairs, and he put his equipment together himself. You'd think maybe by this point he would have earned the right to have someone else take care of that for him, but he wants to be the guy who takes his old-school equipment and make sure it works. I think the viewers will enjoy seeing that as well."

Picker also enjoyed seeing how Chase reacts and greets arena workers and fans before games, even though the cameras were off at the time. Chase knows someone in almost every arena the Komets play in, and in cities like Kalamazoo, Toledo and Indy, he knows almost everyone who's working at the games.

"He's an incredible figure in the game, and it was an honor to get to see how he operates on a daily basis," Picker said. "His relationship to the coaches, players and fans ... he's incredibly enthusiastic and energetic. His stamina is unbelievable. When we left him at the bus in Toledo after the game, my impression was that he could have gone on for another 10 hours if he needed to."

Another highlight was watching and listening to Chase and Emrick call the third period of the Komets' Wednesday win over Rapid City. They had worked together with Fort Wayne legend

Robbie Irons to call a Komets' home game Nov. 9, 2012, but Picker said their coordination and timing was unbelievable.

"Getting the two of them in a booth was like a symphony," he said. "It was lyrical to hear the two of them speak at just the right time. It felt effortless because they know each other so well. It was spectacular."

Another interesting tidbit was the way Chase has become a destination for fans on the road who often come up to say hi to him outside his booth.

"I think Bob's listeners realize he's not just broadcasting the game, but he's a conduit between the fans and the players," Picker said. "The fact is that Bob is an incredible part of the game. His connection to hockey is incredibly important, and hockey is an important part of NBC, and it's the perfect fit to have Bob shown on 'Hockey Day in America,' and we're celebrating him and his accomplishments in the game.

"It was a real honor to spend some time with Bob and see how he does what he's done for 63 years now. It's an incredible part of the game, and the people of Fort Wayne and the Komets and those who play against the Komets are lucky to have a guy like him so closely associated with the team and the game."

As for Chase, he's interested to see the piece, but he's also still a little bit overwhelmed by the entire process.

"It's just me, I guess, but I never thought in a lifetime that things like this would happen to me," he said.

His only regret, he said, was that his parents are not around to share in and enjoy his success. He's already called family members around the country to let them know when to watch.

"All the little things that have happened to me were late in life, and I appreciate all of them," he said. "I just thank God that it all worked out the way it did. I'll take what comes along humbly and be thankful that I'm here to enjoy it."

CHAPTER 63
REMEMBERING BOB CHASE
Nov. 25, 2016

Longtime WOWO Sports Director and Fort Wayne Komets broadcaster Bob Chase died early Thursday morning at Parkview Hospital on Randalia at age 90. As announced in a News-Sentinel story in October, Chase had been battling congestive heart failure for several months.

Perhaps no one in Fort Wayne history did more to promote the city, just as it's possible no one has ever introduced hockey to more new fans or caused more to love it. Chase's voice was known to generations across the country and throughout several countries during his 63-year tenure with WOWO and the Komets.

Throughout the 1950s and much of the 1960s, Chase's broadcast on WOWO was the only one throughout the International Hockey League and the only hockey broadcast throughout much of the rest of the country. During the era of six NHL teams, the game he saw was the only one to visualize for many young fans who'd fall asleep listening to their transistor radios hidden under the covers. Today there are millions of hockey fans because Bob Chase introduced their parents, grandparents and maybe even great-grandparents to the game.

"I think Bob's listeners realize he's not just broadcasting the game, but he's a conduit between the fans and the players," said NBC Feature Producer David Picker while doing a piece on Chase in February. "The fact is that Bob is an incredible part of the game."

Born Jan. 22, 1926, in Negaunee, Mich., Chase's actual name was Robert Donald Wallenstein. However, when he came to Fort Wayne in June 1953, WOWO Program Manager Guy Harris thought Wallenstein was too long. He changed his last name to Chase, his wife Murph's maiden name. Her father, who was blessed with five daughters but no sons, loved it.

Because he served four years in the United States Navy and then spent four years studying at Northern Michigan University, Chase was 27 when he came to Fort Wayne. He started as a co-announcer of Komets games with Ernie Ashley and then took over sole duties in 1954.

This would have been his 64th season with the Komets. The team added his name to the franchise's retired honorees banner at his 40th anniversary in 1992 and honored him again for his 50th year in 2002 and his 60th in 2012.

He received countless awards during his career, highlighted by the Lester Patrick Award from USA Hockey and the National Hockey League in 2012 for service to the sport in the United States. That year he was also given a key to the city by Fort Wayne Mayor Tom Henry and was inducted into the Northern Michigan University Hall of Fame.

He was also named a Sagamore of the Wabash in 2001 and was inducted into the Indiana Sportswriters and Sports Broadcasters Hall of Fame. He was inducted into the Indiana

Broadcasters Association's Broadcast Pioneers Hall of Fame Award in 2000. He was also named ECHL Broadcaster of the Year after the 2013-14 season, adding to similar honors from the International Hockey League, the United Hockey League and Central Hockey League.

During his career with WOWO, Chase interviewed such people as Elvis, the Beatles, Jim Brown, Frank Sinatra, Bob Hope, Vice President Nixon, Gordie Howe, Arnold Palmer. His interview with Elvis is part of the Rock & Roll Hall of Fame in Cleveland.

During his tenure, the Komets have gone through five sets of owners, 25 coaches, more than 1,000 players and 70 different opposing teams. Of the Komets' 532 playoff games during their 64-year history, Chase has called 526 of them. Of the Komets' 4,890 regular-season games, Chase has likely called around 4,500 of those.

Until the Komets left the International Hockey League in 1999, Chase had broadcast every all-star game the league had ever played. Until a heart ailment and quadruple bypass surgery slowed him down in 1998, he had broadcast all 351 playoff games the team had ever played, including nine cup-winning championships. He called his 500th Komets playoff game on April 18, 2015. It's unlikely more than a handful of announcers have called 500 playoff games in any sport, let alone with one team.

Besides broadcasting hockey, Chase announced high school basketball for 17 years, also broadcast Big Ten football for 10 years and covered the Indianapolis 500 for 25 years. From 1954 to 1967 he hosted "The Bob Chase Show" Monday through Friday afternoons on WOWO.

In 2000, Chase was nominated for the United States Hockey Hall of Fame. Among those who wrote letters of recommendation were NHL broadcaster Mike Emrick, U.S. Olympics star Mike Eruzione, longtime ABC broadcaster Chris Schenkel and several former IHL commissioners.

Some highlights from those letters:

"The way he taught hockey and the way he described the sport was his gift to all of us who listened and all of us who were associated with this best game," Emrick wrote.

"Much credit must be given to radio station WOWO and Bob Chase for the tremendous growth and acceptance of our great game in the U.S.A.," former IHL Commissioner Bud Poile wrote.

"As a fellow sportscaster, I'm in awe of Bob's incredible skill in painting a verbal picture of my favorite spectator sport - hockey!" Schenkel wrote. "In addition, Bob is a gentleman, a loyal professional. His voice is second to none as a communicator."

"(Bob) used to say hello to my parents back in Boston whenever we played Fort Wayne," Eruzione said. "WOWO was the only station that my family could listen to a few games on. Bob has not only dedicated his life to the sport as an announcer but also has become a great ambassador of U.S. hockey, always being there for the players and their families."

As beloved as Chase was in hockey, he was even more loved in Fort Wayne where he might have been the most recognizable person in the city. He was never bothered by his fame.

"It's a real privilege to have it," he said in an emotional

statement in 2004. "I have trouble ... I love it. I'm honored to be accepted. I'm a native now. You earn it, you just hope you can keep it. I'm honored and thankful."

Wallenstein is survived by his wife of 66 years, Murph; daughter Karin; and sons Mike, Kurt and Dave. There are eight grandchildren and nine great-grandchildren. Services are pending.

CHAPTER 64
EVERYONE WAS FRIENDS WITH BOB CHASE, AND HE LOVED THAT

To everyone else, Bob Chase was always larger than life but never acted that way.

Chase passed away Thursday morning at age 90, surrounded by friends and family, to complete what was truly a blessed life. There have been many times when I've been awed by Chase, but here are three favorites:

* In 1994, the Detroit Vipers joined the International Hockey League playing in the beautiful Palace of Auburn Hills. One problem, though, was that the press box was eight stories high and the Vipers' teal and light purple uniforms were indecipherable. No one in the press box could tell who the players were — except for Bob Chase whose radio perch was actually one story higher. He could distinguish the players on both teams based on line match-ups and experience watching their mannerisms. Everyone else eventually shut up and just listened to Chase who never missed a goal or an assist that night. It was an astonishing performance.

* In 1993, the all-star game was in Phoenix, and Bob had been

kicked out of his room so he was bunking with Kent Hormann and me. On the night before the game, we sat with the door open on a deliciously warm February evening. As we were grousing about not having anything to drink, this little guy walking past the room heard Bob talking and stuck his head in to say hello. It was Ted Giannoulas, who was performing the next night at the game as the San Diego Chicken and who from his many performances in Fort Wayne knew Bob.

He also knew where to find beer, so we all sat there for a bit shooting the bull. Ted left, and Kent and I futilely tried to match Bob's consumption rate, finally giving up and going to bed about 1:30 a.m., or about 4:30 a.m. Fort Wayne time, or about 24 hours after the day had started.

As per his custom, Bob woke up at 4:30 a.m. fresh as a daisy, doing some voice exercises so he could call into WOWO's morning show. We wanted to threaten bodily harm, but (a.) he was a lot bigger than us, and (b.) we were unable to move for several more hours. So that night, without a nap and working on about three hours' sleep, Bob broadcast a nearly perfect game as Pokey Reddick was a human highlight film, making 13 saves on 14 shots to lead the East to a win.

We were definitely not worthy!

* In 1992, as Chase was setting up to broadcast the 1992 IHL All-Star Game in Atlanta, he looked up to see the stare of an older gentleman of diminutive stature. This was the first time Chase had broadcast a game in Atlanta, as the Knights didn't join the IHL until a year later.

"Can I help you?" Chase asked.

"Nope," the man replied. "You Bob Chase?"

After getting a positive answer, the man immediately left, only to reappear five minutes later with a female companion, obviously his wife.

"See, that's what he looks like," the man said. And then they left. Most people would be flattered to be recognized, but Chase was prouder that these people felt comfortable enough to approach him.

"I never consciously tried to point myself to impact people or impress people," Chase said. "My dad always told me, 'Be yourself, and if you can't, then get the hell out of the business.' I feel flattered that I've had that kind of impact on people."

I've seen hundreds of similar scenes over the last 27 years, with fans coming up to the radio booth before games. Parents wanted to introduce him to their children or others wanted to relive memories, or maybe they just wanted to shake his hand. They all felt like they knew him, like he was a family friend, which is exactly what he was after talking for 63 years in their cars, their living rooms or as they hid under the covers as children trying to stay awake and hear one more period. He was everybody's adopted grandfather.

"Had it not been for the public who accepted me, I wouldn't be here," he said. "Whenever you are in my business, if the radio is on and they are listening it's by invitation only because the minute they don't like you they are on to something else. I have never lost sight of that."

And he never did. Bob Chase/Wallenstein never got too big of an ego, never got too big to talk to anyone and was always very gracious with his time.

The easiest way to make him tear up was to give him – or his children – a compliment. He was emotional, involved in the moment and always real.

Even at 90, he was still the man who always knew exactly who he was and who he represented. In many ways, he represented Fort Wayne and us, and we all met the same person.

CHAPTER 65
EMOTIONAL KOMETS HONOR CHASE WITH WIN OVER WINGS
Nov. 25, 2016

All day Thursday, news of beloved broadcaster Bob Chase's death rippled throughout the hockey world. Former Komet Justin Hodgman checked in from Sweden, Matthew Pistilli from Germany, and Minnesota Wild coach Bruce Boudreau led dozens of other former Fort Wayne players by reaching out, as did ECHL officials and a horde of long-time minor league broadcasters, including Fort Wayne-native Chris Treft from Atlanta.

As everyone tried to somehow process their loss, throughout the day the ripples and emotions never seemed to lose strength, which showed Chase's 63-year effect upon the game and people.

But what about the place where the ripples started, where the impact probably hit the hardest outside of Chase's family? Komets coach Gary Graham said Thursday's pregame speech was the hardest he's ever had to attempt and admitted he couldn't control his emotions enough to get through it. For one of the few times during his 27-year tenure, Komets General Manager David Franke addressed the team, preaching how Chase is really the one who established that being a Komet is about being part of the family.

Heady stuff, and then the Komets, like every other of the 7,181 fans in Memorial Coliseum, watched a seven-minute tribute video. It was raw, understated perfectly, captured the essence of Chase and his life and ripped the tears right out, especially the part where Chase got emotional himself describing a few years ago how he'd like to be remembered. No one was unaffected as tissues were passed around row to row, but the Komets had to quit biting their lower lips, drop the puck and go somehow play a game.

"I never started a game with a tear in my eye before," forward Mike Embach said. "When they turned the lights back on, it was like, `Oh, yeah, we're playing a game. Quick, refocus.' "

Much easier to say than to do. After all, they knew the broadcaster as well as most after riding on some of the ECHL's longer road trips. Several players said they got chills from watching the tribute, and it took everyone a few minutes to refocus.

"I remember my first shift, waiting for the faceoff thinking, `Wow, this is the quietest I've ever heard this place, even when there were 2,000 people in here,' " forward Shawn Szydlowski said.

Somehow, the Komets used the emotion to blitz Kalamazoo 6-1, as the Wings really never had a chance. They were facing the Komets, the crowd and quite a bit of inspiration. Kyle Thomas scored two goals and two assists, Mike Cazzola had a goal and an assist and Jamie Schaafsma had three assists.

"It was tough for everyone," Thomas said. "The guys who have been here for a while got to know him. He lived a great life and did what he loved as long as he possibly could. For him, I think he was happy with that. The best thing we could do for him was go out and get a win for him tonight, and we did that."

After the game, Graham told the players he'd received more than 100 texts from people telling him to tell the team to go get a win for Chase, but he didn't do that. He knew the players wanted a victory as badly as anyone.

"It was like the pressure of Game 7 last year against Cincinnati," Graham said. "We wanted to deliver a win for Bob's family and for Bob, but we couldn't play tight. I didn't want to put too much into their heads. I think Chaser had an influence in the second period when we got a couple of favorable bounces."

Maybe, but Chase certainly would have loved the way the Komets used all facets of their speed, toughness and tenaciousness. It was a game he'd have loved to call and then celebrate with the boys afterward maybe on the bus to tonight's game in Toledo. Instead, Chase was the focus of a team prayer at center ice after Embach scooped up the game puck to present to the family.

"They were playing with a lot of heart and passion, and it was really rewarding to see us have a special night," Graham said.

It was because the Komets honored Chase the best way they could have.

CHAPTER 66
BLAKE SEBRING'S EULOGY
FOR BOB CHASE
Dec. 1, 2016

This will not be a formal service because frankly, Bob did not want one. And he certainly didn't want tears, so please, no tears today. Bob would not want that, either. Plus, it ruins the effects of the jokes I want to tell.

And there should be jokes because no one loved to laugh more than Bob did and he instructed me to tell as many jokes as possible. He could tell the same story 50 different ways and make everyone laugh along with him every time because he was so passionate and infectious.

Hopefully, there will be a lot of laughs and some fond memories you can take with you after today. These memories should all be positive and warm ones.

One reason Bob would not want any tears today is because he wouldn't want to be the focus of all those emotions. That's just not what he was about.

Actually, every time Bob won another award, they were horrible stories to try to write because he was always so humble about them. Every time, he would shake his head in disbelief and wonder what he had done to be so lucky in this life. And he and Murph considered themselves so lucky, so blessed in their lives. It wasn't just professionally, but also personally, especially with their children.

Man, could he ever brag about his kids. I wasn't sure if Mike wasn't the actual inspiration for a John Grisham novel about lawyers. Either Mike never lost a case or the other side always settled whenever they figured out he was the opposing counsel because they feared him so much.

I'm not sure if Philo Farnsworth invented TV or if it was actually Kurt Wallenstein because all I ever heard about were all the innovations Kurt has come up with to push the medium to the next level. At the very least, I'm convinced that you actually brought television to Alabama.

From what I understand from her father, Karin didn't make the Olympic volleyball team because she simply chose not to, though I might be confused on that one a little bit. I'm pretty sure he expected you to coach in the 2020 Olympics so you better get busy.

I am also absolutely sure that David has more holes-in-one than any golfer in history and never lost a tournament he was determined to win. And, oh, Lord, as a hockey player, the greatest ever produced by a university south of the Mason-Dixon line ... Well, that one might actually be true.

I'm pretty sure I could write a book about the Wallenstein kids from memory, maybe even one each. If I was you, I'd maybe be a little embarrassed by all this adulation, but you are probably used to it. It sure explains a lot about you and your quirks.

Maybe Bob's favorite thing in life wasn't the Komets, it was bragging about his kids. He loved you all so dearly and was so incredibly proud of you. You were truly the biggest and best accomplishments of his life. Never doubt that or forget it. Be proud of it, cherish it, and continue to honor it.

You are exactly the people your parents raised you to be and hoped you would become. You are his true legacy.

And thank you for sharing him with the rest of us. He was everyone's de facto grandfather. Who ever spent more frequent time in our cars, living rooms, kitchens or in our bedrooms as we tried to fight off sleep to listen to just one more period? He was basically a part of everyone's family, and we thank you very much for allowing that.

Unlike many people in media, even on the local level, there's the on-air persona and the off-air personality, which are distinctly separate. That was never the case with Bob. We knew him and you knew him, truly. I was with him in dozens of cities when opposing fans would approach to talk and within a minute you'd swear they had been friends with Bob for more than 10 years. The Bob Chase on the air was exactly the same person as Bob Wallenstein off the air. There was nothing false about him, and he made everyone comfortable around him.

The bigger point of today is that no one lived life like Bob did. In the history of the world, have you ever known anyone who was so fortunate to live life on their own terms as Bob? Just think about that for a second. I'm not sure anyone ever successfully told him no, certainly not the nurses at the hospital. Talk about spoiled! And he soaked up every second of it.

And few people were ever as rewarded as he and Murph have been.

As he told me in 2009, "That's why I'm so humble, and I can't believe all the things that are happening to me. What have I done to deserve all this? I'm not that good a guy."

Of course, he was, but he also wasn't perfect. It used to drive me nuts listening on the radio when described the conversations he thought that players were having on the ice. "So and so is about to lose it on this guy. He's had just about enough and it could be all over very soon."

When you listened to Bob, you thought a pier six brawl was about to erupt at any moment, when actually, the players were usually just asking how their wives were doing, or how their golf game was going. Don King was jealous of Bob's ability to hype a fight that never happened. If hockey had fit Bob's reality of hate and aggressiveness, the MMA never would have had a chance to develop. It was like the players were doing all they possibly could not to hulk out on an opponent. In his mind, Bob probably created more penalty minutes than Kevin Kaminski, Steve Fletcher or Andy Bezeau actually did combined.

And everyone knows that a Komet never lost a fight that Bob called. Some guy would lose his teeth, get knocked into next week and have to be carried off the ice, but Bob would talk up the one punch he managed to land as if he was Apollo Creed.

And then he'd say the player was surely coming back for a rematch in about 10 minutes. You just wait.

Bob was also a master manipulator in a way.

During his recent hospital stays, no one could figure out why his numbers were steadily improving. Well, for one thing, he had everybody and his brother convinced he was dying of starvation and desperately needed real food! I'm pretty sure Bob might be the only person in history who actually gained weight during a hospital stay. Cookies, jello, fruit cocktail, pizza, coffee, bagels, hamburgers, frosties ... I'm surprised the Budweiser driver didn't stop and make a direct delivery.

Is it any wonder why Bob was such a wonderful salesman of advertising and hockey and Fort Wayne? Is there anyone in history who has done more to market this city or this game? Just think about how many grandfathers and fathers (or grandmothers and mothers) he made into hockey fans and how that love of the game trickled down to future generations. It's staggering to consider. Then throw Mike Emrick's impact on top of that. It's astonishing to contemplate, but it's also probably true.

Now try to think of anyone who has had a bigger impact on telling others about Fort Wayne. Whose reach was further or longer in time? Who has more on-air time to a larger audience? How many tens of thousands of people came to Memorial Coliseum just to see the building Bob described?

And the thing is, he never lost his enthusiasm. That might be the most unbelievable thing about him, not that he called more than 500 playoff games with one team or that he broadcasted their games until he was 90 or that he likely called 5,000 games. I hope to be half as enthusiastic about anything at age 70 as Bob was at 90. It's just utterly astonishing.

Heck, my goal is to be that enthusiastic tomorrow about anything! That would be a worthy goal.

The funny thing is you knew immediately within five seconds of listening by his tone whether it was a good game or a bad game for the Komets. He just wanted so desperately for them to succeed because though he'd never admit it to anyone, I think deep down he knew he was running out of chances for championships. But he also still loved the players and Gary.

Bob rarely made it to practice anymore, but he'd spend an hour a day talking to Gary or me about what we saw or what was happening or might possibly happen in upcoming games. I had final exams in college that were less probing than talking to Bob about hockey practice. His curiosity and love of the game never waned. It's just amazing. I'd sometimes think, I need to do anything else for just one day rather than talk about hockey some more, to just get away and recharge, but he'd be so honest and passionate it was infectious. By the time we got off the phone, I'd be fired up for the next night's game.

About the only part of hockey I could never get Bob to talk about was his book. When we published it, the idea was that he would talk about it on the air once in a while during a game so people would know it was out there. Free marketing to our prime target audience! But would Bob do that? Heck, no. The only time he ever talked about the book was when he'd have me on during an intermission interview. I'd be like, Bob, it's your book. Nobody cares what I think about it, and nobody is going to know it's out there if you don't talk about it sometime. "OK, I'll talk about it this weekend." Whew! But he never would, and I'd want to bang my head against the wall. I'd even write him up ads to read about the book like any other advertisement and he never would. I know he was proud of the book, but I think that was part of his humble nature. I think it embarrassed him in a way. Maybe he was too humble for his own good, but it was the absolute truth and completely real.

The funny thing is that no one could tell a story like Bob. Some of them were even true! One of the most fascinating days of my life was sitting at a book signing between Eddie Long, Terry Pembroke and Bob. I heard the same story from three different perspectives and wouldn't you know that each person was the focus of their version of the story? My bet is that Eddie was the one who actually had it right. He never forgets anything. Amazing! God, those were fun times!

And that should be the message about Bob's life. He had fun, we had fun listening to him and all of our lives were better because of it.

Who could do any better than that? Who has ever set a better example for the rest of us? We definitely shouldn't be sad today, but we should be celebrating instead.

Many people do not know this, but Bob was a very spiritual person. He didn't have a home church, but he definitely had a home faith. Some of our most fascinating conversations were about matters of faith. I have no doubt where Bob resides today or that I'll get to see him again someday in Heaven - where he will truly try to get the last word.

What a life, and what a man!

Bob truly was larger than life and made all of our lives larger because of it.

CHAPTER 67
SHANE ALBAHRANI'S EULOGY FOR BOB
Dec. 1, 2016

He was an eloquent gentleman, a spectacular talent who had extraordinary loyalty to his family, city, and the Komets organization. He could light up a room and turn grown men into little kids just with his presence. He was also a mentor and a friend to a guy whose life ambition was to someday follow him into the Komets' broadcast booth.

In 1951, my father came to America without being able to speak a word of English. He didn't know anybody, nor did he know where to go once he got here. I heard that story a lot growing up, so I often thought about what kind of courage he had, the commitment he made, and the unimaginable fear he faced. I was never able to comprehend any of that until the evening of November 24, 2016 when I sat in an empty press box at the Coliseum realizing the responsibility I had just been handed. "How am I going to do this?" I asked myself.

Then I remembered something Bob told me years ago... Don't worry about being Bob Chase, you just be yourself." And that's what I did! I broke down a few times, but I got through it, even thanking Bob for my wonderful life. Because without him, I never would have chosen this crazy business, I never would have gotten my first job in broadcasting where I met my wonderful, patient, understanding wife Kathi and had our talented daughter, Riley or met my best friend Andy.

Who knows what I would be doing right now if it wasn't for Bob?

Bob and I spoke a lot in the past few months and we got to share a few special moments together, just the two of us. One of those moments was me interviewing him for a broadcast a few weeks ago. We talked about his health, hockey, and of course, Murph. But one thing my little recorder captured that day was Bob saying... "Fans, take care of this guy because he's your new voice."

That might be true, I may be the new voice, but Bob will always be THE VOICE!

CHAPTER 68
ASHLEY MORELAND'S CLOSING SPEECH AT BOB'S FUNERAL
Dec. 1, 2016

In 2012, Tyler and Ashley Moreland started Lamp Lighters Hockey Ministries, a program that allows kids to play street hockey and learn about Jesus Christ. Ashley was asked to close out Bob's funeral service, and this is what she said:

Some of you may know us, but a lot of you don't, and that's okay. But I will tell you, that I think I know now what it feels like as a player to get called up. Because we sure did not expect to be in your presence today, and we are honored to be here. There are thousands of people who would love to honor Bob in this way. So know how speechless and humbled we were to get our "call-up."

Truth is, we didn't know Bob nearly as well as all of you. We grew up listening to him, idolized him, and considered him the legend he didn't consider himself. It's because of the culture he helped shape for the Komets, and how the Komets made Fort Wayne a Hockey Town, that allows us to coach street hockey to kids and adults who wouldn't otherwise have the opportunity to play the game that Bob loved so much and get to share with them how much God loves them. And for that, we will be forever grateful. Because of Bob's legacy, we will continue to raise up a future generation of hockey players, fans, and Christ-followers.

Four years ago, he interviewed us to help promote our very first fundraiser for Lamp Lighters. In our minds, it was one of those God-moments that solidified this was our calling, gave us validation, gave us hope that our ministry would be accepted into the hockey community, because we thought "How many people get to be interviewed by Bob Chase?!" Turns out A LOT over his 67 years in radio. But it was the way he made us feel, like we were the most important people in the world, that even though we had barely even started our ministry, he gave us a chance, an opportunity. Because that's who Bob was. He put YOU ahead of him. He was the epitome of what it means to serve, exactly what God calls us to do.

I love this quote from Bob's retirement from WOWO:

"I've always said I'm thankful for the listeners because had they not turned the radio on and invited me into their home, whether it be as a disc jockey, commentator, sports reporter or play-by-play man, none of this would have happened. If they turned on WOWO, I came into their homes at their invitation. I've always tried to remember that and maintain humility."

What perspective. I have never thought of it that way, that I was INVITING him into my home, into my life. Invitations are always to the best things, right? Weddings, baby showers, birthday parties. And I know it will be hard to know that there will be no more inviting your dad, your husband, your grandpa, your mentor, your friend to all the important things in your life.

I love Danny Gokey's song, "Tell your heart to beat again," and perhaps you feel like this first verse:

"You're shattered like you've never been before. The life you knew in a thousand pieces on the floor. And words fall short in times like these when this world drives you to your knees. You think you're never gonna get back to the you that used to be. Tell your heart to beat again, close your eyes and breathe it in, let the shadows fall away, step into the light of grace."

I know grief is a journey, a deeply personal journey, and you may not be ready to tell your heart to beat again today, to let the shadows fall away or step into the light of grace and no one will blame you and you have that right. But while still holding on dearly to your memories, one day you will, you'll wake up and tell your heart to beat again. And the light of grace will look so welcoming and inviting."

Jesus invites us in Matthew 11:28 "Come to me, all of you who are weary and carry heavy burdens, and I will give you rest." Our burden of loss is heavy today, and it will be for a while. God doesn't promise to take it away or to make it easier but He promises that we aren't alone. We have each other, we have Him. That he walks with us in the darkest of times and gently guides us back to His light of grace in His own sweet time. He reminds us in the stillness of the night that though we may long for Chaser to still be with us calling play by play from the rafters, that his view is just a little higher now, that his box now reads "Radio Heavenside." And we can rest in the knowledge that one day we can see him again, listen to him to say "Shoots! Scores!" one more time…

Jesus makes another invitation in the form of a parable. It comes from Luke 14:8-11. Which reads. "When you are invited by someone to a feast, do not sit down at the place of honor, since a more distinguished person than you may have been invited by the host, and he who invited both of you will come and say to you, Give this man your place, and then in disgrace you proceed to take the last place. But when you are invited, go and sit down at the last place, so that when your host comes, he will say to you, `friend, move up higher' and then you will be honored in the presence of all who are at the table with you. For everyone who exalts himself will be humbled before others, and he who habitually humbles himself will be exalted."

Didn't Bob just embody that entire passage? His goal was to maintain humility. It's easy to be humble once, but when you make humility a habit, that's a lifestyle. A lifestyle set by Christ that Bob followed after. He was a servant, he took the lowest place at the table by the way he regarded you, by the way, he instilled confidence in you, how he made connections for you, how he invited you into his life, just like we invited him into ours. His actions throughout his whole life invited others: "friend move up higher, you deserve a more distinguished place than I".

Now that his time here is done, all he wanted was to be remembered as a good guy. Well, Bob, I think you did it. And I think it's time to tell you, "Bob, my friend, move up higher" Move up higher, to a place of distinction. Move up higher to a place where you can turn God's ear so to help us understand how putting others first will make this world a better place. Because friends, Bob's work here on Earth is done. But ours is not.

Bob understood this life is all about choices. Which is exactly what a radio knob represents: a choice. To turn it on or off, up or down, or change the channel. Bob knew that we had the choice to invite him into our homes, into our lives. And that he had the choice to live only for himself or to maintain a lifestyle of humility. There's a couple of bowls when you walk out today that have some old radio knobs. If you so choose, please take one and put it somewhere where you'll see it. To remind you of Bob. To remind you of the choice he made every day to be humble that he learned by following Christ's teaching: that the first shall be last and the last shall be first. To remind you that every day you have the choice to live for yourself or to lift others higher up and make this world a better place.

CHAPTER 69
KARIN (WALLENSTEIN) THOMSEN'S SPEECH ON THE DEDICATION OF BOB CHASE WAY
Oct. 3, 2017

Greetings and thanks to everyone who had a part in making this day happen. What a glorious day for a celebration!

Growing up in Fort Wayne there were always two things that seemed larger than life to me. The first was my Dad. As he was 6-feet, 6-inches tall, I was always worried about my Dad hitting his head on the ceiling! He simply towered over me — until I grew... and grew... and grew!

The second was the Memorial Coliseum. From the outside, it was this gigantic structure that was the biggest building I had ever seen! From the inside it was equally impressive — walking up the massive ramp left my heart pounding and the excitement of walking into the arena has never faded. From Alice Cooper to Donny Osmond... to my high school graduation to every Komet game I have attended. The feeling of "being home" has never left me — or others for that matter. Just two weeks ago I met a woman in Evergreen, Colorado who had grown up in northwestern Ohio. When I told her I was from Fort Wayne, she immediately shared with me her fondest memories of growing up were her trips to the coliseum for concerts and hockey games. Such a small world we live in!

As I grew, so did the coliseum. While so many cities were tearing down structures, Fort Wayne made the decision to "raise the roof!" Who else but the people of Fort Wayne would figure out a way to keep their prized possession and make it even bigger and better than before? It has continued to grow and evolve just like our wonderful city... and Dad was there for all of this.

Fort Wayne, WOWO Radio, Komet Hockey, the coliseum and our Dad — Bob Chase. How they all became connected is one of those amazing (and true) stories that Dad told so well.

My brothers Kurt and David and I were not born when Dad started broadcasting for the Komets, but the coliseum soon became our second home as well. My earliest memories of Dad and the Komets were magical. Sitting with no glass by the penalty box, so close that you knew who still did or didn't have teeth, and dodging flying pucks was our routine. I can still see Cal Purinton and Merv Dubchak checking guys into the boards at 100 mph! I see Len Thornson dancing through a crowd, and scoring at will. I see Lionel Repka, Reggie Primeau and Terry Pembroke controlling the puck on both ends of the ice. Dad was there for every call — and perhaps some of you were as well. For 63 years you had Dad there with you and for you... and the coliseum was our living room for the home games.

When Dad passed away last Thanksgiving, we were paralyzed with grief. No words could describe how that day changed us forever. What would happen throughout that day — and actually up to this moment, gave us the strength to carry on. That was... and is the love and support of Fort Wayne, WOWO, the Komets, and the coliseum staff (and Blake Sebring who took the wheel and drove for us).

WOWO did the most amazing "on air" tribute, the Komets took my breath away with their tribute and their victory that night. Randy Brown and the coliseum crew gave Dad the most heavenly send-off — right at center ice. The kind words and cards have continued to bless us. It continues to warm my heart to see how much love so many had for Dad. He felt the same way about all of you.

Now today we are all here to unveil the naming of Bob Chase Way. This is one more honor that Dad would never have expected, and would not have felt "worthy of." I personally love the concept and think it is the perfect name! Bob Chase Way... not Avenue, Street or Drive. I find myself saying "THE Bob Chase Way." I hope it reminds people to enter this historical building and bring a piece of Dad's heart with them.

The Bob Chase way was to represent yourself and treat others with dignity and respect. The Bob Chase way was to put family first, to be loyal and committed — to follow your heart and chase your dreams. I hope each time a car turns on to Bob Chase Way, especially on those hockey nights, that each person gets a little shiver up their spine just thinking about the magical moments and memories they are creating... That each night when they drive home they know that Dad was still there with them. After all, it was his home for 63 years. He will continue to wrap his arms around you each time you visit, as long as you keep him in your hearts. Seeing his name will keep his spirit alive. Maybe someday there might even be a statue of Dad greeting everyone who enters the coliseum... only time will tell!

Thank you for allowing me the time and opportunity to share my feelings and express my gratitude to everyone who made this day possible. God bless all of you!

CHAPTER 70
WHY BOB SHOULD BE IN THE HOCKEY HALL OF FAME

Because he was never a member of the National Hockey League Broadcasters Association, Bob Chase has never been eligible to win the Foster Hewitt Award, presented for lifetime achievement. It's also as close as 99.9 percent of any media members will come to being inducted. Hewitt is the only broadcaster who has been selected for the hall.

So – though he's called more professional games than almost anyone who has won the award – Chase is ineligible. That doesn't mean he doesn't rate strong consideration for hall induction in the builder category.

Consider, Chase called more than 4,500 regular-season games during his 61-year career with the Fort Wayne Komets, the second-longest tenured team in all of minor league sports. That means something now, but it meant even more until 1967 when the National Hockey League doubled from six teams. Though many of whom didn't call nearly as many games, Chase's NHL contemporaries have mostly received the Hewitt Award.

When he missed a game on April 2, 1992, because of food poisoning, it was the first time illness had knocked him off a broadcast since 1958 when he had pneumonia. Until he suffered heart problems in 1998, Chase had called all 351 playoff games the Komets had played. He missed the final 10 regular-season and four playoff games but came back the next season after quadruple bypass surgery to call 70 games.

Chase also called more than 500 Komets playoff games. It's doubtful more than a handful of broadcasters in any sport have ever called as many postseason games, let along for one franchise.

He could easily have moved "up" to an NHL market, and had

several chances, but turned them down. In one instance, he didn't want to stab a friend in the back, and a couple of other times he didn't want to move his wife and four school-aged children away from their home. Both are honest, legitimate and understandable reasons.

He was also plenty good enough in terms of quality, winning Broadcaster of the Year honors in each of the five leagues the Fort Wayne Komets played in, honors that were voted upon by his peers in broadcasting and other forms of media. Until the Komets left the International Hockey League in 1999, Chase had called every all-star game in league history.

Essentially, Chase was the voice of minor league hockey in the Midwest with WOWO's 50,000 watts pushing his voice over the eastern half of North America. Players from every team would ask him to say hi to their parents who were listening throughout most of Canada.

Those are Bob Chase's qualifications on paper which are more than enough for consideration. His quality has never been in question, shown by the respect Chase has received throughout the sport from the countless greats he has interviewed. But his greatest contribution to the sport is a little tougher to quantify, his influence over others, either by introducing new fans to the game or influencing other future broadcasters.

Everyone in hockey accepts that Mike Emrick is the true voice of the sport, and he's universally accepted as the best play-by-play man in all of sports, with all of his Emmys and awards as evidence. He's simply the voice of hockey on television, whether in the NHL or the Olympics. With his enthusiasm, class and energy, Emrick has introduced generations of people to the game.

He's also a Bob Chase protégé, who became a hockey fan as a boy listening to Komets games from his LaFountaine home about an hour south of Fort Wayne. During the era of six NHL teams, the game Chase saw was the only one to visualize for many young fans who'd fall asleep listening to their transistor radios hidden under the covers. Today there are millions of hockey fans because Bob Chase introduced their parents, grandparents and even great-grandparents to the game. Emrick does the same thing in today's era. In today's world of internet and cable television and quick access to every game, it's easy to forget that for at least the first 35 years of his career in Fort Wayne, Chase was the only option for countless people.

When Chase was nominated for the United States Hockey Hall of Fame in 2000, among those who wrote letters of recommendation were Emrick, U.S. Olympics star Mike Eruzione, longtime ABC broadcaster Chris Schenkel and several former IHL commissioners.

Some highlights from those letters:

"The way he taught hockey and the way he described the sport was his gift to all of us who listened and all of us who were associated with this best game," Emrick wrote.

"Much credit must be given to radio station WOWO and Bob Chase for the tremendous growth and acceptance of our great game in the U.S.A.," former IHL Commissioner and Hockey Hall of Fame inductee Bud Poile wrote.

"As a fellow sportscaster, I'm in awe of Bob's incredible skill in painting a verbal picture of my favorite spectator sport – hockey!" Schenkel wrote. "In addition Bob is a gentleman, a loyal professional. His voice is second to none as a communicator."

"(Bob) used to say hello to my parents back in Boston whenever we played Fort Wayne," Eruzione said. "WOWO was the only station that my family could listen to a few games on. Bob has not only dedicated his life to the sport as an announcer, but also has become a great ambassador of U.S. hockey, always being there for the players and their families."

After Chase's death on Thanksgiving morning 2016, Atlanta Gladiators broadcaster Chris Treft – another of Bob's protégés – gathered interviews from almost every other ECHL broadcaster to produce a moving memorial. He pulled it off within a couple of days because everyone wanted to participate with their favorite stories of how Chase had affected their careers.

That's the kind of influence Chase had on others, and just as importantly on the game, which is why he deserves consideration for induction into the Hockey Hall of Fame. Yes, he was primarily a broadcaster, an exceptional one, but Chase was also a builder because he really did help lead the game to what it is today.

The Hockey Hall of Fame is about overall excellence in the sport, and Chase definitely exemplified that. He deserves to be in the hall.

Made in the USA
Middletown, DE
05 November 2022

14048369R00168